POLITICAL PHILOSOPHY NOW

Chief Editor of the Series:
Howard Williams, Aberystwyth University

Associate Editors:
Wolfgang Kersting, University of Kiel, Germany
Steven B. Smith, Yale University, USA
Peter Nicholson, University of York, England
Renato Cristi, Wilfrid Laurier University, Waterloo, Canada

Political Philosophy Now is a series which deals with authors, topics and periods in political philosophy from the perspective of their relevance to current debates. The series presents a spread of subjects and points of view from various traditions which include European and New World debates in political philosophy.

For other titles in this series, please see the University of Wales Press website: *www.uwp.co.uk*

POLITICAL PHILOSOPHY NOW

John Gray and the Problem of Utopia

John Hoffman

UNIVERSITY OF WALES PRESS • CARDIFF • 2008

© John Hoffman, 2008

All rights reserved. No part of this book may be reproduced in any material form (including photocopying or storing it in any medium by electronic means and whether or not transiently or incidentally to some other use of this publication) without the written permission of the copyright owner except in accordance with the provisions of the Copyright, Designs and Patents Act 1988 or under the terms of a licence issued by the Copyright Licensing Agency Ltd, Saffron House, 6–10 Kirby Street, London, EC1N 8TS. Applications for the copyright owner's written permission to reproduce any part of this publication should be addressed to The University of Wales Press, 10 Columbus Walk, Brigantine Place, Cardiff, CF10 4UP.

www.uwp.co.uk

British Library Cataloguing-in-Publication Data
A catalogue record for this book is available from the British Library.

ISBN   978-0-7083-2026-6 (hardback)
           978-0-7083-2025-9 (paperback)

The right of John Hoffman to be identified as author of this work has been asserted by him in accordance with sections 77 and 79 of the Copyright, Designs and Patents Act 1988.

Typeset in Classical Garamond by Prepress Projects Ltd, Perth, UK
Printed in Great Britain by CPI Antony Rowe, Chippenham, Wiltshire

To Chams

Contents

Acknowledgements	ix
Introduction	1
1 The Anti-Utopianism of John Gray	11
2 The Traditional View of Utopia	27
3 Utopia and Dualism	39
4 Marxism and Utopia	55
5 The Problem of the Market	74
6 The Caricature of Marxism	93
7 The Problem of the State	107
8 The Inescapable Character of Universalism	122
9 Globalization	144
10 Egalitarianism and Multiculturalism	162
11 Reconstructing Utopia	175
Conclusion	189
References	195
Index	200

Acknowledgements

The idea of linking John Gray to the problem of utopia was greatly boosted by a conference I attended in Tunis on utopias. I am very grateful to Chamseddine Mnasri (to whom this book is dedicated) and Sadok Bouhalila for inviting me and organizing the conference. I gave a paper that provided the kernel of the arguments for this book.

My thanks to Howard Williams for suggesting that I write a piece for his series, and for his help with the chapters. David McLellan has taken a keen interest in this work, and has been hugely helpful in providing literature and advice. Rob Colls kindly furnished me with his writing on John Gray, and Gray himself gave me extremely valuable bibliographical advice. I am also grateful to James Hamill for helping me with literature.

Rowan Roenisch, my partner, has encouraged me, and I am very grateful to my son Fred Hoffman (who also helped me with literature), and my daughter, Frieda Roenisch, for their support.

Introduction

Introduction

This work is a critical examination of John Gray's work, focusing in particular on his view that the Enlightenment, Marxism and much of liberal theory is utopian in character. Gray operates with a negative view of utopia, so that the accusation that a theory is utopian is, in his view, a claim that such a theory is unrealistic and fanciful. To challenge Gray, I seek to offer an alternative concept of utopia and to explain why he is unable to avail himself of this alternative, but subscribes instead to what I shall call the traditional view of utopia.

I initially shared this traditional concept of utopia. But I can now see that utopias pose a problem, because they are traditionally depicted as static and perfect visions of a society. A utopian society is deemed, according to the traditional view, unrealizable. It is an ideal that is abstracted from reality – an imaginary world, usually pleasant, but fundamentally unobtainable.

This view persists in much writing today and it is the view of utopia taken by John Gray in his critique of the Enlightenment and Marxism and in his attempt to reformulate liberalism. Utopia is seen as an abstract ideal imposed, sometimes ruthlessly, upon the complexities of the real world, and the diversities thrown up by history.

This unreflective view argues that utopia is a static and perfect world. It assumes a duality between ideals and reality, the abstract and the concrete, morality and history (to name just three). The traditional conception of utopia has roots in theological beliefs in a second coming of Christ, a notion of heaven and a world where the lions lie down with the lambs. Theology has traditionally seen the second coming in terms of perfection – a realization of an Eden in which conflict between humans and between humans and the rest of nature will disappear.

But utopias can be secular in form. Marx and Engels attacked as utopians thinkers such as Robert Owen who were staunchly opposed to religion, and Marx and Engels embraced a traditional view of utopias, arguing the case that a socialism could only be scientific if it was against utopias. An attempt will be made to explain why Marx and Engels were so hostile to utopianism. This is particularly necessary since the Marxist view offers significant conceptual resources for reconstructing the concept of utopia. Indeed, I shall draw substantially upon the theory of dialectical materialism (although it is not fashionable to describe it in this way) in order to provide a critique of John Gray and his negative view of utopia. Gray, I shall argue, radically distorts Marxism and, although he is fiercely critical of much of liberalism, he is woefully uncritical of the market and the state. In fact, his work is imprisoned in the very liberal abstractions that he often deplores, and his uncritical attitude towards the market and the state means that he imports into his analysis dualisms between ideals and reality, facts and values, that can be found in the work, for example, of the liberal conservative Hume. Hume's position contributes to the traditional view of utopia.

Gray dismisses humanism, post-modernism, Marxism, conventional religion and the Enlightenment. His argument is militantly one-sided. Indeed, what we see with Gray is a one-sided realism confronting what I would describe as an empiricism turned inside out. Realists (so called) concentrate on the 'is', utopians (traditionally defined) on the 'ought'. If the traditional view of utopia is vulnerable, so too is Gray's critique of this utopia. Traditional utopias are usually radical in their rejection of inequality, oppression and exploitation. But they project a world of perfection, free from conflict and change. Liberal conservative critics, understandably, see this vision as incredible and implausible, and propose instead reconciliation to the world as it is. Both are one-sided, albeit in diametrically opposed ways.

The traditionalist view of utopia is a product of modernism and pre-modernism. By modernism, I mean liberalism, an equation that Gray would sternly contest. In my view, modern societies that are currently authoritarian can only further develop if they adopt liberal norms, but I am not suggesting that they will become more like the West. In his work Gray has shown that German liberalism is very different from, say, American liberalism and I see no reason why as, for example, China becomes more liberal in character, it will not present a Chinese liberalism that is still infused with Chinese culture and values.

Although liberalism is premised upon freedom, equality and self-government, it endorses institutions such as the state and market that contradict its premises. I have elsewhere spoken of the subversive abstractions of the liberal tradition (1988: 150). For, while its premises are (and are seen by its conservative critics as) startlingly subversive, they are also abstract. By abstract, I mean that concepts are abstracted from the social circumstances that account for the resources individuals possess and their regional, religious, gender identity etc. Freedom becomes a veil for exploitation; the self-governing individual can secure order only through the state; equality is interpreted simply as sameness; and liberalism expresses a hostility to difference that manifests itself in colonialism, misogyny and war.

Reconstructing utopia requires a break from modernism. The emancipated society is a world that is free from classes, the market and the state, and is an integral part of history. Emancipation is not the culmination of history, but a step along a path of progress that is infinite. Emancipation is incompatible with class division, for classes divide and privilege some at the expense of others. The market abstracts individuals from their real powers and access to resources, and offers an equality that is hollow and formal. The state is a contradictory institution that promises peace and harmony, but uses force to address conflicts of interest, and is therefore a barrier to, and not an instrument of, democracy and self-government. These institutions promote dualism, by which I mean a division between opposites – a division that invites us to choose one rather than the other. In the terminology I prefer, a division is not the same as a difference because it prevents people from 'changing places' – it embodies an unbridgeable chasm that makes it impossible to relate to the other.

The reconstruction of the concept of utopia proceeds on premises that are post-modern rather than modern. I speak at some length of utopia as a momentum concept – a concept that is *infinitely* progressive and therefore has no culminating end point. Momentum concepts seek to avoid the polarizing and paralysing division between abstractly conceived ideals and reality. They are concrete, by which I mean they are part of history, and are informed by a post-modern logic of 'both/and', rather than the modernist logic of 'either/or'. It is true that some self-styled post-modernists espouse a kind of relativism and subjectivism, but it is hardly the fault of post-modernism if some of its practitioners fall back upon a scepticism that is basically modernist in character.

Gray, it goes without saying, does not succeed in moving beyond modernism, even though he is critical of its absolutist and abstract pretensions. At best, he inverts modernism, attacking humanism, the Enlightenment and Marxism, instead of building upon strengths and jettisoning weaknesses. At worst, he retreats into pre-modernism, inviting us to accept practices that are undemocratic and enslaving. I have a good deal of sympathy with his argument that we must respect diversity and difference, but I have none for the way in which he assumes that these differences must be divisive, generating violent conflict.

The utopia that I advocate is the transformation of the world as we know it. It is not the end of history, but a step forward. Hence utopia is multiple and ongoing. It involves progress, but not towards a fixed goal. If it is revolutionary, it is revolutionary in the sense of inviting change through continuity, not through the sudden and mystical break that revolutions are often taken to imply. My utopia is based on the world all around us, but at the same time it offers an alternative to a globe that will simply destroy itself if it continues to pursue its present path.

In my first chapter I feel the need to introduce the reader to a thorough acquaintance with Gray's views. In this chapter I trace the development of Gray's position from an enthusiastic neo-liberal to a traditional conservative and then to a communitarian critical of conservatism and social democracy. Gray is initially impressed by New Labour but (in my view rightly) becomes indignant with its appalling foreign policy (particularly over the war in Iraq) and its uncritical view of the market. In this chapter I will not criticize Gray's position but seek to expound it in as fair and dispassionate a way as possible.

Since Gray attacks the Enlightenment, neo-liberalism and Marxism as utopian in character, I spend my second chapter looking at the traditional view of utopia and examining what I consider to be its weaknesses. I illustrate the traditional view by looking briefly at Plato's *Republic*, More's *Utopia* and Bacon's *New Atlantis* so that the reader can see what a traditional utopia entails. I argue that the traditional concept of utopia can be espoused both by those who are hostile to utopias and by those who admire them. The problem is perfectionism and abstraction: whether one deplores it or celebrates it, the notion of the perfect society is in my view problematic, and serves simply to discredit critical thinking. It is hardly surprising that the traditional concept often takes a conventionally religious form, although I agree with Gray that traditional utopias may well be secular in character. The chapter hints at an argument developed later in the book – that a way needs to be found of overcoming the dualism between realism, on the one hand, and utopianism, on the other.

In my Chapter 3 I engage with problem of dualism – the idea that there is an unbridgeable gulf between opposing concepts – and examine in detail the Enlightenment. Gray is right to be critical of the Enlightenment, although I argue that he needs to build upon, rather than simply reject, Enlightenment arguments. The Enlightenment is abstract and dualistic, and I argue that these dualisms stem from the Enlightenment's position on a wide variety of issues – property, the market, religion, women and, of course, the state. Gray's position on the Enlightenment is ambivalent. He rejects its strengths and endorses its weaknesses, and I seek to illustrate this point by looking at his views on Hume and Mill. He embraces Hume's conservative scepticism and fails to see the emerging new liberalism in Mill's position. Mill regarded himself as a socialist, and this is clear even in his most apparently liberal tract, *On Liberty*.

In my fourth chapter I tackle Marxism's view of utopia. Ironically it is the same as Gray's – a traditional formulation denoting fantasy and abstraction. Marx and Engels, of course, seek to contrast utopian socialism with their own 'scientific' socialism, and this is unfortunate for a number of reasons. The first is that they tend to downplay the extent to which they relied substantially upon the so-called utopian socialists for many of the ideas that they wove into their own theory – the notion of association, the critique of inequality, their view of the family, indeed, the idea of the withering away of the state. Second, they do not explain why socialists such as Saint-Simon, Owen and Fourier consider their own views scientific and share Marx and Engels's negative view of utopia. Third, Marx and Engels's own theory is utopian in the sense of posing an alternative to the status quo, and I argue that the contrast that they drew between science and utopia probably arose from the tendency (which Engels spoke about in the last years of his life) to present their theory in a somewhat one-sided fashion. The chapter also examines William Morris's attempt to construct a Marxist utopia and argues that the problem with Morris's *News from Nowhere* is not that it is utopian, but that it has many of the features of a traditional utopia.

In Chapter 5 I focus on Gray's view of the market. It is my contention that Gray's uncritical endorsement of the market is at least one of the sources of the dualism that mars his work. Initially, Gray supports the neo-liberal view of the market and embraces the argument of Hayek – that the market constitutes the spontaneous coordination of information that no human mind is capable of grasping. The market lies at the heart of all versions of liberalism and, although it is true that new liberals like Green and Hobhouse saw the need for social reforms and state intervention, they regarded the market as central to social order. Yet the market rests upon an abstract egalitarianism that conceals differentials in social power and position and, although all thought contains an element of abstraction, the market distorts social realities by abstracting from the relationships into which people actually enter. Only as we become aware of these realities can the market be transcended. Gray himself becomes critical of the way in which the market is presented in neo-liberal thought, and he rightly insists that markets are moulded by cultural differences and state intervention. This is why he is sceptical about the notion of rights, since this notion is often abstracted from context and practicality. Nevertheless, at the end of the day, Gray sees no alternative to the market, and the way in which he privileges difference over sameness derives in part from his basically uncritical view of the market.

In the sixth chapter I look at Gray's critique of Marxism. Although Gray appears to have a solid knowledge of Marxism, his critique is unfair and at times grotesque. Gray argues that Marxism follows the Enlightenment and Christianity in presenting a view of history that culminates in a dramatic act of salvation. It is true that Marx up until 1843 does subscribe to the ideals of the Enlightenment, but from then on he becomes increasingly critical of liberal thought, developing a critique of private property, the market and the state. Marx aspires to develop a post-liberal, post-Enlightenment argument. To see communism as the end of history is to ignore Marx's attempt to project communism as an historical society that continually changes and, although it is true that Marx tends to exaggerate the discontinuity between capitalism and communism, it is absurd to suggest that he subscribes to a static and religious-type view of communism.

The same is true of Marx's notion of progress. It is dramatically different from the linear, mechanical view of progress that is presented in the Enlightenment, and Gray completely misses the dialectical and contradictory view of progress that Marx asserts. Moreover, there is no textual evidence for the argument that Marxism is a human imperialism (I will later deal with this in depth) and ignores the limits of nature. On the contrary, contemporary Green thinking presents a view of nature that is not significantly different from Marx and Engels's insistence that nature itself is dialectical in character. Nor is it correct to identify Marxism as a theory that is hostile to the individual. A communist society is defended by Marx and Engels on the grounds that it will liberate, not repress, the individual – treat the individual concretely, as a real person with culture and history, not abstractly as an ahistorical construct.

In Chapter 7, I focus on the question of the state. Although Gray from time to time stresses the limitations of the nation-state, he is basically uncritical of the state per se. Like Marx, he identifies politics with statecraft and sees the state as a civilizing agency. It is true that, in societies deeply divided by violent conflicts, establishing an institution that claims a monopoly of legitimate force (Weber's celebrated definition of the state) represents an important step forward, but the state still remains contradictory in character. It claims something that it cannot possibly possess, and it is not simply 'failed states' in the post-war period that have not been able to successfully implement a monopoly of legitimate force. The gulf between ideals and reality is built into the state itself.

Gray notes the failure of non-statist sanctions to function in highly divided societies like the USA, but it is precisely these social sanctions that can make the violence of the state redundant. Gray eloquently defends the importance of diversity without seeing that it is precisely the state that seeks to impose monolithic and hierarchical identities upon people, while the notion of democracy can only be meaningfully presented as a post-statist development. People can govern their own lives only if there is no institution claiming a monopoly of legitimate force. The idea of the withering away of the state is dismissed by Gray as fanciful and (in the traditional sense) utopian, and yet the notion becomes realistic if we make a distinction between the state and government. The latter constitutes ordering mechanisms based upon social sanctions; government rests upon constraint but not force. As long as the state (like the market) is taken for granted, then not only will our analysis be bedevilled by dualism, but ideals will be projected in traditional utopian terms.

In the eighth chapter, I examine the problem of universalism in Gray's thought. Gray is anxious to avoid relativism and nihilism – the idea that everything depends upon the view of individuals at a particular time and place. A relativist would have to concede that the destruction of Jews, for example, is perfectly valid from a Nazi point of view, while a nihilist would deny that anything really matters. Gray argues that on the contrary there are generic human evils – such as torture and avoidable ill-health – and it is because there are universal values, he insists, that diversity and pluralism are not relativist notions. But this universalism is, he says, a 'minimal' universalism. There are many moralities – there is no morality – just as there are humans, but no humanity. Values are 'incommensurable' even though universal evils do exist.

Gray's argument hinges upon a mechanistic distinction between the universal and the particular. He fails to see that what makes pluralism intelligible is the monism that links different things together: the point about universal evils is that they prevent humans from developing. It is true that development differs according to history and culture, but it still represents a universal value even though this universal value can only express itself in diverse and particularistic forms. Gray, it seems to me, treats the notion of peace and peaceful coexistence as an overriding value. Clearly development, in the sense I mean it, involves the acquisition of attributes that facilitate self-government, and requires peace for its generation.

Gray's notion of a *modus vivendi* between different peoples is an attractive one, but it is torpedoed by his uncritical view of the state and market, and the dualistic understanding of sameness and difference, the universal and the particular, that flows from this uncritical position. It is hardly surprising that Gray is so pessimistic about future developments since he assumes that violence, war, destructive competition and crippling scarcities will remain intact – this despite the fact that all these are generic evils that undermine his *modus vivendi*.

In my ninth chapter, I deal with the question of globalization. I agree with Gray that globalization involves a transformation of the world that is genuinely new. Moreover, Gray is right to be highly critical of the neo-liberal version of globalization and to see it as a thinly disguised version of American hegemony. What Gray calls hyper-globalization, I prefer to label pseudo-globalization, on the grounds that meaningful globalization furthers diversity, global justice and a more democratic distribution of resources. Neo-liberalism promotes in practice rivalries, inequality and fundamentalism. I draw upon Stiglitz's *Globalization and its Discontents* to demonstrate the woeful impact that the International Monetary Fund (IMF) had on post-communist Russia. While Stiglitz is also critical of neo-liberalism, he avoids (rightly in my view) Gray's pessimistic view that globalization itself is responsible for inequality and fundamentalism.

The challenge is to reform the World Bank and the IMF, so that we can move towards a system of global government or governance. Such a government must strengthen common interests between countries, making it possible for global regulations on the economy and the environment to be effective. Gray is sceptical that universal solutions can be forged for global problems. He overlooks the potential that globalization, positively defined, has for developing peace, unity and justice – indeed, the very diversity that lies at the heart of Gray's own *modus vivendi*.

In Chapter 10 I examine Gray's treatment of egalitarianism and multiculturalism. He argues that social democracy (like neo-liberalism) is no longer credible but his argument is not that social democrats have often taken a complacent view of the market and state. It is rather that social democrats are fixated by a monolithic and abstract view of equality. The challenge here is not to abandon the notion of equality (as Gray does) but to reconstruct it so that it is linked to development and is an historically informed and context-sensitive concept. Gray's argument is that equalities (like freedoms) compete. Equality of opportunity may conflict with everyone having an equal amount of wealth, but surely this conflict can be resolved (although not without difficulty and error) by linking it to a notion of development. I accept that different ways of life should be respected, not simply because they exist, but because they are accepted by their practitioners. Where 'differences' involve violence and coercion, then they should not be tolerated, since they involve the kind of evils that Gray rightly argues are universal in character. Gray is sceptical about multiculturalism, but what distinguishes genuine multiculturalism from what I call pseudo-multiculturalism is that the latter is purely relativistic, whereas the former links respect with non-violence, and thus insists that cultural practices must be compatible with democratic norms. Gray also rejects the universal importance of the notion of autonomy, but what makes autonomy a meaningful value is that an autonomous person chooses and accepts a value (that others might find repugnant) whereas, when violence or coercion are involved, a 'way of life' becomes problematic and intolerable.

In my eleventh chapter I seek to reconstruct the concept of utopia. A reconstructed concept of utopia must persuasively address the deficiencies of the traditional concept and, to do this, the notion of utopia must become what I call a momentum concept. Momentum concepts are those that develop infinitely – they are eternally progressive – and can never be realized. The idea builds upon an insight of Tocqueville when he noted how democracy transforms itself from a bourgeois into a socialist 'ideal'. The point about momentum concepts is that they are essentially historical. To regard utopia as a momentum concept is to see it as a state of affairs that develops from stage to stage. It is emphatically not an all-or-nothing ideal, but a change that points to a future in which people can increasingly govern their own lives. In no situation can one say that the utopia has been 'realized' since utopias are real changes that are partial and transitional.

For this reason, to identify a utopia with perfection – with an absence of tragedy or evil – is absurd since tragedies are the inevitable consequence of entering into relations independent of our will and, without the notion of evil, progress would be impossible. It is not credible to project a society without prejudice either, since conflict arises from difference, and differences cannot be perceived in a way that is wholly transparent and thus unprejudiced. Gray aspires to post-liberalism since he is fiercely critical of liberal absolutes – the belief in reason, universal freedom and the sharp gulf between humans and nature. But it is not a question of rejecting liberalism but building upon it. In my view, a meaningful post-liberalism eludes Gray because he accepts the institutions that lie at the heart of the liberal tradition – the market and the state – and therefore he cannot bring utopianism and realism together as a set of dialectically linked concepts.

In my conclusion, I note that Gray's analysis is stimulating and interesting, and he is surely right to emphasize the importance of diversity. However, his analysis can be consistently sustained only if he charts a way beyond the institutions that produce the series of dualisms that cripple Gray's argument.

1 • The Anti-Utopianism of John Gray

Introduction

There is an important thread of continuity that runs through John Gray's work, but there is also change. As Colls puts it, 'he has been remarkably loyal to his mentors' (1998: 61). Gray is a conservative academic who seeks to reformulate liberalism and who writes intelligently and cogently on political theory, although one of his critics refers to his 'authoritarian/conservative/realpolitik political analysis' (Barry, 2006: 259). He is sceptical about the narrowness of much academic political theory, and feels that crucial topics – of passionate interest to people in the real world (ethnicity and nationalism, for example) – are ignored by many theorists because these topics don't fit into prevailing liberal orthodoxy. He is hostile to 'isms' since they prevent political philosophers from making a hard-headed appraisal of reality.

In his early writing Gray is a Hayekian liberal, but he becomes increasingly critical of what he regards as free market fundamentalism, and embraces a kind of post-liberal conservatism. His initial admiration for Blair and New Labour rested on his view that Blair had broken with social democracy but more recently he has become absorbed with the environment. He is highly critical of New Labour's foreign policy and can be found reviewing knowledgeably a wide range of books in the *New Statesman* and the *New York Review of Books*.

In this chapter I shall attempt to summarize Gray's development, noting his arguments as dispassionately as I can.

His life and career

Gray was born in 1948 into the working class of Tyneside. This is a world that the market has utterly changed. His father was a shipyard joiner in South Shields, a town that earned its living by coal mining, shipbuilding and factory work. Gray is remembered by (Professor) Robert Colls as 'a brilliant boy living in a mixed area of town'. Gray told Colls that 'the world in which I grew up, which I found both claustrophobic and restrictive and attractive, has gone' (Colls, 1996: 69). This experience impressed upon him just how easy it is for a community to disappear. His family were relatively impoverished, and he went to a (working-class) grammar school where Colls (a year younger than Gray) remembers him as a prodigy, an astonishing intellectual (who disliked sport), 'a beautiful flower in a carboniferous place' (personal communication).

Colls recalls debating with Gray, who was a Buddhist at 14, on the question of God's existence. Colls narrowly won the debate, but Gray, ever the iconoclast and sceptic about majority decision-making, told Colls that he might have won the debate yet 'God still does not exist!' (ibid.). Gray was spotted by the senior history master, Charles Constable, and groomed for Oxbridge. Constable was a fierce realist who had been badly treated by the establishment and had, as Colls puts it, 'iron in his soul' (ibid.). In 1968, Gray went up with a scholarship to Oxford. As a student he was on the left, and his formidable grasp of Marxism (though I shall later query many of his specific judgements) has a former insider's 'feel' to it. At Oxford, he was, like so many, greatly influenced by Isaiah Berlin. Gray read Philosophy, Politics and Economics, completing his B.A., M.Phil. and D.Phil. He was a lecturer in political theory at the University of Essex before becoming fellow and tutor in politics at Jesus College in Oxford. He was visiting professor at Harvard between 1985 and 1986 and Stranahan Fellow at the Social Philosophy and Policy Center in Bowling Green State University from 1990 to 1994, and he has also held visiting professorships at Tulane and at Yale University in 1991 and 1994. He is currently Professor of European Thought at the London School of Economics.

From liberalism to post-liberalism

Gray saw working-class culture as supportive, on the one hand, and yet, on the other, as imposing an orthodoxy, 'which invaded personal privacy and distrusted difference'. Social networks were torn apart in the 1960s when bulldozing began (Colls, 1998: 70). Labour culture, Gray tells Colls, was oppositional – its terms were set by others (1996: 71). In the middle 1970s he came to the conclusion that the Labour Party (which he had supported) was incapable of facing up to new realities and 'it was time to change tack' (Colls, 1998:

59). New Right intellectuals were particularly attractive in the mid-1970s. They were rigorous, spoke a language of fundamentals, and saw themselves as revolutionaries (ibid.: 60). They were concerned with intellectual issues that made a practical political impact.

Initially, Gray is enthusiastic about Hayek and neo-liberalism. He argues that the creation of money should be privatized in order to stabilize monetary values, and he sees the market as the source of incentives, innovation and novelty. However, even though Gray speaks fulsomely about the free market and its spontaneity, what attracts him to Hayek is the fact, as he puts it, that Hayek has purged 'classical liberalism of its abstract individualism and uncritical rationalism' (1984: x). Hayek's defence of liberty reconciles the modern sense of individuality with the claims of tradition. Rational criticism comes to a stop when it reaches the tacit component of our practices (O'Sullivan, 2006: 288).

Gray is already suspicious of abstraction and a universal belief in free and equal individuals. He likes the fact that Hayek stresses the importance of the inarticulate, and Gray praises Hayek for synthesizing the concerns of conservative philosophy – that the human individual is a social achievement and that reason is no more than an element in the growth of culture – with the central concerns of classical liberalism (1984: 124, 130). Hayek's position, he will argue later, derives from some of the most profound insights of conservative philosophy, and Hayek puts them to work in an original and uncompromising fashion (1996a: 32).

In his book *Liberalism* (1986) Gray is hostile to Benthamite theory, arguing that Benthamite utilitarianism is committed to the constructivist fallacy – the idea that social institutions can be the object of successful rational redesign (a critique that Gray takes from Hayek). He also attacks John Stuart Mill's new liberalism, having defended Mill's *On Liberty* in his (later published) doctoral thesis. Both Bentham and J. S. Mill (he argues in 1986) broke with the liberal tradition (1986: 29–30), and he refers warmly to Burke as a figure with whom 'liberal values are preserved but liberal hopes chastened' (1986: x). Gray's liberalism already has a conservative hue. It has no truck with natural rights theory or abstract individualism, and is sympathetic to Hume and Smith rather than Locke or Rousseau. He sees Hayek, more than any other figure, as responsible for the revival of classical liberalism in the post-war period (ibid.: 39).

Gray will later argue that Hayek makes the mistake of assimilating freedom to other goods such as the rule of law and social stability (1989: 97). It is possible, he argues, as Singapore demonstrates, to have the rule of law and social stability in an authoritarian society. In 1989 Gray is still enthusiastic about free markets, but stresses a theme that will predominate in his later writings: the need to establish a civil society that enables persons and communities with different and incompatible values to coexist without destructive conflict (ibid.: 22). The scene is now set for developing a 'post-liberalism' that acknowledges that liberalism does not have the universal authority its admirers claim, even though he later insists that there can be no return to the conservative tradition (1996a: ix). The New Right, he complains, subscribes to the 'unrealizable and dangerous utopian project of a minimal or neutral state enforcing a regime of common rules that is not underwritten by a fund of common culture' (1996a: 273).

Beyond conservatism

In *Beyond the New Right* Gray identifies with the conservative truth that humans are imperfect and political projects ultimately vain (1993: xii). He is still in favour of private property and the market but now seeks to stress the importance of historical context and the need to respect diversity. In *Beyond the New Right* Gray does distance himself from those conservatives who seek to restore an organic national community (ibid.: 51) but two years later he takes the view that it is impossible to detach conservatism from the neo-liberal tradition (1995: viii). Neo-liberalism has destroyed conservatism as a viable political project. Tainted by an uncritical belief in free markets, which inevitably requires a strong state, Conservatives, he complains bitterly, have become Maoists of the Right, pursuing a managerialist cultural revolution that seeks to refashion the entire national life on the impoverished model of contract and market exchange (ibid.: 88). What initially appealed to him about the New Right – its apparently revolutionary character – now repels him.

The decline of the British Conservative Party is one of the unintended consequences of the neo-liberal project: a new class of Tory nomenclaturists has sprung up as the quango state has devastated local government, and a market corporatism has taken root (1997: 2–3). Gray refers to this process as 'market Bolshevism' (ibid.: 28). The attempt to 'Americanize' Britain has ignored the basic cultural differences between the two countries (ibid.: 7). He refers to neo-liberal policy from Thatcher to the present as one of 'neo-nationalization' with regard to intermediary institutions (ibid.: 27). The Conservatives have created a Leviathan 'with unfettered market institutions sheltered by the authoritarian apparatus of an unaccountable quasi-governmental apparatus' (ibid.: 104). New Right policies in New Zealand saw increased poverty, massive economic inequalities and the growth of an underclass. Gray also paints a dramatic picture of the 'socially destabilizing effects' of neo-liberal policies in Mexico (1998a: 42, 49).

One of Gray's doubts about the free market is its ability to tackle the problem of the environment. 'No market solution exists, as far as I know, for the greenhouse effect' (1993: 112). Global warming arises from billions of separate acts, each of which is individually innocuous or imperceptible. Market pricing of each of these acts will not prevent the totality of them generating this phenomenon (ibid.: 133). Environmentalism taught Gray to stress the limits of the humanly possible and to respect, in Burkean fashion, the importance of tradition and authority (Colls, 1998: 60), although it should be noted that one of his critics complains that Gray needs much more acquaintance with Green thinking (Barry, 2006: 248).

Social contract doctrines attribute to pre-social abstract individuals qualities that they could only acquire by living in society (1989: 36). To suppose that society could be created by agreement is to neglect the fact that agreement, like language, is a form of social life (1996b: 130). People live in communities, and it is crucial that we tolerate their own particular customs and values. A universal language is just an ideal, a creature of the human imagination, whereas the universal reality is that of the diversity of tongues (ibid.: 131).

We must live with conflict and violence, and attempts to deal with them through an unthinking application of liberal values can only make a bad situation worse. Gray remarks in an essay on Mill that, if there is such a thing as an experiment in living, it is collective and not individual; it is conducted by social groups held together by common traditions and practices and it is tried, not over a single generation, but across the generations (1989: 226). As he puts it crisply in 1993, one of the basic needs of human beings is membership of a community (1993: 122). Human individuals are artefacts of social life; in short, exfoliations of the common life itself (ibid.: 136). At times he appears to reject liberalism, and on other occasions to reformulate it. In 1989 he insists that no liberal can (without ceasing to be a liberal) accept that liberal practice embodies only one among 'many ranges of often conflicting and sometimes incommensurable varieties of human flourishing' (1989: 239). He insists that central liberal values like autonomy may be relevant only to our kind of society. But even in 1993 (as part of his disillusionment with the thinking of the New Right) when he tells us that he seeks to return to the 'homely truths of traditional conservatism' (1993: xv), he never repudiates liberal institutions. Traditional conservatism appeals to Gray because it stresses community, tradition and continuity with the past. Not surprisingly, therefore, Gray is not impressed by the publication of Rawls's *Theory of Justice,* seen by many as inaugurating the rebirth of classical political philosophy. Political philosophy may have been reborn in 1971, but it was a 'stillbirth' (1995: 2). But, critical as he is of Rawls, Dworkin and other 'new liberals' (as he calls them), his mission, nevertheless, is to reform rather than transcend liberalism.

The rejection of utopianism

Gray is strongly opposed to the Enlightenment and what he sees as its extension into Marxism. Gray had had personal experience of the corruption, waste and authoritarianism of Eastern Europe and takes the view that workers suffered the most in Communist Party states (Colls, 1998: 60). Both Marxism and the Enlightenment are examples of utopianism. The modern utopia, Gray argues, seeks to marginalize local identities and is the common patrimony of all political movements spawned by the Enlightenment, liberal as well as Marxist (1997: vi). The roots of Marxism are to be found in the Enlightenment, and it is not plausible to insist upon a sharp break between Marx and the Soviet experience. The introduction of war communism by Lenin embodied 'an authentic Marxian vision' (1998a: 134), and in their arrogant attitude towards nature, the Bolsheviks were faithful to Marx (ibid.: 149). Marx, he tells us, was inspired by a fusion of technological Gnosticism with Enlightenment humanism (2002: 138). Marxism is only a radical version of the Enlightenment belief in progress – itself a mutation of Christian hopes (ibid.: 7). Marxism is seen by Gray as promising the 'final perfection of mankind' and 'the end of history' (2004: 1). It is a commonplace, he argues, that Marxism is a secular version of a Christian view of history (ibid.: 27).

The 'West' has become an obsolescent and indeed a substantially contentless notion (1997: vi–vii). Gray's work of 1995 is revealingly entitled *Enlightenment's Wake,* and here he flays a 'shallow optimism' that ignores the entrenched character of evil and national and ethnic particularism (1995: 16–18). The biblical myth of the Fall is closer to the truth than this shallow optimism (2004: 6). Malthus rather than Marx is a much better guide to understanding conflict. The idea that we can abolish prejudice is futile and counter-productive, and it encourages extravagant notions like the setting up of a federal Europe or even worse, the idea that we can go beyond the nation-state. The market and liberal institutions such as the rule of law are important, but they must be judged in terms of the practical contribution they make to individual well being: they are not magic wands that can transform every possible situation.

Just as Gray is hostile to what he sees as the utopian character of the Enlightenment and Marxism, so he is highly critical of the notion of progress. He sees progress as an Enlightenment notion involving the idea of movement for movement's sake. He pithily describes belief in progress as the Prozac of the thinking classes (2004: 3). What fascinates him about Voltaire is that the latter exposes not only the contradictory character of the Enlightenment but its peculiarly problematic notion of progress (1998b: 13). The doctrines of the Enlightenment show a blithe disregard for cultural difference and diversity, and wrongly assume that there is a universal humanity that espouses liberal values. We live, as Gray puts it, in a post-Enlightenment age (1995: 100). The problem with the notion of equality is that it ignores diversity, and assumes that all fit one universal model.

Pluralism and incommensurability

What attracts Gray to the work of Isaiah Berlin is the latter's stress on pluralism and his acceptance of conflict and division. Indeed, Gray describes the idea of pluralism as one that is 'subversive of the dominant tradition in Western thought' (1989: 64). It is an illusion to imagine that we can eliminate tragedy and pain, and that all problems are amenable to a rational, universal solution. Indeed, where Berlin parts company with Karl Popper is in rejecting monism in methodology – the view that the subject matters of the natural and the social sciences can be approached in the same way (1996b: 12).

Berlin's famous distinction between negative and positive liberty recognizes the importance not only of diversity but of the fact that sensible policies require a mixture of logically incompatible concepts. Negative liberty for Berlin is not an 'absolute' value, so that trade-offs between liberty and other values are often legitimate and unavoidable (ibid.: 27). Berlin's position goes well beyond that of Rawls, who sees justice and rights simply as regulative principles. For Rawls's theory is a version of those traditional liberalisms that Berlin seeks to challenge: it presupposes that principles of right can be sealed off from conflicts within the good (ibid.: 146–7).

Gray's point is this. People choose, but they need not choose liberalism: it is not irrational that some people are not liberals. Gray is fond of Raz's comment that incommensurability is the only ultimate or absolute truth. Incommensurability marks the inability of reason to guide our action (ibid.: 52). The problem with Berlin, as far as Gray is concerned, is that he does not go far enough. It is not, as Berlin supposes, choice-making that is central to human nature, but simply variability and propensity to cultural difference – very different things (ibid.: 25). Although Berlin's liberalism is agonistic (a liberalism that admits competition and conflict), it still makes universalist claims – a position in tension with his own insistence on valuing pluralism (ibid.: 2). Conflict and rivalry enter into the ideal of liberty itself, as our liberties disclose themselves to be 'rivalrous and incommensurable values' between which we must choose, without the benefit of any overarching rational standard (ibid.: 25). Logically, liberalism should not be able to claim any universal authority, but Berlin shrinks from this conclusion by postulating choice-making as a universal human propensity (ibid.: 120). Indeed, Katznelson even argues that Berlin's pluralism, *contra* Gray, rests, albeit sceptically, on Enlightenment foundations (1994: 618).

Admitting incommensurate values does not mean that we have to tolerate logical contradictions. We need merely to be pragmatic, rejecting the abstract rationalist insistence that everything is either true or false. Gray is in favour of what he calls 'irrealism' – the idea that we can identify errors without there being a single reality that our ethical beliefs track (2000: 62). He defends what he calls an 'objective pluralism' – a belief that ultimate values are knowable. But these values are multiple, often in conflict and uncombinable, and there is no overarching standard in terms of which conflicts can be rationally arbitrated (1996a: 291). Gray is generally critical of Aristotle, and his vigorous rejection of Aristotelianism arises because the thought that there may be many incommensurable forms of human flourishing is alien to Aristotle's outlook (1989: 260). Gray does not deny that a 'minimal' universalism exists – but this is to do with a rejection of violence and disease, a fear of death and destruction. We all seek security from violent death or from starvation (1998a: 110), but the point is that we do so in different ways. This universalism does not involve the embrace of liberal values, however self-evidently desirable these may seem to be in the West. We have a common human nature: however, this does not involve doing everything in the same way. Universal evils do exist. They are much the same for human beings whatever their ethical beliefs – genocide, persecution, avoidable ill-health, poverty – but these universal evils do not create the basis for a universal morality. Universal values are compatible with many moralities (2000: 66–7). Because they are practised by human beings all ways of life have some interests in common (ibid.: 136). These commonalities are all the more effectively recognized if they are not forced into some kind of Procrustean universal morality. Indeed, if Berlin has a weakness, it is that he mistakenly privileges his particular version of liberalism, whereas Gray's argument is that, if we are wedded to respecting diversity, then we must deny that even liberalism, in whatever form, has a claim to our allegiance (1995: 2). The point is that value pluralism is true all the way down (1996b: 168). Gray is not (in the last analysis) opposed to liberalism, but he argues that liberalism can be renewed only if it embraces diversity and accepts the fact that ideals of life in different cultures cannot be fused into one all-encompassing human good (2000: 39)

The problem of fundamentalism

Gray is acutely aware that the attack on the Enlightenment and liberalism may promote fundamentalist and pre-modern thinking. He is not so much – although he does not really develop this distinction – anti-Enlightenment as he is post-Enlightenment. He argues that the historical theodicies of the political religions, such as Marxism, have been supplanted by resurgent fundamentalisms as threats both to individual liberty and minimal human decency

(1996a: 166). If the 'dreary modern utopia' has been brought about by the self-undermining Enlightenment project, fundamentalism seeks to re-enchant the world (1997: vii). Gray characterizes the ruling view of the age 'as a sort of scientific fundamentalism allied with liberal humanism' (1993: 128). The danger with an abstract liberalism is that it creates a cultural void that fundamentalism can easily fill. Fundamentalism and nihilism are conjoined: the former is a dialectical negation of the latter (ibid.: 176). The New Right has everywhere tended to cultural and familial fundamentalism (1997: vii). Gray is surely correct to insist that in the United States, as elsewhere, fundamentalism is not a return to tradition, but an 'exacerbation of modernity' (1998a: 106).

Gray defines al-Qaeda rather crisply, as a post-modern organization serving pre-modern values (2002: 176), and he argues that its closest precursors are the revolutionary anarchists of late nineteenth-century Europe (2003: 2; 2007: 70). 'Modern western influences are fused with Islamic themes' (ibid.: 79). Fundamentalism is like totalitarianism, and it can be said that both follow the goal of a world without conflict or power (ibid.: 9). In rejecting what he calls 'the free market utopia' of Hayek and Friedman, Gray argues that the free market seems able to achieve what socialism was never able to accomplish – the euthanasia of bourgeois life (1998a: 72). In contrast to his position in 1993, Gray sees British Toryism as a 'cultural kitsch' (1997: vii–viii) – a nostalgic yearning for a mythological golden age.

An enduring understanding of human needs has passed to Green theory and New Labour, while post-modernists (for all their stress on diversity and difference) are trapped by the illusions of the modern age. Post-modernism is simply humanism in a 'late and radical form' (1995: 159). It is not a genuine effort to grasp the post-modern condition in which some cultures find themselves, but is a 'dying echo of the ruling projects and illusions of the modern age' (1997: x). Indeed, in his *Straw Dogs*, Gray defines post-modernism as just the latest fad in anthropocentrism, i.e. human arrogance (2002: 55).

Liberalism in its American version has become a cultural fundamentalism. It is a crankish and sectarian species of Enlightenment ideology (1998a: 104). But traditional social democracy does not offer a solution to our problems since it fails to see that there is a clash not only between countries, but within policies themselves between desirable goals – for example, between equality of opportunity and social mobility (1997: 18). The market remains necessary, but so does human security, and we must accept that a compromise between the two has to be reached. Politics is the negotiation of unavoidable conflicts (ibid.: 21), a messy process involving compromise and a smudging of ideals.

A good example of this can be seen in the fact that protecting people from racist abuse entails curbing freedom of speech. The two freedoms are logically incompatible (2000: 79) and, rather than insist upon one or the other, we need to accept the need for both. In the same spirit of compromise, Gray favours communitarianism, but a communitarianism based on shared understandings of communal life (not upon universal principles). The objective of such a communitarianism: raising the competence of individuals and their capacity to participate in the community.

Fundamentalism ignores these complexities. It either worships or rejects the state, whereas in fact we require a state that is conscious of its limitations. We are part of nature and the danger with emancipatory projects is that this linkage is forgotten. Humanism, says Gray in a particularly memorable sentence, can be easily equated with human imperialism (1997: 174). Low-impact technologies follow a respectful agenda: we must abandon fundamentalist beliefs in progress – an arrogant and abstract idea that is brought down to earth with Kraus's sobering dictum that 'progress makes purses out of human skin' (Gray, 1997: 161).

The position of rights

In a world of diversity, we need a *modus vivendi* that respects differences. Common institutions rather than common values are crucial (Gray, 2000: 6). When different ways of life cease to be antagonists and simply become alternatives, this *modus vivendi* arises as a political ideal (ibid.: 68). It is true that we can be at odds only if we have something in common but, when universal values collide, there are no universal principles for settling conflicts. Gray does not doubt the existence of universal human rights, but these cannot be realized within a universal regime (ibid.: 21). Human rights simply embody minimum standards of legitimacy: instead of searching for (and imposing) some kind of universal theory of political legitimacy (ibid.: 106), we should confine the role of human rights to protecting individuals against universal evils (ibid.: 110). We need a more modest view of democracy, a kind of neo-Hobbesian liberalism. Democratic government ought to be seen as an expedient to enable divergent communities to reach common decisions without violence (ibid.: 105). One of the reasons why Gray favours the state – its withering away being simply a utopian vision – is that the sad truth is that justice and rights can be upheld, in the last resort, only by force. This is a truth that recent liberal philosophy with its illusion of a universalist morality has found it convenient to forget (ibid.: 132). The problem is not that we have a state, but rather that in the last decade of the twentieth century, in many parts of the world, the state's monopoly of violence broke down (2003: 72). We should stop demonizing the state (2004: 114). In fact, we are beginning a new era of state sovereignty (ibid.: 164).

The appeal to abstract rights becomes a substitute for taking meaningful action to defend real interests. The question of rights cannot be insulated from the content of human well being and the relative place of different human interests (1995: 72). Disputes over rights are in fact disputes over human interests. The problem with Mill's argument that intervention can only be based on harm is that what constitutes harm depends upon a person's concept of the good (2000: 87). Rights should not be seen as theorems that fall out of theories of law and ethics. They are judgements about human interests whose content shifts over time as threats to human interests change (ibid.: 113). The grim truth is that the culture of unconditional rights can only speed the United States towards ungovernability (1998a: 109). Here there has been what Gray calls 'a ruinous inflation of the rhetoric of rights', a virus that prevents compromise, bargaining and the political arts from being brought into play (1996a: 14–15). Indeed, Gray even refers to 'a sort of chronic, low-intensity civil war' in the US (ibid.: 238) reflected by this rights discourse.

This is why Gray is so critical of Rawls: the central institution of his 'political liberalism' is not a parliament, but a court of law. Legalism has proved powerless to prevent the erosion of the rule of law that has occurred in a contemporary USA captured by fundamentalism (2007: 169). Rawls's self-description of his doctrine as political is supremely ironic, since his doctrine is a species of antipolitical legalism (2000: 16). It appeals not to compromise, but to rights, and without the content that can be given only by a concept of the good the notion of right is empty (ibid.: 19).

The ecological challenge

In 1993 Gray argues that concern for the environment is quite compatible with traditional conservatism (1993: 124). He speaks enthusiastically of Lovelock's concept of Gaia, a counterweight to the dominant humanist heresies of modernism (ibid.: 139). *Straw Dogs* (2002) is devoted to linking Gray's strictures on humanism and the Enlightenment with the problem of human relations to the environment. The earth is much older and stronger than humans will ever be (2004: 37). Humans are often besotted with an arrogance that ignores the needs of other animals, and ignores their own natural needs as well. The fact is that science enables people to satisfy, but not change, their needs. These needs are no different today from how they have always been (2002: 155). Gray is not opposed to science and technology, but he argues that they should be used to seek peace and uphold freedom – without believing that these things can be attained permanently (ibid.: 194). Here Gray reiterates his view that 'humanity' does not exist. There are only humans, driven by conflicting needs and illusions, and humanism is a religious type of doctrine promising the salvation of humankind (ibid.: 16). Gray acknowledges his indebtedness to Lovelock's ecological critique of modernity, and breaks still further from ethical liberalism by arguing that freedom of will is itself an illusion. It is myth to think that we are authors of our lives, since nearly everything that is important in our lives is unchosen (ibid.: 109–10). The notion of free will, Gray argues, comes from religion, not science (2004: 109). For Socrates, Aristotle and Plato, Descartes, Spinoza and Marx, consciousness is our very essence and the good life means living as a fully autonomous individual (2002: 111). However, humans may think that they are free, conscious beings, but in truth they are deluded animals (ibid.: 120).

Far from humans abolishing war, war will continue, and future wars will be fought over dwindling natural resources (ibid.: 180). Ethnic and religious differences will persist, and the scarcity of natural resources and the collision of rival values are permanent sources of division. Such conflicts cannot be overcome; only moderated.

The critique of modernity

We inhabit an historical context, Gray tells us, which is that of 'the no-man's land between the late modern age and early post-modernity'

(1995: 176–7). Although Gray is sceptical about post-modernism, he identifies modernity with the Enlightenment, Marxism and unregulated capitalism. He speaks of the 'sceptical dogmatism of the modern liberal mind' (1996a: 21). The flaw in the modern myth is that it tethers us to a hope in unity when we should be learning to live with conflict (2004: 103). Nevertheless, he sees himself as a modernist when all is said and done. There is much, he comments in 1993, that is amiss in modernism, and much to reject in modernism, but we can only hope to temper the modern age and its ills (1993: 126). He notes (but rejects) the modernist idea that each of us is here only once, as an embodiment of the 'one generational world view' (ibid.: 136).

Gray is scathing about what he sees as the hopelessly doctrinaire free market policies applied to post-communist Russia, and he presents a graphic picture of the social and economic collapse that took place in Russia in the 1990s (1998a: 150–1). He shows the uniqueness of Japan's path of modernity, and stresses the role of small-scale family enterprise in Chinese capitalism (1998b). He is fiercely critical of the 'criminally stupid' (2004: 157) war in Iraq, seeing it as the embodiment of all that is arrogant, foolish and abstract in a belief in universal models of democracy and progress. He is scathing about the 'war on terror' and vigorously condemns Blair's foreign policy. The Bush administration will go down in history as the gravedigger of the global free market (2004: 58). Its policies have discredited capitalism and unleashed fundamentalist forces at home and abroad. His most recent book is devoted to a fierce attack on what he sees as the neo-conservative utopianism that has led to the adventure in Iraq, with a 'willingness to use intolerable means to achieve impossible ends' showing 'the utopian mind at its most deluded' (2007: 160). He is scathing about the ignorance that led to the invasion, and about the torture, chauvinism and erosion of freedoms that the invasion has brought about.

Conclusion

Gray is initially impressed with Hayek and his version of liberalism. Gray admires Hayek's rejection of rationalism and abstract individualism, and his argument that the idea of planning rests upon a fallacious notion of a society that can be designed. Although Hayek insists that he is not a conservative, his work seeks to draw upon conservative notions of the individual and reason.

But Gray becomes increasingly critical of the New Right and Hayekian liberalism. The New Right presents the market in an abstract and ahistorical manner and Gray is drawn to the traditional conservative critique of liberalism. Neo-liberalism is a form of market fundamentalism and fails to take sufficient account of tradition and diversity. This is why Gray is critical of Rawls's work: Rawls presents a liberalism that is basically American in its inspiration despite its universalist pretensions. Indeed, so problematic is the New Right that Gray comes to the conclusion that it has even contaminated conservatism in general, and he argues that the British Conservative Party has been destroyed by Thatcherism.

The New Right draws upon the abstractions of the Enlightenment and presents a utopian vision that is shared ironically by Marxism. Both ignore the importance of culture and context, and present a vision of the future as salvation. Humanism may see itself as a secular doctrine but in fact it draws upon Christian notions of redemption. The notion of progress is a theme that unites humanists, Marxists and the neo-liberals. What is required is a pluralist approach that accepts liberalism as a doctrine relevant to many countries in the 'West', but that can claim no overall authority and superiority. It is simply one outlook among many. Crucial to Gray's argument is the notion of 'incommensurability'. Values are incommensurable – they cannot be meaningfully compared – so that, although there are undoubtedly universal evils, these are minimal in character. There are many moralities – there is no morality, just as there are many diverse humans, and there is no humanity.

Diversity and pluralism are denied by fundamentalists but one should not think of fundamentalism as simply Islamic or Christian in character. Secularists can also be fundamentalist and Gray is as comfortable with the notion of 'market fundamentalism' as he is with the idea of a religious fundamentalism of the kind that underpins the anarchist outlook of al-Qaeda. His opposition to universalism makes Gray sceptical about the notion of rights, which in the USA has led to courts being more important than the political process of compromise and negotiation, and he sees humanist hubris manifesting itself particularly with regard to nature. What makes Gray sympathetic to ecological arguments is his opposition to the arrogance that underpins anthropocentrism – the idea that humans are superior to animals and can treat nature wilfully and recklessly. Indeed, Gray comes increasingly to question the notion of choice and autonomy since these notions assume that human volition is unlimited and that free will exists.

The Iraq War is a supreme example of universalist arrogance – the attempt to impose upon other countries the values and institutions of the USA – an effort that tramples upon diversity and thoughtlessly exalts sameness. Gray's latest book (2007) is devoted to showing the utopian character of this war.

2 • The Traditional View of Utopia

Introduction

Gray's political theory hinges upon a negative view of utopia, and I want to argue that he wrongly identifies utopia with what I call the traditional view of utopia. The traditional view, for all its diversity, involves a vision of a static, perfect world, in which there is no further change. More's *Utopia* is a case in point. Not only is it authoritarian and depicts a society that is divided but it is static and frozen in time. More's society is without unfinished business. Plato's *Republic* is rather more conservative than More's *Utopia,* but rests upon a timeless notion of the Good. So does Bacon's *New Atlantis.* Utopias can be praised or condemned but, if they are premised upon static and perfectionist notions of the good society, then they are inherently problematic. Whether we approve or reject their static virtuosity, utopias are generally regarded as abstract ideals hanging lifelessly and impotently over the real world.

Attempting a definition

There is no doubt that utopia and utopian thought have taken a dramatic variety of forms. The number of utopias runs into many thousands. Goodwin and Taylor argue that the attempt to generalize amid such diversity produces somewhat platitudinous formulae that give no precise idea of the special nature of utopian theory. Of course, utopias can be opposed or supported, and those who oppose them often impute characteristics to utopias that distort the actual position of utopias (Goodwin and Taylor, 1982: 70, 92). But none of this avoids the problem that the traditional view of utopia is of a world that is timeless and perfect, a world without the kind of conflict that generates continuous change. I shall attempt to reconstruct the concept of utopia so that it embraces change, is rooted in the present and ceases to have the status of an ultimate society.

A terminological point: the concept of 'utopianism' is sometimes preferred to that of 'utopia' on the grounds that the latter embraces all forms of thought embracing a utopian element without purveying a 'utopian' blueprint (ibid.: 16). This distinction is not particularly helpful since it can be argued that 'utopianism' surely contains reference (however implicitly) to some kind of utopia. I shall use the term 'utopianism' simply to mean a belief in utopias.

The traditional presentation of utopia is of a world that is static and timeless. Hence utopias have often been located on islands or in distant lands and in dreams. A common formula involves a shipwreck or chance landing on the shores of what turns out to be an ideal commonwealth. The idea is to try and insulate the 'perfect' society from historical processes so as to allow the imagination free rein. Levitas refers to utopias as imaginary worlds freed from the difficulties that beset us in reality (1990: 1). Wells declared that he intended his to be not impossible, but 'distinctly impractical, by every scale that reaches only between today and tomorrow' (Kumar, 1991: 3). This is reminiscent of Mucchieli's definition, that utopia evokes 'in the imagination an other or a nowhere where all obstacles are removed' (Manuel and Manuel, 1979: 12).

This problematic presentation has given rise to a problematic conception. Utopias have been traditionally presented, whether by those who applaud or deplore them, as visions of a static and perfect society. Sargisson quotes a number of writers who take this view. She cites the words of Davis, who sees utopia as a society without change: 'the dynamic utopia is a myth'; a vision that is incapable of further progress, so that, in the words of Goodwin, utopian states have 'a static quality, which detracts from their credibility' (Sargisson, 1996: 19). Utopia is defined as an elaborate version of the 'good life' 'in a perfect society which is viewed as an integral totality', so that utopianism and surrealism are seen as similar modes of thought (Goodwin and Taylor, 1982: 16–17). The traditionalist view takes it for granted that to pursue utopia is to pursue perfection. In a later chapter I will examine William Morris's attempt to present a Marxist utopia.

I offer three examples of traditional utopias that have been particularly influential in both formulating the traditional view and the critique of this view.

Plato's *Republic*

The Peloponnesian War (between Athens and Sparta) lasted until Plato was 23. Plato witnessed what he described as 'troublous times' (1955: 12), including the execution of his friend, Socrates. The *Republic* is 'a word picture of an ideal state' (ibid.: 232). Although Plato did not call this ideal state a *utopia,* his work greatly influenced More, and Plato sets out to achieve a perfect state.

In this perfect state, there are three distinctive class systems. There are the Guardians who are the rulers themselves; there are the Guardians that serve the rulers (some of whom may become rulers when older); and there are workers, who may be farmers, artisans or simply unskilled labourers. The rulers are famously philosophers who are deemed to be a kind of craftsperson (they can be men or women) who are public-spirited in temperament and skilled in government. They are absolute rulers who know what is best for society. Indeed, says Plato, without them, there is 'no other road to happiness, either for society or the individual' (ibid.: 233).

Philosophers, as Plato sees them, have the capacity to grasp 'eternal and immutable truth' (ibid.: 244), grasping things in their entirety. No state can find happiness unless the artist drawing it uses a divine pattern (ibid.: 263). The philosopher rulers are capable of pure thought, finding assumptions that are 'steps in the ascent to the universal, self-sufficient first principle' (ibid.: 277). Philosophers deal with Forms and, in his famous simile of the cave, Plato speaks of ordinary people as the prisoners of delusions. Philosophers are able to grasp pure numbers and pure figures that are perceptible to reason and thought but not visible to the eye (ibid.: 298). All this leads to what Plato calls the dialectic – the only activity whose method rests firmly on first principles (ibid.: 302). Opinion relates to the world of becoming, knowledge to the world of reality. This constitutes the 'perfect state' (ibid.: 312).

However, because society is composed of humans and is 'created', it must decay and, as it does so, war sets in, and private property and profit contaminate the purity of the rulers. What Plato calls 'timarchy' results, a military aristocracy that degenerates into oligarchy, rule by the wealthy. There is a transition from 'the ambitious, competitive type of man to the money loving business-man' (ibid.: 322). Democracy develops when the poor win, exile or kill their opponents (ibid.: 329) and, although democracy seems to be charming and relaxed, in fact it is a society in which insolence appears as good breeding, licence as liberty, extravagance as generosity and shamelessness as courage (ibid.: 333). In a democracy, says Plato, rulers behave like subjects and subjects like rulers. The father stands in awe of his son, there is no distinction between citizen, alien and foreigner, the teacher panders to pupils, the young argue with their elders and the 'extreme of popular liberty is reached' when slaves have the same liberty as their owners. In fact even Greek democrats took slavery for granted, so it can be said that Plato allows his distaste for the subversive logic of democracy to erase historical evidence. Not only do men and women have complete equality but the spirit of liberty permeates private life and in the end even the domestic animals are affected with anarchy (ibid.: 336)! The point is that 'excessive desire for liberty' leads inexorably to tyranny, the tyrant being furthest removed from true and proper pleasure, the philosopher king nearest to it (ibid.: 363).

Plato's *Republic*, though a conservative utopia, embodies traditionalist notions of perfectionism and purity – the aversion to property and privacy that characterizes traditional utopias. It is deeply and explicitly religious, identifying the good society with a divine pattern that embodies values that can never change.

More's *Utopia*

Thomas More drew in part upon Plato's *Republic* to depict a world in which medieval asceticism blended with astonishingly modern ideas about marriage and death. His *Utopia* provides a graphic picture of the misery resulting from the enclosure movement and speaks of the futility of punishing people for theft while leaving their poverty intact. The ideal society is a communist one: 'as long as you have private property, as long as cash is the measure of all things, it is not really possible for a nation to be governed justly or happily'. There are no lawyers, and among the Utopians everything is shared equally (1992: 13–15, 28).

This equality, however, is of a remorselessly abstract kind. All the cities are exactly alike and everyone puts on the same style of clothing. Throughout the whole island, everyone wears the same colour of cloak (ibid.: 33, 37, 40). It may be a communist world, but it is one in which the freedom of citizens rests upon colonialism, slavery and patriarchy. Where natives don't make use of their land, the

Utopians drive them out and claim the land for themselves. Women are subject to their husbands, children to their elders: husbands chastise their wives, and parents their children. Marketplaces may exist where people help themselves, but slaves do the slaughtering of domestic animals. These slaves are not only captives in war; they are also criminals. They work as a punishment, are dressed differently and have one ear slightly cropped. Slaves do all the heavy and dirty work in food preparation and the cooking is done by women alone (ibid.: 16–17, 41–3).

Equality is combined with due respect to seniority, and there is stern discipline. A person who leaves his district without permission is severely punished, and on a second offence is made a slave. There is a fierce and witty contempt for precious metals: all the humblest vessels – including chamber pots – are made of gold and silver. Gold and silver are used to make the fetters of runaway slaves, and iron is deemed far more valuable (ibid.: 45–8). Women (despite the somewhat menial role allocated for them) are encouraged to educate themselves; they can become priests, and both sexes have a healthy contempt for liberal abstractions such as 'men in general' (ibid.: 49). Religion is obligatory, 'serious and strict', 'almost stern and forbidding': there is a law against any person who thinks that the soul perishes with the body, although, on the other hand, assisted suicide is common (ibid.: 50, 74). When war takes place, women are allowed to accompany men on military service; we are told that members of a 'disgusting and vicious race' are employed as mercenaries. Although prospective partners to a marriage are to see each other naked, pre-marital intercourse is severely punished, and adulterers are punished with the strictest form of slavery. Slaves who rebel are instantly put to death.

Utopia is, More assures us, the only commonwealth worthy of the name: where there is no private business, every man zealously pursues the public business; with the disappearance of money comes the disappearance of anxiety and greed (ibid.: 82–3). More's *Utopia* is often cited as the paradigm case of a static and perfectionist utopia, and indeed Jerome Busleiden told More that he had drawn a portrait of a 'perfect state', one that devoted its energies less to setting up perfect laws than to putting the very best men in charge of them (ibid.: 116).

But it is sometimes said that *Utopia* is not a utopia, that his work is part of a critical debate and it is open-ended (Sargisson, 1996: 25).

It is certainly true that More describes 'utopia' as the best state of a commonwealth, and it is not clear that he regards it as perfect (despite what Busleiden says) although he would like to see many of its features 'in our own societies'. He ends his book saying that 'there are many things I wish our country would imitate – though I don't really expect it will' (1992: 85). It could be argued that More's *Utopia* derives from 'outopia' meaning 'nowhere' rather than 'eutopia' meaning the 'good place'.

Nevertheless, not only is More's Utopia militantly anti-liberal, 'subduing', as Elton puts it, 'the individual to the common purpose and setting each man's life in predetermined, unalterable grooves' (ibid.: 199), it is certainly static. The Utopians, More tells us, have made their community capable of lasting forever (ibid.: 84), and it is difficult to disagree with Frye when he argues that More's Utopia is a final or definitive social ideal, a static society (ibid.: 210).

Bacon's *New Atlantis*

New Atlantis (Bacon, 1974) was written in English in 1624 and continues in the same vein as More's *Utopia*. Yet, where More emphasized the importance of religion, Bacon emphasized that of science – its power over nature that government can use for the improvement of humanity. *New Atlantis* centres on the Bensalemites who convert to Christianity, a conversion brought about by the House of Solomon. Christianity gives a moral underpinning to science, which searches for causes and thereby enlarges human empire.

The role of the House of Solomon, the 'very eye of the kingdom', is to maintain order and harmony: to keep people happy through meeting their needs. *New Atlantis* demonstrates the greatness of human ingenuity and the way in which science can tackle human want. Although Bacon builds upon the tradition begun by Plato, H. G. Wells referred to *New Atlantis* as the first of the modern utopias and 'the greatest of the scientific utopias' (Kumar, 1987: 30). Indeed, Plato had already referred to Atlantis, although the connection between Bacon's work and Atlantis itself is somewhat tenuous. Atlantis was a mysterious city about which many utopians wrote – the perfect society, the Paradise Lost that humanity must regain.

A ship lands, and the sailors are welcomed into the city, where they are lodged in spacious chambers, and those who are sick are particularly well housed. Six people attend to them – food and drink is provided and medication for the ill. The visitors are then tenderly addressed by the warden of the House for Strangers, who tells them of how the city converted to Christianity and how the laws of nature are God's own laws. The visitors venture out and are well received. They find that Jews are treated with respect and prostitution does not exist. The visitors meet one of the fathers of the House of Solomon – a great honour – who informs them about the great scientific advances they have made – in astronomy, horticulture, mining, animal husbandry, food production, medicine, printing, microscopes, music etc. There are even aeroplanes and submarines. The inhabitants maintain contact with other countries. (The text of the *New Atlantis* can be found on the internet.)

Utopia and the problem of stasis

Does a utopia have to be static? It is true that from the sixteenth century in Europe utopia designated a society on earth and not some otherworldly paradise, but utopia is still a world that is ideal and perfect. As Manuel and Manuel have pointed out, there is growing concern with the 'mode of access', of reaching utopia. This raises prickly questions of revolution, violence, determinism and free will. But utopia itself remains a 'perfectly reconstructed society' (1979: 5). It is hardly surprising that, if utopia is defined in this way, it lacks credibility and is an easy target for scepticism. It may be thought to have moral worth, but such a proposition places morality outside of the historical process, and in my view diminishes it. Goodwin and Taylor argue that utopianism tries to free itself 'from many of the compromises often associated with political power and its exercise' and that, in utopias, people achieve complete happiness and fulfilment (Goodwin and Taylor, 1982: 9, 138). A complete absence of politics and power sounds thoroughly implausible, and the notion of 'complete happiness and fulfilment' makes it appear as if further change and progress is impossible. What stands out, Manuel and Manuel note, in both monastic rule and utopia is 'their changeless character' (1979: 50). Tillich in arguing for a religious socialism identifies the religious principle as representing 'an ultimate concern', the unconditional (Marsden, 1991: 110). But this is to place religious (and utopian) inspiration outside of history.

The question that arises then is this. Can the concept of utopia be reconstructed so that it avoids the static and perfectionist bias that afflicts traditional ideas of utopia? Geoghegan declares himself 'in praise of utopianism'. He is only too conscious of traditional objections: utopianism is frequently characterized as the defence of an activity that is 'unrealistic', 'irrational', 'naïve', 'self-indulgent', 'unscientific', 'escapist' and 'elitist'. Geoghegan premises his praise on support for an 'ought' that is in opposition to an 'is' (1987: 1–2). But does this mean that utopias can never be realized?

Here we need to make a distinction between utopia as an abstract blueprint and utopia as a critique of the present that arises from existing realities. The abstract blueprint is problematic – for, although it is critical of the present world, it suggests that an imaginative leap must occur. The utopia is an island – it is 'no place'. It is a kind of heaven on earth so that like Bacon's *New Atlantis* it has a theological finality about it. Winstanley asked: 'why may we not have our Heaven here (that is, a comfortable livelihood in the Earth) and Heaven hereafter too?' (Goodwin and Taylor, 1982: 144). Andreae actually called his utopia Christianopolis, an idealized Christian commonwealth, and it is interesting that, in Bellamy's utopia, religious faith still continues, with a preacher saying that, for the first time, humanity has 'entered on the realization of God's ideal of it' (1967: 205).

Marsden, who seeks to bring Marxian and Christian utopianism together, sees modern utopianism as 'a secularized form of millenarianism' (1991: 12). Indeed, Manuel and Manuel refer to utopia 'as a hybrid plant, born of the crossing of a paradisiacal, otherworldly belief of Judeo-Christian religion with a Hellenic myth of an ideal city on earth' (1979: 15). They argue that, although utopia proper is a creation of the world of the Renaissance and the Reformation, the vision of the two paradises (Eden and the World to come), of the Messiah and the millennium, have made a huge impact on utopian thought (ibid.: 33). They describe utopia as 'a man-made paradise on earth, a usurpation of His [i.e. God's] omnipotence' (ibid.: 112).

It is not clear from Geoghegan's argument whether utopianism is an 'ought' permanently at war with an 'is', or, as he puts it, the problem lies with the critics of utopianism, who are guilty of a 'sad dualism': unreality, error and subjectivity on the one side; realism, truth and objectivity on the other (1987: 22). The latter option is far more fruitful because it suggests that the very notion that an 'is' and an 'ought' are at loggerheads is problematic. The key to a new and sustainable view of utopianism involves overcoming this dualism so that critical thought is both realist and utopian at the same time. A reconstructed notion of utopia seeks to improve society without taking the view that perfection is possible or desirable. Perry Anderson comments that utopianism typically involves 'overshooting the limits of the realizable' (1980: 175) but, if this is so, then utopias are always and necessarily problematic.

Utopia and perfection

Bauman argues that we should view utopias positively – as a necessary condition of historical change (1976: 13). But is it possible for a utopia to avoid the charge that it is inherently unrealistic? Bauman insists that a utopia 'sets the stage for a genuinely realistic politics'. It extends the meaning of realism to encompass the full range of possible options (ibid.). Utopias make conscious the major divisions of interest within society: the future is portrayed as a set of competing projects (ibid.: 15).

Goodwin argues that many utopians are 'perfectibilists' – that is, 'thinkers who believe that human nature is not immitigably bad, or marred by original sin' but is 'capable of improvement, and even perfection' (1987: 534). Bauman draws a distinction between perfection as a stable and immutable state, and perfectibility that, he argues, paves the way for utopia. The latter concept, in his view, stresses movement rather than end point and 'sets no limits to development, refusing even to discuss its supposedly final frontiers' (1976: 19).

The problem is, however, that perfection as a concept remains. To say that humans are 'perfectible' does imply that they can, not merely improve, but become perfect – like gods. Godwin commented that humans are perfectible, 'in other words, susceptible of perpetual improvement' (Marshall, 1993: 202) but does this mean that the perpetual improvement is leading to an ideal end? Perfection, whatever form it takes, is a theological concept that inevitably contrasts utopia and reality. It is impossible to disagree with Gray when he says that the concept of a perfect person, like that of a perfect society, is incoherent (1989: 47–8). The concept of pluralism destroys the very notion of perfection (1996a: 291). The incoherence of the concept of perfection arises out of the problem of its emergence: if it has a beginning, it must have an end, in which case it can hardly be perfect.

Gray's problem, as we shall see, is that, although he embraces what he calls the lesson of imperfectability (1993: xi, 47), he does not go beyond institutions such as the market and state that enshrine (as we shall see) perfectionist abstractions in their very being. Because, Gray argues (in his pro-conservative phase), conservatives reject the evanescence of imperfectibility, they also reject the Procrustean politics of the utopian blueprint (ibid.: 48). The idea that all institutions are imperfectible is itself 'an exceedingly ancient truth' (ibid.: 119). But that does not preclude injecting into the notion of imperfectability a subversive and new meaning so that the notion challenges the existence of market and state. It is true that the idea of a perfect society has been linked to traditional views of utopia (1996a: 1), but the challenge is to reconstruct the notion of utopia so that we can dispense with the undialectical and incoherent notion of perfection.

The question of reality

Bauman argues that utopias are little concerned with 'pragmatically conceived realism' and they do not seem logical and immediate steps from what is in existence at present (1976: 13). This surely implies that a utopian critique does not work through the present, but somehow stands outside it. As Mannheim put it, utopia is an idea that is 'situation transcending' or 'incongruent with reality': it 'breaks the bonds of the existing order' (1960: 173). This suggests that utopias stand outside reality, with the term 'transcendence' implying not just a going beyond but a mysterious leap. This is precisely the archaic formulation that stands in need of reconstruction. Mannheim argues in a famous passage that, without a utopia, humans would become mere things, mere machines without will and an ability to change history (ibid.: 236). But the problem here is that he identifies utopia with reality-transcending perspectives as though to be a utopian is to reject science and 'matter of factness' (ibid.: 236). Mannheim sees a positive role for utopia, but he depicts it in traditional terms.

Goodwin and Taylor speak of the fact that utopias 'transcend the ubiquitous, seemingly unassailable present'. 'They help us to escape from the existent.' 'They involve an instant or immanent transition from the present system: a break with history.' But, although Goodwin and Taylor defend utopias, their argument reproduces rather than transcends the opposition between 'is' and 'ought'. While they see utopianism in political theory as a 'dynamic force', they regard it as haunted by the problem of the leap from theory to practice (Goodwin and Taylor, 1982: 9, 31, 26, 55).

It is one thing to argue that there is a necessary tension between ideas and reality – ideas are abstractions, and therefore they necessarily simplify the complexities of the real world. It is quite another to see an unbridgeable gulf between ideals and reality, so that utopias are abstract in a pejorative sense: they are necessarily unrealistic, unhistorical, static, perfectionist etc. Gray, as noted above, adopts this traditional view of utopia. He describes Marxism and neo-liberalism as utopian. His critique of neo-liberalism is persuasive (as far as it goes), but neo-liberalism is problematic not because it is utopian, but because it is a very abstract form of utopia. Unlike reforms, for example the abolition of slavery, utopian projects are those, in Gray's opinion, that cannot be realized in any circumstances (2007: 20).

Gray's view that utopias are necessarily unrealistic, unhistorical, static, perfectionist etc. shows that, as I shall argue, he succumbs to the very dualism upon which the traditional view rests. Instead of the abstract 'ought', he argues for the abstract 'is'. His rejection of utopianism arises from an uncritical attitude towards the institutions, the market and the state, that lie at the heart of liberalism.

Conclusion

It is true that the number of utopias that have been constructed goes into many thousands, but the traditionalist view of utopia, like traditionalist utopias themselves, depicts a static society that is perfect and timeless in character. In Plato's *Republic*, for example, the rulers are philosophers who demonstrate their superiority through their capacity to divine the Good and the True. More was impressed with Plato's utopia (where private property is abolished for the two classes of Guardians) and he, too, depicts a world in which private property has been banished. Although More argues for equality among the Utopians, in fact his society is patriarchal, rests upon slavery and war, and is repressively religious. It is also timeless and changeless in character.

It is not surprising that pre-modern utopias are explicitly and conventionally religious since they depict an otherworldly promised land that somehow exists on earth, but even modern secular utopias have an aversion to change and history. The idea of locating the utopia on a faraway island or in a dream stresses this fantastical aspect and utopias, in their traditional formulation, are deemed perfect societies. Even when they are described as 'perfectible', the static and ahistorical concept of perfection remains. To reconstruct the notion of utopia, this is the problem that needs to be tackled. How can we have a utopian concept that is dynamic and historical?

It is no use praising utopia for its purely ethical or normative character, because a meaningful notion of society has to be empirical and realistic as well. Whether the 'ought' is deplored or celebrated, the dualism between 'ought' and 'is' has to be overcome if the concept is to be reconstructed. Admirers of utopia also subscribe to traditional concepts if they see utopia as a world that is somehow outside of reality. Gray is right to challenge the notion of perfection and the traditional view of utopia but wrong to leave two of the main institutions intact (the state and the market) that generate these abstract and perfectionist notions. A utopia simply represents a critique of the status quo, and therefore a poor or flawed utopia is a critique that is itself unpersuasive.

3 • Utopia and Dualism

Introduction

In this chapter I seek to examine the conceptual problem that underpins the traditional concept of utopia and the relationship of this problem to the Enlightenment. Anatole France declared that 'out of generous dreams come beneficial realities. Utopia is the principle of progress, and the essay into a better future' (Levitas, 1990: 17). Gray's critique is consistent in that he rejects not only the traditional concept of utopia, but also the concept of progress. However, the problem that Gray fails to engage is whether progress is statically realized (and therefore contradicted) by utopia, or whether a concept of utopia can be formulated that is dynamic and historically informed. Gray condemns the Enlightenment, but the difficulty with his argument is that, while he is right to see the Enlightenment as deficient, he does not see that, as I shall argue, it must be built upon and not simply rejected.

The Enlightenment, although diverse, can be defined, and its unifying premises are the postulates of classical liberalism. Its premises are subversive but abstract, and it is because of its abstract character that the Enlightenment endorsed property, the market and patriarchy. Enlightenment thinkers perfected rather than looked beyond the state.

Defining the Enlightenment

The Enlightenment has a tremendous appeal since it embodies modernity against pre-modernity. The Enlightenment thinkers had a revolutionary view of nature and a thoroughly subversive view of people as individuals. All this, I want to argue, is positive, but the problem with the Enlightenment is that this revolutionary view of nature and subversive view of the individual involves an abstract humanism that has dualism at its heart.

It is true that there is much that appears attractive in pre-modern thinking in a world that has experienced the deficiencies of the liberal tradition. Indeed, Gray's hostility to the Enlightenment leads him to argue that pre-modern thinkers did not expect any secular transformation of human affairs, and in this they were closer to the truth than those who came after them (2006: 339). Pre-modern thinkers in ancient Greece saw history as cyclical whereas Christianity adopted a linear view of history, seeing historical movement as deriving from creation and fall through redemption to the Second Coming. It is true that pre-modern thinkers take a view of people as part of a wider community, of people always in relationships with one another. Pre-modernity argues that to exercise power is not to advance one's interests as an individual, but to work for the good of others.

However, the problem with this pre-modern view is that, while it presents a relational view of society, the relationships with others that it points to are unequal and enshrine a 'natural' domination of the many by the few. The community was deemed explicitly divisive and repressively hierarchical, and the community was embodied by a monarch whose right to rule came from on high. It is not surprising that ethical justifications for rule in pre-modernist thought appeared pompous and hypocritical to those of lowly status: if the individual was disdained, particular members of an elite were not. Indeed, it can be argued that pre-modernity scarcely had a concept of the individual at all, since people fulfilled particular roles that were incommensurate with one another, and therefore people took their place within a hierarchy that distinguished explicitly between ruler and ruled. But can we speak of the Enlightenment, given the fact that Porter has argued that the Enlightenment was 'necessarily rather amorphous and diverse' (2001: 9)? Lassman complains that Gray's notion of an Enlightenment project is polemical rather than historically or philosophically accurate (2006: 212). But the thinkers of the Enlightenment have, it seems to me, enough in common for the collective term to be meaningful. Hence, we are entitled to say that the Enlightenment sought to enshrine freedom and equality in the place of repressive hierarchy and particularistic difference. It identified humans as individuals who were everywhere the same in the sense that they were all rational and capable of self-government and enjoyed a 'natural' right to freedom.

The Enlightenment and liberalism

I see the Enlightenment as a movement that enshrined the principles of classical liberalism. In my view, despite his authoritarian proclivities, Hobbes should be seen as the founder of liberalism and a precursor of the Enlightenment (Gay, 1967: 17). In that sense Rousseau's critique of Hobbes in the *Social Contract* (1968a: 51), where Rousseau accuses Hobbes of treating humans as cattle, is unfair. It is true that Hobbes justifies the authoritarian activity of the state as a mortal god and argues that a commonwealth could be acquired through conquest. But the premises of Hobbes's system are impeccably liberal and (from a pre-modern point of view) dangerously subversive, for Hobbes argues that every person has a natural right to survive. Servants are not slaves: they have made a promise to obey their masters and therefore they have authorized rule over themselves through consent. Hobbes was a conservative politically, but he was no Aristotelian. Bees may be numbered amongst the political creatures, he argues, but people are not. Distinctions between master and servant are purely conventional, since there are few so foolish as would not rather govern themselves than be governed by others (1968: 225, 211). The point is that people are naturally free and equal, in stark contrast to the pre-modern view, expressed by Aristotle, that repressive hierarchy is natural so that by nature, people are divided into citizens and slaves (Hoffman, 1988: 150). Gray identifies Hobbes as the kind of liberal of whom he approves (2000: 25).

It often comes as a shock to undergraduate students to discover that Locke, a key founder of constitutional liberalism, justified slavery and had shares in a company that owned slaves (Gay, 1969: 410). How is it possible for a writer who champions freedom and equality to defend slavery? Locke argues that people who have lost their rights in a state of war can be generously treated as slaves rather than killed outright. Porter characterizes Locke as a Whig philosopher who was no democrat (2001: 27).

The problem of slavery is evident in the work of most liberals at least until the end of the eighteenth century. Rousseau in part 1 of the *Social Contract* explicitly denounces slavery. Yet later in the same work he appears to link slavery with citizenship, arguing with astonishing ambiguity that 'a citizen can only be perfectly free if a slave is absolutely slave' (1968a: 143). Even where the *philosophes* rejected slavery (as they generally did), they adopted racist attitudes, regarding blacks as inferior to whites (Gay, 1969: 416). They preferred secular rather than religious justifications for colonial expropriation (Outram, 1995: 72).

Religion, the market, patriarchy and property

It is true that Rousseau scandalized conservatives of his day by arguing that pre-Christians had sensibly linked their conception of God to the laws of the state. Christianity is condemned for the way it divides life into a kingdom of this world and a kingdom of the other world, and Hobbes is praised for 'uniting the two heads of the eagle' 'although he should have seen that the dominant spirit of Christianity was incompatible with his system' (1968a: 180). Rousseau is vehement in his condemnation of Christianity, stating that 'true Christians are born to be slaves; they know it and they hardly care; this short life has too little value in their eyes' (ibid.: 184). Nevertheless, he argues that the state should allow people to have any religion they please, provided they have one. For religion entrenches 'sentiments of sociability' and, Rousseau insists, 'no state has ever been founded without religion at its base'. Atheists should therefore be banished from society and hypocrites put to death (ibid.: 186). Rousseau argues for a civil religion – a religion that is tolerant of other religions but is a religion nevertheless.

What makes Rousseau a liberal in the last analysis, despite the charges of collectivism so often brought against him, is that he sees people as individuals whose nature inclines them to own property (1968b: 208). Once that point is grasped, then there ceases to be a problem about the ownership of people as property and the domination of women as the property of their husbands and fathers. For, once property is conceived of as an atomistic expression of abstract individuality (property as a commodity that is marketed and that gives power over others), then, conceptually at any rate, people can be treated as things.

The Enlightenment not only subscribed to a divided society but, despite attacks from the established church, saw humanity in a way that was at least implicitly religious in character. Gay describes the *philosophes* as 'modern, secular philosophers' (1967: 27), but it is not difficult to see that, while (some) liberals rejected conventional theology, there is an important sense in which the ownership of property as an individual expression of natural right rests upon assumptions about a Supreme Creator. Human nature is static because the individual is created. Most thinkers of the Enlightenment were deists rather than atheists (Porter, 2001: 31), and some members of the Enlightenment did not attack religion but preferred to argue for toleration (Outram, 1995: 36).

The link between liberalism and patriarchy and property is rooted in the premises that liberalism adopts. The very concept of the abstract individual presumes a rational male who dominates others. The link between domination, abstraction and possession is brilliantly demonstrated by Horkheimer and Adorno when they argue that 'everything is subsumed in the same matter' (1973: 10). What is generally true of 'Western' political thought is also true of the Enlightenment: it is patriarchal in the sense that it enshrines the domination of women by men – since patriarchy is encapsulated in all abstractly individualistic and atomistic theories (Mendus, 1987: 40).

The Enlightenment and feminism

It is revealing that Gray embraces the patriarchal custom of referring to 'man' when he means humankind; hence in *Straw Dogs,* he presents the bizarre view that 'man', like other animals, 'wants food and success and women' (2002: 28). This makes sense only if we assume that 'man' is a heterosexual male! Whatever his differences with the Enlightenment and liberalism, this kind of sentiment is fully in line with the traditions that Gray so sternly berates. Peter Gay stresses the ambivalent attitude of the Enlightenment towards women. The *philosophes* were, he says, 'feminists with misgivings' (1969: 33). Although opposed to 'male tyranny', they still saw women as everything men were not. Porter comments that the Enlightenment valued reason but helped to launch a cult of idealized motherhood, thus leaving 'an ambiguous legacy for women' (2001: 46). In fact, Rousseau's *Emile* is notoriously patriarchal: abuse, molestation and predatory activities are justified since women constitutionally are unable to speak the language of consent. In *Emile* Rousseau argues that the woman who is a victim of force must 'permit or arrange it'. In other words, women who are raped are asking for it. No 'real violence' is involved in 'that sweetest and freest of all acts' since while the mouth says no, the eyes, the colour, the breathing, the soft resistance – the language of nature – says otherwise. In the *Social Contract* Rousseau argues that wives who commit adultery are guilty of treason since marriage is deemed crucial for the state. Presumably, they should be put to death (Hoffman, 2001:105).

Helvetius takes it for granted, when he talks about the impact of education on 'everyone', that those who receive education are men (Gay, 1969: 514). Manuel and Manuel comment that, even in their most expansive moods, most *philosophes* regarded women as either frivolous or lesser human beings (1979: 619).

It is true that modern feminism springs from the Enlightenment assumption that all humans are free and equal individuals. But the relationship between liberalism and emancipatory theories like feminism has always been a problematic one. For, while it is true that liberalism rests upon premises that are subversive, these premises are also abstract, by which I mean that they are abstracted from concrete reality. Classical liberals excluded women from the suffrage, and women were seen to inhabit the private sector of a public/private divide. Hence the very construct of a liberal or Enlightenment feminism is debatable. It should also be noted that Kant (another great Enlightenment thinker) also adopted a derogatory view of women, and this is not some kind of personal quirk. It stems from his 'perfectionism', and support for the state and private property. Baumeister has sought to defend the relevance of Kantian views for feminism, arguing that Kant's concept of imperfect obligations captures the notion of context, situation and difference – concepts crucial to modern feminist argument (2000: 65). Yet 'imperfect' duties are contrasted with 'perfect' duties – abstractly conceived as 'universally' acceptable. Although Kant sought to establish a regulatory world of categories (which Kant believed was an answer to Hume's empiricism), his work is still dualistic. He accepts a Humean view of nature and experience, so it could be argued that Kant's categories are abstractions that hang lifelessly above the real world.

Wollstonecraft's *Vindication of the Rights of Women* is often described as a classic exposition of liberal feminism, but Wollstonecraft challenges the 'divine right' of husbands in the way that the liberals challenged the divine right of kings. She also contends that Rousseau's natural woman is as much an artificial construct as Hobbes's 'naturally' aggressive and competitive man. Women are deemed rational and autonomous beings and, when

Wollstonecraft takes the view that recognizing that fact would make women better wives, mothers and domestic workers, she adds significantly 'in a word better citizens'. There is no doubt that her rationalism has statist and abstract residues; she is reluctant to make the case for political rights for women and sees motherhood as a 'natural' feminine vocation. But the point is that, in so far as she advances the case for feminism, she is beginning to move beyond the positions of the Enlightenment.

The same is true with Mill's *Subjection of Women*. Mill is in many ways an unusual Enlightenment figure and Gray is highly critical of Mill's defence of progress. It is true that much of his (and Harriet Taylor's) text is almost painfully uncritical of women's traditional roles. He argues that women are most suitable for the position of domestic worker and child rearer, and his defence of female suffrage is linked to the contention that having the vote would assist wives in supervising domestic expenditure. But there is no doubt that his views on marriage and the family (which he argues should become a school for freedom) implicitly challenge Enlightenment notions of the public/private divide and the statist view of politics (Hoffman, 2001: 44–6).

In general, as Outram comments, the thinkers of the Enlightenment were unable to handle questions of difference – whether 'difference' related to non-European peoples, women or the poor (1995: 89, 122). Built into the entire tradition is a conflict between theory and practice. Because the universalism is abstract, it presupposes and necessarily engenders concrete hierarchies of a repressive kind – whether colonial, patriarchal, ethnic or other. Behind the abstract individualism of contract and property, for all their positive potential, lies the concrete misery of exploitation and inequality.

Rousseau might have denounced property as embodying alienation and division, but he felt that it was impossible to look beyond it. Gay is surely right to argue that, at the end of the day, the Enlightenment was bourgeois in character (1969: 4; Porter, 2001: 20). As Horkheimer and Adorno put it, 'The burgher, in the successive forms of slaveowner, free entrepreneur, and administrator, is the logical subject of the Enlightenment' (1973: 83).

The dualism of the Enlightenment can be seen vividly in relation to the state.

The Enlightenment and the state

Carter argues in her nuanced exposition of the Enlightenment's view on colonialism, citizenship and war that, in general, Enlightenment thinkers accepted 'the reality of the system of sovereign states'. It is true that she argues that their immediate goal was to create 'a cosmopolitan society which in crucial ways transcended state boundaries through learning and exchange of ideas, through acceptance of universal humanitarian values, and not least by the cosmopolitan and civilizing effects of commerce' (Carter, 2001: 48–9). But, alas, 'transcending state boundaries through learning' and civilized commerce is not the same as transcending the state. The state, as Outram makes clear, was taken for granted (1995: 112).

Hutchings has argued that Kant's notion of politics is based upon moral universality, and yet for Kant 'nature' dictates that we must be framed within a non-moral order, 'the juridical realm of the state' (1996: 16). With an uncritical view of empiricism comes an uncritical view of the state. For Kant, as with Locke and Pufendorf, the moral law is partially fulfilled through the positive law of a sovereign state (ibid.: 121). Modern Kantians, such as the international relations theorist Linklater, have sought to make the case for a cosmopolitan citizenship but, as Walker rightly notes, this is still trapped in what he calls 'the official discourse of states' (1999: 187).

The politics of the Enlightenment, as I have argued above, were the politics of liberalism. Gay is correct to note that the *philosophes* had a contemptuous view of the mass of the population (1969: 450, 520; Porter, 2001: 24). They invariably argued that religion was needed to secure deferential attitudes among the masses. Even though Gay argues (1969: 552) that Rousseau was not representative of the Enlightenment, his views on the state are the most challenging because the paradoxes and problems of the liberal tradition are sketched with memorable and startling explicitness. In my view, he is the most advanced thinker of the period.

Rousseau demonstrates with particular sharpness what is in fact the general problem of the state: the impossibility of combining legitimacy with force. Rousseau captures memorably the dilemma of the liberal tradition as a whole when he regards the use of force as inimical to freedom, on the one hand, and yet defends the necessity of the state. Rousseau describes force as a physical power – 'I do not see how its effects could produce morality' (1968a: 52) – and yet, of course, he argues famously that those who refuse to obey the general will shall be 'forced to be free' (ibid.: 64). As I have argued elsewhere, it does not get round the problem to contend (as Pateman does) that Rousseau simply means that people should be 'strengthened' to be free, since (as we have seen) Rousseau appears to argue that adulterous wives, like hypocritical unbelievers, are to be subject to capital punishment (Hoffman, 2001: 105). It is not that Rousseau's references to the need for force 'contradict the basic principles of his theory' (Pateman, 1985: 160): it is that the state itself (which he idealizes) is a contradictory and paradoxical institution.

As I shall argue in more detail later, the state poses an ideal of community that its concrete reality as a divisive institution, an institution that uses force to settle conflicts of interest, necessarily belies. The Enlightenment can be said to have perfected statism – as in the notion that we force ourselves to be free by obeying laws that we ourselves prescribe – but it is woefully unable to challenge it. Along with an uncritical attitude towards the state goes a whole series of dualisms that reflect a statist mode of thinking. The fact that the state asserts an ideal of community that it necessarily contradicts means that a dualism between theory and practice is built into its very constitution. So is the dualism between the abstract and the concrete, freedom and necessity, subject and object, the ideal and the real etc. The force of circumstance, Rousseau argues, tends always to destroy equality: the force of legislation always ought to preserve it (1968a: 97). No wonder the state is such a contradictory body, for it seeks to achieve what is impossible – harmony through division, freedom through force. I shall later argue that the state cannot be abolished, as conventional anarchists argue; it must gradually disappear as negotiation and common interest replace force and division.

There is no article on utopia in the *Encyclopédie* and Diderot, for example, frequently mocked utopianizing: yet it could be argued that not only did Enlightenment thinkers subscribe to utopias but, as their views on the state and property indicate, this utopianism was static and problematic. Gray's own uncritical view of the state means that, although he rejects what he sees as the perfectionism of utopia, his own position is thoroughly dualistic as a result. It is all very well to insist upon 'the imperfectability of all human things, and the ultimate vanity of all political projects', but this is not simply 'a conservative truth' (1993: xii). It is a radical stance as well, for anti-perfectionism can be sustained only if we challenge the market and state – the source, as we shall see, of perfectionist thinking.

Gray and Hume

Gray is enthusiastic about Hume, regarding him as the 'greatest representative of the Scottish Enlightenment' (1996a: 134) or, as he puts it a little earlier, the 'greatest conservative philosopher of all' (ibid.: 65). It is true that Gray is critical of Hume's universal view of human nature and his relative neglect of particularity and culture. Nevertheless, the traditional view of utopia, it will be argued, is linked to an acceptance of a 'Humean' dualism between 'is' and 'ought'.

Hume's argument is that our ideas derive from experience (with the exception of mathematical principles). This experience is seen as the passive contemplation of 'sense data' – and out of these contemplations emerge 'facts'. Values, on the other hand, are mere beliefs that derive from habit and tradition: there is no empirically based reason that transcends sense data and establishes the necessary connections between things. Abstract reasoning concerning quantity and number coexists with ideas derived from experience. Between the abstract and the concrete, there is an unbridgeable gulf. Gray, as we shall see, is a great admirer of Hume and inherits this dualistic outlook. Gray, as Kateb points out, is 'too impressed' by Hume's dissolution of the mind into 'successive perceptions', a scene of disconnected occurrences (2006: 316–17).

There *is* a distinction between facts and values but it is what I want to call a relational distinction. Facts refer to relationships that are not contested; values to relationships that are. In other words, the evaluative character of a factual statement arises from the relationship that it necessarily implies. To give an example of a contested fact that thereby becomes a value: the statement that people of low income participate in politics less frequently than those of higher income ceases to be a factual statement when it is contested. Critics point to its normative 'bias' since it suggests the kind of action (or non-action) that could be taken to improve the rate of participation. The distinction between facts and values is therefore relative: a statement can be factual or evaluative, depending upon whether it is contested.

Empiricists, on the other hand, see the distinction between facts and values as absolute, and not relative. They believe that facts can be sharply separated from values because they see facts as atomistic entities unrelated to each other and the world around. They express the distinction between facts and values in dualistic terms.

This dualism is linked to an uncritical view of the market and the state, and accounts for the idea that utopias are the inspiring 'ought' confronting the mundane world of the 'is'.

Values, Gray argues, are only human needs, or the needs of other animals, turned into abstractions. 'They have no reality in themselves' (2002: 196). But this is a curious comment. For if, as I have argued, human values express contested human relationships, then, however distorted, they identify some element of the real world.

The dualism between facts and values needs to be comprehensively challenged, and not simply inverted, if a critical and dynamic view of utopia is to be forged. It is no good merely objecting that alongside a conservative realism we need a utopian idealism, for this argument still preserves the dualism between the two. This, in a word, is the problem with Goodwin and Taylor's account. They argue that the study of utopia should be deemed part of political theory on the grounds that it is 'an orthodox empiricist and positivist view of political science' that rejects attention to the 'unverifiable and unreal'. They assume that the empiricist simply attends to the world of the 'is'. This, they contend, seems to be a peculiarly Anglo-American obsession since the French feel that it is perfectly acceptable to attend to 'speculative theory': a genre of thought not susceptible to 'simple truth-tests or empirical verification'. Value judgements must be made, and they rest upon perfectionist ideals. Such ideals enable us to evaluate imperfections by reference to notions such as perfect justice and ideal liberty (Goodwin and Taylor, 1982: 19, 20, 22, 99). All would-be predictive or progressive thinking must free itself in part from the present. This kind of critique merely inverts empiricism, it does not transcend it.

Gray himself rejects what he calls 'restrictivism' – the idea that it is possible to tackle the question of freedom, for example, in a non-evaluative fashion (1989: 64). There is no question that utopians employ a normative and rationalistic (in Gray's term, an anti-restrictivist) approach (Goodwin and Taylor, 1982: 22, 218), but the problem is this. Does a normative and rationalist approach have to be abstract in character? Does it have to abstract itself from the world of the present and the concrete rhythms of history? Although Goodwin and Taylor are sympathetic to utopianism, they present a view of utopia that is one-sided and abstract in character. Whereas most condemn utopia, they praise it, but they still present it in dualistic form.

Gray dismisses Marxism and the Enlightenment as 'utopian' in character. It is not difficult to see that the Enlightenment rested its premises on a dualistic view of the world. This dualism is deepened by thinkers such as Hume who embrace a sceptical attitude towards the ideals of autonomy and freedom that the Enlightenment poses. But Gray is wrong, in my view, to reject the Enlightenment. It needs to be built upon and it is just this transcendence that Marxism attempts, even if it fails to be wholly consistent in its 'transcendental' endeavours. Interestingly, Gray traces his growing disenchantment with the New Right (which he initially embraced) to the latter's sectarian spirit, which belongs, he says, to the rationalist doctrines of the Enlightenment (1993: xii). Rationalism, in Gray's view, encourages a Manichean division between what is true and what is false. However, the answer to this problem is not support for a kind of liberal conservatism, but a movement beyond the whole dualism between abstract rationalism, on the one hand, and local particularity on the other.

Gray approves of Hume's scepticism towards the existence of the self. The self is simply a collection of perceptions. Gray likes Rees's view of the individual as a Mr Nobody (Gray, 2002: 75–6), but it seems to me that this embraces the same problem that postmodernism sometimes suffers from. Of course, the self is not the absolute identity that many liberals think it is – unchanging, god-like, composed of sheer continuity. The self is plural and changeable, but this does not make it any the less a 'self'. Like Hume, Gray knocks down a dogma, producing an equally one-sided concept in its stead. On the one hand, Gray argues that we must believe in the self, even though, on the other hand, he sees it as no more than an illusion (ibid.: 78).

The defence of Mill

In *Mill on Liberty: A Defence* (1996c), Gray tackles the conventional view that Mill is divided against himself, espousing a liberal moral theory and yet still retaining a utilitarian standpoint. If liberty can be limited only to avoid harm, then how can we retain the view that liberty can be limited if such a limitation does not have good consequences? Liberty and happiness often conflict: which is the overriding principle?

Gray argues (in 1983 when the first edition of his work is published) that in fact Mill's principle of utility is axiological – i.e. a principle that cannot yield judgements about what ought to be done. Mill's *On Liberty* in fact contains a coherent and utilitarian defence of liberal principles about the right to liberty. His utilitarianism is indirect so that there is room for weighty second principles, including principles to do with justice and moral rights (1996c: 14). Neither general happiness nor the agent's happiness is the object of direct pursuit, and utility contains many systems of precepts, among which moral codes have central but not exclusive interest (ibid.: 38–9). For Mill, a higher maximum of utility is attainable where policy is bounded by the constraint of the principle of liberty than could be attained by the direct and unconstrained pursuit of utility (ibid.: 65). Mill's notion of interest must have a developmental or historical aspect (ibid.: 51). Gray usefully quotes Mill's distinction, developed in *Principles of Political Economy*, between authoritative and non-authoritative use of government authority, the first being prohibitive or coercive, the second simply giving information and advice (ibid.: 62)

Mill assumes that higher pleasures are enjoyed by those who have a distinctive capacity for autonomous thought and action (ibid.: 72). Gray argues that Mill takes the view that no one can interfere with the fully voluntary choice of a mature rational agent concerning matters that affect his own interests (ibid.: 91). He gives the bridge example: a person may be prevented from going on an unsafe bridge on the assumption that he or she did not want to fall in the water (ibid.: 191). A weak form of paternalism is permissible where an individual's action is not the result of considered rational deliberation (ibid.: 92). There is, of course, a divergence between Mill's utilitarianism and value pluralism, since Mill does rank vital interests over people's other interests (ibid.: 127).

The point is that because there are utilitarian reasons for according the vital interests in autonomy and security a privileged immunity from utilitarian trade-off, Mill's theory is superior to liberal doctrines that see the right to liberty as self-evident (ibid.: 128).

Gray's critique of Mill

This defence is deceptive because Gray elsewhere (and later) is much more critical of Mill. In his Postscript Gray takes the view that the attempt to reconcile a theory of liberty with utilitarianism is impossible – utilitarianism might lead to discrimination against minorities, an objection that Mill's indirect theory of utilitarianism is no more successful than any other utilitarian theory in answering (ibid.: 137). Gray now holds that the purely axiological character of the utility principle cannot be sustained, and he argues that the theory of liberty has (in reality) a perfectionist rather than a utilitarian basis (ibid.: 140).

The distinction between higher and lower pleasures is seen as unsustainable, and the notion that human flourishing requires autonomy and individuality ignores the fact that security, for example, might be seen as more important than self-development. Mill's theory is in fact rooted in a culture-bound particularity (despite its universalist pretensions), i.e. European individualist societies (ibid.: 145), and, given all these problems, the notion of value-pluralism is seen as devastating for Mill's argument which ignores that fact that conflicts between the ingredients of human well being are uncombinable (ibid.: 146).

Gray (curiously in my view) argues that a ban on paternalist interventions does not allow us to prohibit 'seriously self-harming' behaviours. Elsewhere he takes the view (1989: 3) that Mill would rule out 'paternalist' restrictions on liberty of the kind, for example, that is involved in the legal prohibitions of hard drugs. But this criticism arises because, in my view, Gray ignores here (though not elsewhere – see 1996c: 93) Mill's concern with the liberty of retraction (Mill, 1974: 173), in which Mill offers a socially developmental notion of freedom, arguing that only those actions from which we can retract ought to be tolerated. This argument emerges in the context of a discussion that women should be free to decide that they married the wrong man, and can therefore divorce. The principle of freedom cannot allow that a person should be free not to be free – it is not freedom to be allowed to alienate freedom.

This principle, as Mill acknowledges, is of wide application (1974: 173) and would mean that drugs that impede a person's liberty of retraction (i.e. are addictive) can be legitimately regulated. How can a person *learn* from a mistake if they are not free to change their minds and behaviour? Riley in his critique of Gray gives the example of an individual learning that his girlfriend is a cocaine user and exercising his own liberty by ceasing their friendship (2006: 124). But if cocaine use infringes upon the liberty of retraction (as it may well do), then her action ceases to be self-regarding and her boyfriend is not restricted to invoking natural penalties as a result of his discovery. Riley considers that drug use is a self-regarding activity but ignores the problems that the liberty of retraction may create. Smoking and consuming alcohol (where they impede liberty of retraction) do not count as self-regarding actions. Mill is not simply concerned about harm to others. Where the harm to oneself contravenes the liberty of retraction, it becomes problematic for Mill.

Gray also complains that Mill's harm principle ignores the fact that, if we harm ourselves, we harm those who take care of us or depend upon us (1993: 52). But Mill is not an old liberal who sees people simply as self-contained atoms. His notion of harm assumes that people can do as they please, provided that they can learn from their mistakes, and that they do not injure the interests of others. Strictly speaking, we can be said to harm ourselves only when our action infringes the liberty of retraction – our capacity to learn from our mistakes. Moreover, Mill allows those who offend others (as opposed to injuring their interests) to be subject to what he calls natural penalties (Hoffman, 1988: 121).

Gray's Postscript to *Mill on Liberty: A Defence* is thus far more critical of Mill than the work itself. Mill's theory of liberty is now seen as 'defenceless and without foundation' (1996c: 132). It rests upon a Eurocentric philosophy of history that conflates modernization with Westernization, and places him squarely in the treacherous sands of the Enlightenment tradition. Gray condemns the abstract individualism that permeates contemporary political philosophy in the West (1995: 6). He speaks of the legacy of the Enlightenment project as a world ruled by calculation and wilfulness which is 'humanly unintelligible and destructively purposeless' (ibid.: 146). And yet abstract individualism is inherent in all forms of liberalism, and it has, as we shall see, its roots in the market. Whether he challenges or endorses classical liberalism, the problem is that Gray's attitude towards liberalism is ultimately uncritical.

Conclusion

I see the Enlightenment as embodying modernity and liberalism. It is tempting when confronted with the abstract premises of the Enlightenment to embrace the tenets of pre-modernity. After all, medieval and ancient thought saw people as social beings who played particular roles rather than possessed universal rights, but it needs to be remembered that pre-modernity also stressed the 'naturalness' of repressive hierarchy.

The Enlightenment was, of course, diverse in its reach, but it united, in my view, around the endorsement and elaboration of classical liberal principles. Although we think of the Enlightenment as developing with the French *philosophes*, in fact its origins can be traced back to Hobbes, who despite Rousseau's denunciations had an abstract and universalist notion of the individual. Hobbes was a conservative but he was also a rationalist: his notion of a sovereign state is quintessentially modern in character.

Some of the early liberals (such as Locke) accepted slavery and even Rousseau, though he denounces slavery, is remarkably ambivalent about its linkage to citizenship. The thinkers of the Enlightenment upset the established church and were deists rather than conventionally religious; the source of their abstractions lay in a defence of property and the market as mechanisms of freedom and autonomy. They supported perfectionism and patriarchy, and where they offered alternatives to a despotic status quo they did so in a manner that was remorselessly dualistic in character.

Benevolent abstractions about humanity in general concealed support for colonialism and contempt for 'others'. Every Enlightenment thinker took the state for granted and, even when legitimacy was seen as self-authorization, the need for an institution claiming a monopoly of force was regarded as essential. The state was perfected rather than challenged. This is why Gray's own critique of the Enlightenment is defective. He arguably endorses what he should challenge, and rejects what he should build upon.

It is revealing that he is a great admirer of Hume's scepticism, and fails to see that Hume's response to abstract rationalism is an abstract empiricism – as militantly one-sided as the position he rejects. The dualism that is central to Hume is also accepted by Gray and his treatment of Mill's liberalism ignores the developmental emphasis that Mill (somewhat inconsistently) seeks to establish. We conclude that, although Gray targets the Enlightenment for his fiercest critique, his own argument embodies the weaknesses of the tradition that he denounces.

4 • Marxism and Utopia

Introduction

In this chapter I seek to explore the view of utopia embraced by classical Marxism, by which I mean the Marxism of Marx and Engels. Gray dismisses Marxism as utopian, but ironically he shares the same traditionalist view of utopia that Marx and Engels adopted when they championed the notion of 'scientific socialism'. The idea that the notion of utopia cannot be 'scientific' rests upon a dualism that Marx sought to banish but that residually remains in his work. Dualistic aspects of Marxism are identified in terms of a notion of revolution that necessarily polarizes society and necessitates authoritarian rule. Marx, it is often argued, attempts to suppress the market, and certainly his followers in Eastern Europe did. But this means that the market comes in through the back door (in informal and particularly damaging forms), so that the alternative to capitalism is an inversion and not a meaningful transcendence of capitalism. In the same way the notion of class war and the 'dictatorship of the proletariat' both in theory and (more so) in practice perpetuates the need for a state, and reproduces the dualism between the ideal and the real that Marxism sought, but failed, to wholly overcome.

William Morris's intriguing attempt to develop an explicitly Marxist utopia will be considered in the light of the classical Marxist rejection of utopian socialism. Classical Marxists embrace the notion that scientific and utopian socialism are 'opposites' that exclude one another. However, if we reconstruct the concept of utopia to overcome the is/ought and science/utopia dualism, then Marxism can be itself identified as utopian, and the concept of utopia ceases to be pejorative in character.

Marxism can be characterized as advocating a utopia, but the problem with the theory is not that it is utopian, but that this utopia is flawed. Its notion of communism is inadequately historical, and its concept of revolution is statist and authoritarian. Not surprisingly, a traditionalist view of utopia is adopted by Marx and Engels, and contrasted to a notion of science that is often taken by Marx's critics (Gray included) to be positivist in character. What is implicit in Marx becomes explicit in Bernstein's 'revisionist' socialism memorably characterized, as we shall see, as a utopia (in the traditional sense) minus utopian expectations. Bernstein was a German socialist in the late nineteenth century whose book on *Evolutionary Socialism* (English title) caused a wave of protest in orthodox circles.

Marxism: an anti-utopian politics?

There is some ambivalence in the literature about whether Marx and Engels were utopians. Heywood describes communism as 'a utopian vision of a future society envisaged and described by Marx and Engels'. On the other hand, he notes that Marx and Engels supported 'scientific socialism' and rejected what they called 'utopian socialism' (1992: 115, 127). It is worth noting how strongly influenced Marx and Engels were by the 'utopian' socialists, and 'utopian' notions of 'harmony', 'association', 'community' and 'cooperation' appear in their own work (Goodwin and Taylor, 1982: 161).

Marx and Engels adopted a traditional view of utopia. So, indeed, did those – if we follow Geoghegan's account – who were characterized by Marx and Engels as 'utopian socialists'. Indeed, Geoghegan shows that Saint-Simon regarded himself as a hard-headed scientist who saw the rule of the producers (in whose ranks he included industrialists) as deriving from the historical realities of a modern society. Saint-Simon's formulations sound astonishingly 'Marxist': not only does he refer to administration replacing the state, but he speaks of scientific decisions taken 'independent of all human will' according to historical necessity. 'Everything is relative, that is the only absolute' (Geoghegan, 1987: 10). The comment could have been written by Hegel or Marx.

What makes Saint-Simon a utopian, in my view, is not that his views are problematic, but the fact that he poses an alternative to existing society. One could argue that his utopianism is contentious, given the fact that he ignores the conflicts of interests between workers and capitalists. But this is because he is a poor or flawed utopian, not because he is a utopian per se.

The same is true of the other two socialists who are regarded as utopians in Engels's famous *Socialism: Utopian and Scientific*.

Fourier, as Geoghegan again makes clear, defined utopia traditionally – a 'dream of well-being, without the means of execution' (ibid.: 17) and saw his libertarian communities, in which work was done freely and enjoyably, as the product of a scientific analysis of the present 'ripe with the future'. A youthful Engels referred to Fourier's 'scientific research, cool, unbiased systematic thought' (cited ibid.: 23). As for Robert Owen, he regarded his village communities as eminently practical, and the young Engels described Owen's proposals as 'the most practical and the most fully worked out' (ibid.: 20, 23). The point here is that Fourier's ideas, stimulating as they are, are unworkable. Likewise, Owen's village communities are naïve in the way they ignore the need for people to involve themselves in the struggle to change their lives. Owen's theory of character is one-sided. It is true that human behaviour is affected by the circumstances in which people find themselves, but it is not true that they lack agency and cannot change the circumstances moulding their character. There is a dialectical and not merely a mechanical relationship between circumstances and conduct. Owen assumes that ordinary people are the victims of the circumstances beyond their control: only the great reformer (Owen himself!) can rescue them from their environmental fate. It is true that one must recognize the constraining nature of circumstances; but it is through this recognition that circumstances can then be changed.

Marx and Engels's critique of the three 'utopians' is basically sensible, but what is problematic is the idea that they are seen as utopians whereas Marx and Engels are not. People like Saint-Simon, Fourier and Owen ignored the need for a political struggle to achieve their objectives; they overlooked the conflicts of interest involved in posing a socialist solution; they ignored the need for allies; they overlooked the importance of designating stages, and the fact that a resort to violence is justifiable under certain conditions, i.e. where no constitutional transition to communism is possible. But these arguments – developed passionately by Engels in *Socialism: Utopian and Scientific* – make them unrealistic utopians, not utopians per se.

Marx and Engels did much to overcome the negative features of the so-called 'utopian socialists'. They followed Hegel in adopting a view of dialectics that rejects the dualism of traditional liberal and conservative (and much socialist) thought. In his early critique of Hegel, however, Marx demonstrates brilliantly that Hegel's entire logic is the demonstration that abstract thought is nothing in itself – that the absolute idea is nothing in itself; that only nature is something (Marx and Engels, 1975a: 343). It is true that the young Marx prefers the term 'naturalism' to 'materialism', but with his formulation of a dialectical or consistent materialism (in 1845) he argues (I think persuasively) that ideals as a reflection of reality point to a future possibility buried in the present. In his famous afterword to the second German edition of *Capital*, Marx comments that his dialectical method is the 'direct opposite' of that of Hegel. Instead of the real world being merely the 'external, phenomenal form of "the Idea"', the ideal is nothing else than the 'material world reflected by the human mind, and translated into forms of thought' (1970: 19).

I have elsewhere argued at some length that a reflectionist theory of ideas does not mean that ideas are the passive 'copies' of an external world. Indeed, a passive notion of ideas leads inexorably away from materialism since, if our ideas do not change the external world (Hoffman, 1975: 100–1), how can we be sure that such a world exists at all? Reflection is a practical process that enables us to reconstruct (partially and imperfectly) external reality in our thoughts. As far as Marx is concerned, what makes dialectics 'critical and revolutionary' is that they let nothing impose itself upon reality. Every 'historically developed social form' is 'in fluid movement' and a dialectical approach takes 'into account its transient nature not less than its momentary existence' (Marx, 1970: 20). Even in the *1844 Manuscripts*, Marx stresses that, while communism is 'the necessary form and dynamic principle of the immediate future', it is 'not itself the goal of human development – the form of human society' (Marsden, 1991: 26).

This approach creates the basis for overcoming the traditional view of utopia. Marx frequently referred to communism as 'the real movement which abolishes the present state of things' (Marx and Engels, 1976: 29). It has been argued that Marx made 'an ideal future' dialectically necessary (Goodwin and Taylor, 1982: 26). In his defence of the Paris Commune, Marx notes that the working class have no 'ready made utopias' to introduce by decree, but they know that in order to secure their emancipation 'they will have to pass through long struggles, through a series of historic processes'. They have, he argues, 'no ideals to realise', and must avoid 'ignorant platitudes and sectarian crotchets' made in 'the oracular tone of scientific infallibility' (Marx and Engels, 1971: 76). This argument creates the basis for overcoming the dualism between 'is' and 'ought', fact and value etc. that lies at the basis of the traditional view of utopia, and therefore Marxism provides the tools for reconstructing the concept, even if Marx and Engels did not do so.

In *What is to be Done?* Lenin defends 'dreaming' on the grounds that dreams may simply 'run ahead of the natural march of events' (he is quoting the Russian writer Pisarev). Dreams can be a stimulus 'to undertake and complete extensive and strenuous work'. They constitute 'an entire and completed picture', the product to which a person's hands are only just beginning to lend shape (1961: 509). Although the notion of 'an entire and completed picture' has a somewhat static ring to it, the idea that dreams or utopias can represent a future within the present is, in my view, valid and exciting. Indeed, Mannheim argues that the 'socialist idea' (by which he must mean the socialist idea as formulated by Marx) sees itself as a 'tendency' within the matrix of reality that 'continuously corrects itself with reference to this context' (1960: 221). This can only be taken as 'reducing the utopianism of utopia' (Levitas, 1990: 74) if one defines utopia in traditional terms. Marx and Engels's rejection of the notion of utopia assumes that utopias must be abstract. Marx told Beesly in 1869: 'The man who draws up a programme for the future is a reactionary' (Manuel and Manuel, 1979: 698). But Marxism is, in my view, utopian simply because it poses an alternative to a particular status quo. Marx objected not so much to the creation of social harmony as to the reliance upon gradual reform (Goodwin and Taylor, 1982: 166). He is still seen as presenting social harmony as an ultimate vision, thus creating problems for the Marxist analysis of history and its case for communism. Although Bloch is particularly fascinated by the *Paris Manuscripts* of 1844, there is justification in his contention that 'Marx teaches us to find our All precisely in the Nothing of this zero point. Alienation, dehumanization, reification . . .' (1986: 1358). The absolutist contrast between alienation and non-alienation, humanization and dehumanization, etc. constitutes what post-modernists call 'binary' thought. Whatever we call it, the point is that it is undialectical. How can humans continue to progress and change if there is no alienation whatsoever? It is true that it could be argued that, under communism, humans 'externalize' rather than 'alienate' but, unless this externalization is problematic, what is the incentive to continuously move forward?

The problem with the concept of alienation is that it implies that a human alternative is an abstract ideal brought to concrete reality. Marx's famous comment in the *Economic and Philosophical Manuscripts of 1844* demonstrates the problem when he speaks of communism as a 'true resolution' of the strife between freedom and necessity, existence and essence – 'the riddle of history solved' (Marx and Engels, 1975b: 296–7). Marsden is right to see this passage as not really credible – as far too sweeping and romantic – and he makes the point that personal strife, existential anxiety, disease and other ills basic to the human condition would still continue to exist under communism (1991: 27).

Marx's comment here expresses in sharp terms what is a general problem within Marxism: the tendency to underplay the historical (and thus historically limited) character of communist society.

William Morris: an old or new utopian?

Morris is an important figure in this discussion because he is regarded by Geoghegan as the 'first self-consciously utopian Marxist' (1987: 68). Does he succeed in bridging the gulf between science and utopia that is central to the classical Marxist position? Some see Morris as a traditional utopian. Pierson takes the view that Morris reverted to the utopianism from which Marx believed he had rescued socialists (Kinna, 2000: 22). Others argue that Morris pioneered a notion of utopia that was consistent with classical Marxism. Thus, A. L. Morton says of Morris's *News from Nowhere* that 'it is the first Utopia which is not utopian' (cited by Thompson, 1977: 697), and Thompson in his work on Morris refers to *News from Nowhere* as a 'a Scientific Utopia', a work in which the world of dream and the world of reality are reunited (ibid.: 695). Kinna comments that for Morris, 'as an imaginary ideal, utopia is compared to the idea of paradise' (2000: 198). But she insists that, although he had written an essay dealing with 'the Promised Land of Socialism', he saw his utopia as a realizable goal (ibid.).

The question I want to pose is not whether Morris is a utopian, since I have argued that the notion of utopia, when reconstructed, ceases to designate a static, idealized society of the kind that Marxism, not entirely successfully, challenges. The real question is whether Morris subscribes to a static or dynamic concept of utopia – an old, traditional concept, or the new, critical and historically conscious one.

It is clear that some of his commentators are uncertain. Hence Morton's paradoxical formulation – that Morris wrote a utopia that is not utopian – and Thompson's comment that *News from Nowhere* embodies a scientific utopia: 'And yet it is still is a Utopia, which only a writer nurtured in the romantic tradition could have conceived' (1977: 695–6). In his Postscript Thompson concedes that he sought in his original argument to somewhat dogmatically assimilate Morris to the classical Marxist tradition, and he argues that Engels's rather disdainful view of Morris (he saw Morris as a 'sentimental socialist') reflects a tendency by Marx and Engels to dismiss romanticism as 'moralism' and 'utopianism' (ibid.: 786).

But why should we praise Morris only if we can show that he has classical Marxist credentials? There is no doubt that Morris was greatly influenced by Marxism, but he is also an independent thinker – and whether we call him a Marxist or not is less important than how we evaluate his communism. The French critic Abensour objects to the formula 'scientific utopia' on the grounds that it implies a paradox – a work cannot really be scientific if it is utopian (ibid.: 787). Morris, Abensour argues, espouses a new utopianism: he is concerned with the liberation of desire, the idea that we must desire in a different way (for example, we can desire to forget relationships rather than possess things) (ibid.: 791), not with the static, perfectionist models of traditional utopias. It is certainly true that *News from Nowhere* breaks from the traditionalist concept of utopia in significant ways. It is worth examining the text in a little more detail.

William Morris's *News from Nowhere* is set in England about a hundred years after capitalism has been overthrown through violent revolution. The central figure goes to bed in winter and awakes in mid-summer, and takes a walk along the Thames. The boatman, who takes him up the river, is astonished and puzzled by the money that is offered. The visitor is transported through Hammersmith – now with pleasant country lanes and fields. The buildings are exquisite, the women beautiful and poverty vanquished. He travels to Kensington and passes on to Piccadilly. He is treated with great generosity in shops that no longer take money. In Trafalgar Square he notes the elegant and ornamented houses. There is no formal education, the Houses of Parliament are used to store dung, and prisons do not exist. Work is enjoyable. The central figure visits an old man who has a house near the British Museum, who tells him that courts of law have disappeared and the country overall has become a garden full of beautiful and tasteful dwellings. There is no state or criminals, with majorities deciding matters of common interest. The country is living under a tolerant and agreeable communism. There are 'markets' but they are institutions through which people obtain what they need. People who act anti-socially are 'punished' simply by the remorse they feel. There is certainly little social conflict. Transgressions are treated as the 'errors of friends' (Kinna, 2000: 211).

Guest (as he is called) returns to Hammersmith and is taken by boat up the Thames, stopping at Hampton Court for a meal, and continuing on to Runnymede, where he is told about the revolution and civil war. He then travels to Oxford, and the dream (or vision as Morris prefers to call it) ends. The work not only acknowledges the existence of non-violent conflict, but allows for the occasional murder. The use of social sanctions in *News from Nowhere* to handle serious ethical infringements is interesting and challenging. It is clear that the past has left its mark on the communist society since there are still a few eccentrics who hanker after the capitalist society of old. Women are treated in a mildly sexist manner – they still manage the house and wait on men, and Levitas is surely right to say that Morris continues to support the sexual division of labour (1990: 114). But to what extent can we say that Morris has broken from the traditional concept of utopia? Centrally problematic to his whole portrait is that Morris aggravates the static implications of the classical Marxist view of communism by identifying his future society as 'an epoch of rest' (the subtitle of the book, which Morton omits from his edition of *News from Nowhere*), and he sees communism as a society of 'fulfilled aspirations', a 'vision of all my longings for rest and peace'. As Thompson comments, 'Unceasing criticism, boundless curiosity in the ways and thoughts' of the past has gone (1977: 696). In *News from Nowhere* the narrator is told: 'We have been living for a hundred and fifty years at least, more or less in our present manner' (ibid.: 697). The vision is almost that of traditional religion.

Morris tends to be anti-capitalist rather than post-capitalist. Thompson points out that Morris doubted that 'bourgeois' individualism had made any real contribution to human consciousness and his reference to the great artists of the past four hundred years was without any warmth. He disliked Puritanism so intensely that he could not bring himself to read Milton. Indeed, Anderson argues that Morris repressed and rejected (rather than built upon) the history of capitalism (1980: 168). Kinna argues that *News from Nowhere* drew upon a 'well-developed model of medieval England' (2000: 201).

Morris's *News from Nowhere* is problematic, not because it is utopian, but because it has static and ahistorical features that make it implausible as a portrait of the future. 'This is not the age of inventions', says one of the characters (Morris, 1970: 146). Morris speaks of having moved 'into the present rest and happiness of complete Communism' (ibid.: 160). Levitas refers to Morris's goal, like that of Bloch's, as the transcendence of alienation (1990: 110), and I see the idea that we can end alienation once and for all as a perfectionist rather than a realistic idea. It is revealing that Morris viewed the impressionist painters as 'drifting into the domain of empirical science' (ibid.: 659–60), a comment that suggests a dismissal of science rather than a meaningful integration of science and utopia. If the distinction between science and utopia is to be overcome, then it needs to be argued that, because science is critical, utopianism (in our reconstructed sense) is part of science: it is not external to it. Thompson, however, even in his Postscript, argues that there are disciplined and undisciplined ways of 'dreaming' but even disciplined dreaming is a work of imagination, not of science (ibid.: 793).

Thompson takes the view that in *News from Nowhere* the ideal and the scientific coexist and argue with each other (ibid.: 802), but it is clear that he sees them as separate and conflicting modes of interpretation. Science, Thompson suggests, cannot tell us what to desire or how to desire, since knowledge and desire are two operative (and unrelated) principles of culture (ibid.: 806–7). The notion of 'desire' is taken from Abensour's comment that the role of desire is to 'teach desire to desire', and Anderson is right to warn that this notion, when placed in contrast to scientific analysis, is obscurantist and irrationalist. As Anderson comments later, morality is not simply affective sensation: 'it is always a matter of intellectual conviction as well' (Anderson, 1980: 160, 164). Although Thompson sees utopianism as a legitimate enterprise, it is, in his view, separate from, and in contrast to, science.

If classical Marxism is wrong to see science as incompatible with utopia, Thompson is wrong to continue with the divorce, since, as we have asked above, why should the critical function of a reconstructed notion of utopia be alien to science? It is difficult to disagree with Goodwin and Taylor that the utopia/science distinction is a false dichotomy that serves merely to exclude non-favoured theories from the charmed circle (1982: 77). The so-called 'utopian socialists' are dismissed in a peremptory way that bodes ill for later debates. Morris's *News from Nowhere* is problematic, not because it is utopian, but because it has static and ahistorical features.

Utopia and science

Marx and Engels were anxious to present their views as scientific. From the Marx of 1844, who identifies science with humanism and the transcendence of alienation, to the Marx of *Capital*, science is seen to be a rigorous and disciplined view of reality at odds with superficiality and mere indulgence. Indeed, the entire analysis of *Capital* hinges on the distinction between the 'essence' of commodities and the way they appear, and he tells us that science would be superfluous if 'the outward appearance and the essence of things directly coincided' (1966: 817).

In *Wages, Price and Profit* Marx comments that 'scientific truth is always paradox, if judged by everyday experience which catches only the delusive appearance of things' (Hoffman, 1975: 93). The notion of science is crucial to Marx, and it is a view that embraces values and does not see science, to quote Gray, as 'that practice whose goal is control of nature' (1995: 145). The role of science is to develop nature, not merely dominate it. But to the extent that Marx endorsed a concretely humanistic view of science – a broad German notion of *wissenschaft* – it seems all the more problematic that he should identify utopianism as escapism and fantasy.

Why did Marx and Engels contrast science and utopia? It is arguable that this contrast arose from a tendency to rather abstractly polarize opposition to positions that they rejected. We can draw an analogy here with 'philosophy' and 'ideology' (I also comment on this below). Marx and Engels appear to oppose the latter as such, but in fact they are opposed to idealist presentations of philosophy and ideology, rather than philosophy and ideology per se. In the same way, it could be argued that what they really opposed was fantasy (i.e. ideals unrelated to the real world) and they (in my view wrongly) identified utopia as being inherently fantastic in character.

The contrast between science and utopia is unfortunate and misleading, and reflects what I would describe as a residual modernism within Marx and Engels' theory – a tendency to think at times in binary opposites, according to an undialectical logic of either/or.

The state and revolution

The best way to demonstrate this residual modernism is in relation to the state. Reconstructing the concept of utopia requires tackling the problem of the state, for I shall argue that there is a necessary link between the traditional view of utopia and an uncritical view of the state. Traditional utopians thought in terms of an ideal state (Kumar, 1991: 53). Yet the state is a highly problematic and indeed contradictory institution. Goodwin and Taylor take the view that, 'although logical propositions have contradictions and contraries, there is no such thing as a contradictory institution' (1982: 30). I would argue, however, that the state is just such an institution. I define the state in Weberian terms as an institution that claims a monopoly of legitimate force for a particular territory. Marx refers to the state as a 'theological concept' (Marx and Engels, 1975b: 150), and this is true because the state embodies a dualistic relationship between theory and practice, the ideal and the real, the 'ought' and the 'is'. The state is an 'illusory community' because it presents the common interest in a way that is divorced from real individual and collective interests (Marx and Engels, 1976: 46). The notion of perfection – central to the traditional notion of utopia – is essentially a statist idea. It is true that Saint-Simon sought a society without the state (and indeed Marx and Engels took their argument from Saint-Simon), but statism is still inherent in Saint-Simon's astonishing statement that 'it would be blasphemy to presume that the All-Powerful One founded his religion on several principles' (Manuel and Manuel, 1979: 609). This notion of oneness is inherently statist in character, for the state demands monolithic and ultimate allegiance, and writing can have a traditionally theological (and statist) tone even if the state itself is apparently rejected.

Marx and Engels were certainly correct to identify communism as a classless and a stateless society, but there are a number of features in classical Marxism, as I shall argue below, that prevent the state from withering away. To look beyond the state, it is crucial to be able to address conflicts of interest through social pressures rather than force, so that, as I have argued elsewhere (1995: 40–7), what replaces the state is government – i.e. the arbitration and negotiation of conflicts of interest through compromise. Of course, this is only possible when conflicts of interest allow disputing partners to understand each other's point of view – to change places – and class division, as Marx and Engels rightly pointed out, makes this kind of empathy extremely difficult. But not impossible – as Marx himself acknowledged in a remarkable letter to Henry Hyndman when he said that in Britain if the 'unavoidable evolution' turned into 'revolution' then this 'would not only be the fault of the ruling classes but also of the working class'. Every peaceful concession has been wrung out through pressure, and the workers must wield their power and use their liberties 'both of which they possess legally' (Marx and Engels, 1975c: 314). It is revealing that this letter is omitted from the English (and I would think Russian) edition of the *Selected Correspondence* published in the Stalin period. Presumably Marx could not have possibly meant what he said!

What is true is that this comment is atypical of Marx – he continued to hold with Engels that revolution was inevitable, although it could be peaceful and constitutional. This is the first of the modernist residues in Marx's thought – the idea that conflicts of interest require a revolution. For revolution polarizes and is, in Engels's famous formulation, the 'most authoritarian thing there is' (cited in Hoffman, 1984: 168). It makes it more difficult to cement common interests, which are crucial if conflicts of interest are to be settled governmentally. The 'dictatorship of the proletariat' is a form of the state that, despite Marx and Engels's contention to the contrary, refuses to wither away because it is the product of revolution, and therefore finds it impossible to cement consensus and common interest. Indeed, even two centuries after the French Revolution, there is still a sharp conflict of interest between Catholics and secularists. It is logically possible to formulate the dictatorship of the proletariat as a purely democratic state that like any state only employs force against those who break laws, but in practice the notion of 'dictatorship' has been construed in a more conventional manner.

It might be argued, for example, that the liberal state regularly and systemically uses force against those who break its laws. On this argument a dictatorship of the proletariat can be said to act 'illiberally' only when its use of force extends to those whose opposition to the new government is not violent but peaceful and constructive.

Lovell (who argues that revolutions are inherently illiberal in character) acknowledges that such illiberalism can be limited where the suppression of 'fundamental opposition' coexists with the flowering of non-fundamental opposition (1984: 67–8). In other words, the revolution is not acting illiberally when (like any 'normal' liberal state) it protects itself against terrorism and subversion. But if revolutions are to be successful then they must polarize and make it impossible, as Marx commented on the Paris Commune, to keep up the 'decencies and appearances of liberalism as in a time of peace' – a policy that, Marx adds, involved a shameful betrayal of trust (Marx and Engels, 1971: 81).

It might just be argued that the suppression of the Constituent Assembly by the Bolsheviks in 1918 would have been justified if it had been acknowledged that this was a (temporary) suspension of democracy to be followed at some point by the summoning of a constituent assembly that was more representative than the one that had just been dissolved. Or – to continue the fantasy – if a system of soviets had been established that articulated the wishes of the population more accurately and meaningfully than would have been possible by a more conventional parliamentary body. But, of course, the dissolution of the Constituent Assembly was justified as a *victory* for democracy, a democracy far higher than, and qualitatively different from, the despised bourgeois parliamentary democracy. Indeed, while Lenin tried to argue that the Constituent Assembly was not representative, Trotsky saw it as a counter-revolutionary democracy (Hoffman, 1984: 186). Rosa Luxemburg put the matter precisely when she spoke of Lenin and Trotsky making a virtue out of necessity, and presenting dictatorial practices as though they were somehow higher forms of democracy (1972: 250).

Abstraction and class

The concept of class that Marx embraces is abstract. Class tends to be defined in terms of structure rather than agency, so that how we experience exploitation and conflict is not built into the notion of class. Class should be seen, in my view, as the content rather than the form of a social relationship. It is true that Marx does stress the importance of form, as in the famous comment in his Preface to *The Critique of Political Economy* where he speaks of 'ideological forms' in which people become conscious of the conflict between the forces and relations of production and 'fight it out' (2000: 426). But class can be seen only in political and ideological forms where the class content of a relationship seems to be belied by its universalist and otherworldly character. Thus, the oppression of women by men is a class relationship but one that does not present itself as such. There is, in other words, an inherent tension between the content and the form.

Marx's tendency to define class in structuralist terms makes it tempting to mechanistically place gender, nationality, religion etc. alongside class rather than to see class as an exploitative relationship that can be visible and experienced only when it expresses itself in gendered, national, regional, religious terms etc. In a well-known comment, Marx stated that, in class-divided societies, social relations are not 'relations between individual and individual, but between worker and capitalist, farmer and landlord, etc. Wipe out these relations, and you annihilate all society' (Marx and Engels, 1975c: 159). This comment is fine as far as it goes, but it does not go far enough.

The problem is that people do not relate to each other simply as worker and capitalist. They 'concentrate' their interests in forms that embrace gender, nationality, sexual orientation etc. It is only through gender or national or religious oppression etc. that we see class. The narrowness of Marx's definition of class as form and content is compounded by the argument that the proletariat is the class that leads, an argument that stands in tension with the wider notion of emancipation. In my view, people from widely variant backgrounds seek self-development and are marginalized by the market and by capitalism. To expect them to have to accept leadership from the 'working class' is silly and counter-productive.

The argument for revolution and the abstract view of class arise through a tendency to reject, rather than go beyond, liberalism or modernism. The concept of the individual – central to liberalism – is replaced by the notion of class. Rejection implies that a body of thought is merely turned inside out – it is not meaningfully transcended. Hence I speak of the residual modernism in Marx and Engels (here expressed as a tendency to anti- rather than post-liberalism) and it is this residual modernism that may explain why they employed a traditional view of utopia as a perfect and static society.

Communism as an historical society and the nature of conflict

Marx and Engels also do not say enough about the status of communism as an historical society. By this I mean that they are taken by critics and supporters alike to imply some kind of grand culmination of social movement beyond which it is impossible to go. In my view, there is an historical view of communism in their writings, as in the comment that, under communism, social evolutions will cease to be political revolutions (Marx, 2000: 232). Communism continues to evolve but revolution becomes redundant. But this dynamic view of communism is insufficiently emphasized. It is also true that, as Marsden notes, Marxism too readily assigns humanity's 'prehistory' to insignificance (1991: 178). The discontinuity between communism and capitalism is stressed, but what about the continuity, which is also important? In volume 3 of *Capital* Marx shows some concern with the socialized character of joint stock companies but the implications of these developments are not integrated into his overall theory.

There is also a tendency in Marx and Engels's writing to speak of conflict as linked to class division (and not part and parcel of society). Conflict can be violent, but it does not have to be. Conflict, in the sense of difference, is inherent in society and is perfectly compatible with the kind of common interest that enables people to 'change places' when tackling disputes. The notion that conflict is always rooted in class division is reinforced by a modernist use of the term 'politics' that ties it to the state. This implies that going beyond the state involves going beyond 'politics', and to many readers – not to mention theologically minded followers – the notion of communism as the end of politics translates easily into the idea of communism as the end of history. It is true that the *Manifesto* does state that public power will lose its political character (2000: 262) and this implies that public power, rather than the state, continues under communism. But the divorce of power from politics seems strange and contradictory.

It is difficult to disagree with Marsden's point that Marx did not give sufficient consideration to how conflicts of interest under communism would be resolved, and Marx has little to say about 'the form which the state [I prefer the term 'politics'] should take' (1991: 176). One does not need to be a theologian to note Marx's silence on the question of death and evil in his texts. Goodwin and Taylor express the traditional view of utopia when they speak of an assessment of utopia in terms of 'the familiar political polarities, for example the egalitarian/elitist distinction' (1982: 9–10). An opposition to elitism of any kind constitutes a denial of relationships, and equality can be dialectically understood only if it involves the recognition that people are *both* the same *and* different. Hence equality and elitism are not mutually exclusive concepts – unless by elitism one means a dictatorial tendency. Goodwin and Taylor identify utopias as ideas in which there are no differences of opinion and interest, and therefore no power struggles (ibid.: 34). The utopian mode, they argue, is one of power without politics.

Social democrats (in their post-1917 form) accepted the dualism between science and utopia that Marx and Engels had presented, but inverted it, seeing socialism as a piece of the beyond – something that 'ought' to be but is not (Gay, 1962: 158, 163). Like Goodwin and Taylor, they took a positive but abstract view of utopia. Socialism becomes 'ethical' rather than scientific so that it leaves intact class divisions, the state, the market and capitalism, with Berki rather mischievously characterizing social democracy as a 'utopian socialism minus utopian expectations' (1974: 101).

Marx and the negative view of utopia

Marsden cites the words of Bonino: 'Utopia without political science is romantic, ineffective daydreaming; science without a mobilising dream is inhuman or merely functional' (1991: 180). Marx was right to stress the importance of science, and, as we have seen, he identifies being scientific with being human. In his preface to the French edition of *Capital*, Marx speaks of the fatiguing climb to the luminous summits of science (1970: 21).

It is entirely understandable that one way of stressing the importance of a scientific socialism, i.e. a socialism that is systemic, coherent and realistic, is to contrast it with utopia. Marx after all saw himself as creating an argument that was new and different, and Engels's comment after Marx's death, that he and Marx had laid more stress on the economic determination than is due to it (1964: 396), has relevance here. In order to distance themselves from the superficial and uncritical utopias of socialists such as Owen and Fourier, it was tempting to dismiss utopianism as fantasy, and to contrast it with science. The problem is that such a contrast creates the impression that Owen and Fourier were purely fantastical, and Marx and Engels purely realistic. This dualism fails to capture both their own indebtedness to the 'utopians' and the necessarily speculative elements that characterize their own view of communism.

The same one-sidedness that leads to a dualistic view of the scientific and the utopian is evident in Marx and Engels's apparent dismissal of philosophy and ideology. In my view, what Marx and Engels were rejecting was not philosophy or ideology per se, but the idealist version of them. They were not opposed to a materialist analysis of philosophy or ideology. But, since philosophy and ideology were often rooted in idealistic premises, it was convenient to put them in capital letters and dismiss them.

The same could be true of their negative attitude to utopia. Because utopias have been traditionally regarded as perfect and static societies, utopianism is denounced as inherently unscientific. In my view, this contrast impoverishes Marx's own view of science since Marx rejected a positivist view of science – the idea that science must be value-free. It is clear from his comments on science that he regards his doctrine of communism as 'scientific' in character, and had no problem linking science to an 'ism'. Marsden is correct to insist that any value/fact dualism is alien to his work (1991: 59) – and therefore there is no reason why the division between science and utopia should not be overcome as one of the dualisms that characterize an uncritical view of bourgeois society.

It is hard to disagree with Bloch's comment that, the more scientific socialism is, the more it is concerned with the elimination of human alienation. Science is linked intrinsically to ethics and, given its moral impulse, it can be argued that utopian thought does not contradict but enriches historical materialism (ibid.: 94). Provided, of course, this is a reconstructed notion of utopia, and one that goes beyond the dualistic and implausible alternatives postulated by utopianism in its traditional form.

Conclusion

Like Gray, Marx and Engels espoused a traditional view of utopia and they contrasted their own 'scientific' socialism with a utopian socialism (which they rejected). Ironically, those whom they pilloried as 'utopians', such as Fourier, Saint-Simon and Owen also embraced the science/utopia dualism and considered that their own view of socialism was 'scientific' in character.

It is true that Marx and Engels create the basis for overcoming dualistic concepts in general. The notion of reality as essentially historical and their view that ideas ultimately reflect material reality enables us to construct a dialectical concept of the world in which dualism has been overcome. Yet their own theories can be criticized for not being consistently dialectical in character and the sharp contrast that Marx drew between alienation and communism is problematic. Marx and Engels's own view of socialism is also utopian in character (although commentators sometimes equivocate on this point) because they pose an alternative to the status quo. What makes their position vulnerable is not that it is utopian, but that their notion of utopia and conception of communism are themselves vulnerable.

Morris is an intriguing figure since he is sometimes presented as a 'utopian Marxist' because he sought in his *News from Nowhere* to argue the case for a communist society in terms of a dream. His argument has a number of interesting features – a stress on the importance of social sanctions in securing order, a recognition that the past influences the present, some stimulating insights into the nature of criminality – but, at the end of the day, *News from Nowhere* is a predominantly traditional utopia. The communism it portrays is essentially static and changeless, and there is a strong case to be made for seeing Morris as a romantic who sees communism as an idealized version of medieval England. Morris himself is anti- rather than post-capitalist and he tends to ignore the importance of the bourgeois epoch and the importance of the empirical.

It is true that Marx and Engels stress the importance of science and their view of science is refreshingly non-positivist in character. But why contrast science and utopia? It seems to me that this residual dualism arose from their insistence upon revolution as a concentrated political event – a notion that meant that their critique of the state comes to grief in an argument that, since socialism or the first phase of communism arises from revolution, it requires a dictatorial state to protect it. All this is part of a tendency to overemphasize the discontinuity between communism and capitalism. Engels conceded towards the end of his life that he and Marx had tended to neglect the problem of form in their general presentations of historical materialism, and this arose, it seems to me, out of a desire to present the gulf between their own theories and those of their opponents in a rather absolutist fashion.

Just as ideology and philosophy appear to be rejected because they are seen as inherently idealist in character, so it is arguable that science and utopia are presented in dualistic terms, rather than as a unity in which each strengthens the other.

5 • The Problem of the Market

Introduction

The traditional conception of utopia is founded upon dualism, and it will be argued that this dualism stems from an uncritical attitude towards the market and state. Here I will deal with Gray's attitude towards the market, and argue that accepting the market uncritically promotes a dualistic view of the individual and society, agency and structure. It assumes a theoretical harmony between the individual and society that reality belies.

Gray (as we pointed out in Chapter 1) initially embraced the neo-liberalism of Hayek, and he is hostile to the social liberalism of John Stuart Mill (having initially defended Mill's *On Liberty*). Increasingly, however, he becomes sceptical of the classical liberal tradition (and neo-liberalism) and, after a period in which he defines himself as a conservative, he becomes a sympathetic critic of New Labour. Although Gray is sharply critical of neo-liberal views of the market, he ultimately accepts the market as an institution that is here to stay. He fails, in my view, to get to grips with the interesting critique that Marx makes of the market in *Capital*.

Hayek's sceptical Kantianism

In his work on Hayek, Gray quotes Kant approvingly to the effect that, while we can avoid a dualistic attitude towards ontology – Kant sees everything as ultimately mental – dualism in practical thought is unavoidable (1984: 9). Hayek also sees a dualism between the natural and social sciences, a position that Gray endorses – the data of the social studies being themselves subjective phenomena (ibid.: 12, 17). It should be noted, however, that Gray embraces a version of naturalism that sees humans as (deluded) creatures of nature. This would seem to point in a materialist direction – that the human mind has evolved from the natural world. But Hayek's view (which Gray supports) is that order in the world is the product of a creative human mind. However, intellectual life is always governed by inarticulable laws or principles (ibid.: 21–3). For Hayek, as for Kant, philosophy is reflexive and critical rather than transcendental and constructive; it plots the limits of human understanding but cannot hope to govern it (Gray, 1996a: 32).

In the market process itself Hayek argues that there is a constant tendency to self-regulation via spontaneous order. Gray sees this notion as an explanatory value-free schema for natural and social phenomena. It has no normative or liberal content even though the spontaneous order concept does show the futility of planning (1984: 120–2). Gray continues to share Hayek's view that planning inevitably concentrates power in the hands of unaccountable bureaucrats, but Femia has rightly argued that planning can be democratic if a socialist society accommodates a diversity of independent power centres: local government, churches, trade unions, industrial and professional associations (1993: 150). Surely a system can be devised in which major planning decisions can be responsive to the wishes of the people's elected representatives? It is defeatist to assume that the planning process is inherently incompatible with a democracy where popular control permeates the economic sphere (ibid.: 152). Colls pleads with Gray to recognize that planning can exist within intellectual traditions to do with liberty and equality (1996: 73).

Hayek approves the system of natural liberty of the sort Adam Smith advocated, and Gray praises Hayek for synthesizing the concerns of conservative philosophy – that the human individual is a social achievement and that reason is an element in the growth of culture – with the central concerns of classical liberalism (1984: 124, 130). The organizing categories of the human mind express evolutionary adaptations to a world that is unknowable (1996a: 33).

The market and the liberal tradition

Although Hayek is praised for purging classical liberalism of its abstract individualism and uncritical rationalism (Gray, 1984: x), accepting the market involves of necessity embracing abstraction and dualism. The notion of the market is rooted in classical liberalism. Hobbes assumes that people are naturally competitive and self-interested, and this possessive individualism stems from a belief that market relationships are themselves built into human nature. The war of all against all is the free market without the state.

In Locke, the assumptions of the market are even more dramatic and explicit. Although Locke's state of nature assumes initially that people should only appropriate what they can use, the invention of money enables people to accumulate wealth that goes far beyond their usage. People, Locke argues, consent to the role of money even while outside the social contract (1924: 139), and he takes it for granted that part of an individual's labour is 'the turfs my servant has cut' (ibid.: 130). From premises of freedom and equality, Locke ends up with the differential view of consent and power, the most important end of the state being the protection of property. Locke makes it clear that the 'inconveniences' that necessitate the formation of society and the state are linked to the development of class divisions.

Even when liberals have rejected the notion of a state of nature, they continue to assume that market relations are natural. Adam Smith's famous comment in *The Wealth of Nations* bears this point out, where Smith argues that individuals naturally exchange things with one another (1970: 117). James Mill and Jeremy Bentham may have rejected the notion of natural rights, but the pursuit of utility was rooted in the view that individuals seek pleasure and avoid pain through market relations. For Bentham, the incentive to produce arises from the desire to avoid starvation, and to enjoy the pleasure of abundance, and James Mill saw the market as providing an extractive power that enables us to render the person and properties of human beings subservient to our pleasures (Hoffman, 1988: 166–8). James Mill accepted suffrage for male adults in Britain on the grounds that, in his view, the vast majority of the working class will follow the advice of the middle rank – the class in society that gives science, art and legislation their 'most distinguished ornaments' and is the chief source of all that is 'refined and exalted in human nature' (ibid.: 167).

It is true that the new liberals like Hobhouse and Green were critical of the market in that they advocated welfare policies to offer workers a measure of social security, but they still considered the market itself indispensable to freedom. As Arblaster has rightly noted, their objective was not to abolish capitalism but rather to diffuse it among the community as a whole (1984: 288).

Neo-liberalism and equality

It is often said that the rise of neo-liberalism, associated in particular with the British Prime Minister Margaret Thatcher and the US President Ronald Reagan, involved a return to classical liberalism. Gray himself speaks of the classical liberal inheritance and classical liberal orientation of much of Thatcherite policy (1996a: 275). But, although there are similarities between the two, there is also a crucial difference. Neo-liberalism questions equality as a value, and a classical liberal could never have spoken, as Thatcher did, of the 'right to be unequal'.

Classical liberal thought, of course, regards equal individuals as individuals with property and a male gender etc. but equality was a guiding value linked to freedom. Classical liberals were targeting the champions of medievalism and absolutism who argued for explicit repressive hierarchies, whereas neo-liberals are reacting against socialists and social liberals who have extended classical liberal notions in a social direction. As noted above, the distinction between negative and positive liberty – freedom from and freedom to – is meaningless to classical liberalism, which takes it for granted that individuals can do things and have power: the problem is the space to exercise this capacity.

Gray characterizes Rawls's notion of the original position (in which we are asked to imagine individuals ignorant of their wealth and personal strengths) 'as a metaphor ruined by its internal contradictions' (1989: 42), and argues that, 'like that of any other universalizing in liberal thought', it intends simply to entrench the liberal form of life (ibid.: 251). What is revealing, however, is that Gray goes along with the objection that Rawls is guilty of 'asset egalitarianism' – the idea that all the skills of society belong to a common pool to be distributed (ibid.: 31). Hayek, appointed a Companion of Honour on Thatcher's advice, not only makes it clear that freedom must be construed in militantly negative terms but he argues that equality cannot rest upon 'the factual equality of all men'. Equality can only mean equality before the law (Hayek, 1960: 86). Indeed, some neo-liberals are willing to support authoritarian regimes of the right (both Thatcher and Hayek have expressed admiration for Chile's General Pinochet, who led the military coup against Allende's elected but radical left-wing government in 1973). Reacting against social liberalism and socialism, neo-liberals reject any values of the classical liberal tradition that might have provided an unwitting basis for left-wing politics.

Faulks has commented that Hayek is really an authoritarian elitist, and his version of liberalism is difficult to distinguish from authoritarian conservatism. Neo-liberal policies have led to the creation of vast inequalities and, in so far as modern America approximates to a neo-liberal utopia, this is a society that marginalizes its inner-city areas and is afflicted by high rates of drug abuse and organized crime (Faulks, 1998: 71–2). The situation in New Orleans following the devastation of Hurricane Katrina has been likened to a Hobbesian state of nature – but a Hobbesian state of nature without the equality. Although the coexistence of the free market and a law-and-order state seems paradoxical, in fact, as Gilmour (a Tory critic of the New Right) has remarked, the establishment of a free market state is a 'dictatorial venture' that demands the submission of dissenting institutions and individuals (ibid.: 89).

It is revealing that Gray is strongly opposed to multi-national corporations and he accepts that they are institutions that share the same vices as the central state. Yet these multi-national corporations are themselves the product of the market and market competition, and Gray argues that they are too powerful to be controlled by sovereign states. The way in which the Swedish parliament was destabilized by global bond markets demonstrates the truth that no nation-state can resist the multi-nationals (Colls, 1996: 72–3). Two points need to be made here. First, Gray seems unduly fatalist about large-scale enterprises: the fact is that they have been – although far more needs to be done here – pressurized into operating according to social and ethical criteria. The reputation and image of large companies abroad are tarnished by adverse publicity around issues like pollution, the use of child labour and support for regimes with poor human rights records. Second, they represent concentrations of power brought about by the logic of market – the very institution that Gray accepts, even though he does not like the consequences.

The problem of abstraction

It might be objected that it is wrong to identify the market with abstraction, since all thinking involves abstraction. One can argue that the ideas that we have always oversimplify the real world and in that sense they are abstract. We could not think or speak without abstraction, since communication can only occur when the complexities of the real world are ordered and simplified. In this sense, abstraction is inevitable and positive.

But the notion of abstraction linked to the market should be differentiated from the kind of abstraction that is inherent in thought. Marx is right to identify this negative kind of abstraction as mystification and distortion – as inherent in the exchange process and the market. When a commercial exchange occurs, we have to find something that two (or more) very different things have in common. Imagine a barter situation in which a polished stick exchanges for, say, a bow and arrows. This is possible only because the actors are able to abstract something that equates the two very different things they are exchanging. Marx argues that Aristotle was unable to find the 'common' substance that equated two very different objects because this is possible only when human equality has acquired 'the fixity of a popular prejudice' (1970: 60). The commodity as an object of exchange seems obvious enough, but it is, in reality, a 'very queer thing, abounding in metaphysical subtleties and theological niceties' (ibid.: 71).

Money is even more 'abstract' since its purpose is simply to facilitate exchange. Marx in *Capital* took the view that what makes it possible to exchange different objects is the labour that both embody, even though this labour is 'abstract'. It is not the labour that produced a particular object such as a stick or a bow but it is a generalized or abstract labour that both have in common.

But we do not need to be wedded to a labour theory of value in order to pursue this theory of abstraction. In my view, goods and services are the product of activity of a kind that goes well beyond labour as it is usually understood. This activity includes the unpaid work of a parent and the risk-taking of an investor, but the point remains. The exchange process abstracts from the particular kinds of activity that produce things that are exchanged. But why is this a problem?

Take the Cape apple during the period of South African apartheid. As a piece of fruit, it fulfils a need, tastes good and may be relatively cheap. Open the apple in any way you like and you will not see the poverty and oppression, the discrimination and inhumanity inflicted upon those who produced it. This is because the market abstracts from the social relationships without which no object could be produced. For Marx, of course, this problem becomes even more acute when humans work for each other in a contractual way. When one sells one's services to an employer, the employee and employer are equated even though the amount of social power that each commands is very different. The contract that is formally or informally entered into does not register the differential facts about each party: that one partner to the contract may be, say, poor and female, the other male and prosperous. The two contractual partners are equal in a way that abstracts from the particular circumstances that make them what they are.

Emancipatory movements seek to make visible the conditions that the market renders abstract. They ask for the kind of concrete information that the exchange process conceals – the age, the sex, the wages, the safety, the health etc. of those whose activity brings the object exchanged to fruition. Thus, feminism argues that women as well as men are individuals and it is rightly suspicious of abstractions that appear to denote humankind but in reality relate only to men. Socialism, for its part, is concerned about the plight of the poor – the individuals without property – and wants to know who is left out when ringing declarations declare that all men are equal etc. Anti-racists are concerned about the 'whiteness' that abstractions can conceal.

Smith in a celebrated comment argued that it is not humanity but 'self-love' that motivates people (1970: 119) but this approach abstracts production from its impact upon natural and social relations. What of the unintended consequences of the kind in which cars, aeroplanes, factories etc. lead to the destruction of the environment? Economists have been compelled to pay heed to externalities – the unintended consequences that self-interested actions have on the life of others. Addiction to abstraction means that it is not surprising that champions of the free market are very reluctant to admit the realities of, say, global warming since the destruction of the environment is the product of an invisible hand that is supposed to lead to the well being of all. Ecological and environmental movements seek to render market relations more concrete and transparent so that one can see the wider social and natural realities that result from exchanges. All solutions to these problems, from the most moderate to the most extreme, involve going beyond the market as narrowly and abstractly conceived. Thus, air flights in Britain might be cheap as far as the market is concerned, but what if the notion of consumption is extended to take account of problems of noise, congestion and the depletion of the ozone layer?

Gray himself defends the proposition of social market theory that the market is 'an abstraction from an enormous miscellany of practices and institutions having deep roots in social life' (1996b: 24), but this abstraction is more mystifying and problematic than Gray admits. He praises Oakeshott for his insight into the fact that principles are invariably impoverished by the process that produced them (Gray, 1997: 86) without seeing that it is precisely the market that undermines 'the primacy of practice'. It produces consequences that conflict with its 'ideals'.

The market and freedom

Liberals have assumed that the market is indispensable to freedom. Gray argues in *Liberalism* that the coordination that the competitive market effects is non-coercive in character (1986: 69). During his Hayekian phase, he takes the view that the market demonstrates that social order does not depend upon any hierarchical structure. Norman Barry sees the market as a mechanism that allows consent but no power. People who exchange goods and services can be said to exercise their will autonomously (1981: 72). Now it is true that in order to enter market relations a person has to exercise choice, but whether this 'choice' is compatible with freedom surely depends upon how constraining the circumstances are under which such a person works. If the choice is between starvation and, say, working for another, does this constitute an *authentic* choice?

Macpherson argues, in a critical assessment of Friedman's *Capitalism and Freedom*, that exchanges in a capitalist society cannot be said to be free and voluntary when workers lack sufficient capital to work for themselves. Choice surely implies meaningful alternatives, and a worker (with no capital of their own) has no choice but to enter the labour market. In Macpherson's view, this constitutes 'coercion', not choice, and only when – in what he calls a simple market model – a household can produce sufficient goods and services to be self-reliant can it be said that the decision to enter the market is one of meaningful choice (1973: 143–5).

This raises the question of the market and determinism, because it can be argued that, even in the simple market model, circumstances still 'compel' a person to enter into exchange relations. Marx, for example, speaks of capitalists themselves being coerced by the laws of competition, and commodity producers being subject to what he calls 'the coercion exerted by the presence of their mutual interests' (1970: 356). It seems to me that it is problematic to speak of coercion in this context, since coercion implies, in my view, the threat of force, and neither capitalists, commodity producers nor, indeed, workers are necessarily, in this sense, coerced into market relations. Indeed, Marx speaks of humans entering into relations of production 'independent of their will' by which he means, not that humans are mere automatons, but that the need to be involved in production is central to the 'human condition' and no human can abstain from this process.

The real question is not whether the market constrains – since this is true of all circumstances – but whether it constrains in a way in which human development is advanced or retarded. The problem with the market is that it is liable to conceal circumstances, so that the exchange process appears to rely merely upon the will of participants, and not upon the resources and personality that each has, and the conditions in which each works. It is widely recognized, for example, that women who 'choose' to sell their bodies as prostitutes are invariably responding to circumstances of a dire and inhuman kind. The more that exchange relations become transparent, the more that choice can be said to be genuine. Transcending the market involves, therefore, not an act of arbitrary and doctrinaire suppression, but a system of regulation that increases transparency, and our knowledge of cost and consequence.

The notion that freedom must be restricted, since, as Riley puts it, 'nobody has a moral right to *complete liberty* with respect to social conduct' (2006: 127), assumes that freedom is non-relational. I can be free even when I harm you. However, once we define freedom in relational terms – I am free only if you are free – then the notion of freedom to harm becomes a contradiction in terms, and the way that the market conceals relationships involved in exchanges is a serious problem.

Gray, the market and liberalism

In his *Liberalism*, Gray sees private property as the embodiment of individual liberty in its 'most primordial form' and argues that 'market liberties are indivisible components of the basic liberties of the person' (1986: 62). It is true that Gray becomes increasingly hostile to Hayekian liberalism. But three years after he last praised Hayek he still argues that a free market is desirable although its legitimacy rests upon a reasonable spread of endowments (1989: 68). There is, he insists, no sustainable alternative to the institutions of liberal capitalism (1997: 50). Civil society, he comments, is the matrix of the market economy, which both history and theory show to be the precondition of prosperity and liberty in the modern world (1996a: 246).

The greatest problem of the age is, Gray argues, reconciling the demands of an efficient and dynamic market economy with the human imperatives of fairness and security (1997: 103). He does, however, see the market as frail, fallible and as imperfect as any other institution (1989: xv). As he puts it in 1993, 'the market is made for humans, not humans for the market' (1993: 63). There are important contexts – health care and urban planning for example – in which non-market institutions should be protected as a matter of public policy (1997: 18). Free markets, he comments, are creatures of state power, and they persist only as long as the state is able to prevent the human needs for security and the control of economic risk from finding a political expression (1998a: 17).

Gray links the concept of the sovereign state with the notion of the free market, and he is surely right to argue that by itself market exchange makes no contribution to human autonomy. It depends upon whether people come equipped with the capacities, resources and options needed for an autonomous life (1997: 79). But what is absent from Gray is a coherent and critical view of the market. Gray tends to veer between seeing the market as inadequate to human well being and arguing that the market provides autonomy and self-determination. Critics of the market, he argues, want to transform individuals into 'passive and powerless consumers of impersonal bureaucracies' (1993: 15). Either we have the market or we have reliance upon the state. But why can't we go beyond the market by making the exchange process more visible and transparent? The task of the age, Gray argues, is that of 'reconciling the human need for security with the permanent revolution of the market' (1997: 19). But his is a binary opposition of a classically modernist kind. Two conflicting principles – we must simply hope for some kind of reconciliation!

Gray assumes that we have to make a choice between Soviet-style planning and market pricing. If we reject the former, then we must embrace the latter (1993: x). In 1993 he argues that the market is at least one dimension in which individuals make choices and exercise responsibility (ibid.: 63): private property is a precondition for individual autonomy (ibid.: 76). Planning, he is fond of arguing, is an epistemological impossibility (1996a: 35–6), but why do we have to choose between abstract planning and abstract spontaneity? I have already noted Femia's argument above that planning can be democratic if it accepts a diversity of independent bodies of power. Why can't there be what Gramsci considered to be a *disciplined* spontaneity (1971: 198)?

Although Gray argues in his later work that the market is culturally conditioned and circumscribed and is not a panacea for all problems (he mentions in particular environmental degradation), he sees markets as integral expressions of histories and parent cultures (1997: 30). Encumbered markets, as he calls them, are the norm in every society (ibid.: 17), and he takes it for granted that we need a 'dynamic market economy' (1996b: 11). Market exchanges, he argues, are universal and perennial (or they may be) (1997: 183) but it is precisely this ahistorical assumption that makes it impossible to develop a critical view of the market itself.

Markets may differ significantly, but human society without the market is as unimaginable to Gray as it was to Adam Smith. Gray argues that we are living in a post-socialist age in which the choice we face is not between central planning and the market economy, but between varieties of capitalism. In Britain, our task must be to make our liberal market capitalism friendlier to human needs (1996b: 14). Gray champions a communitarian liberal view that takes the view that 'there is no sustainable alternative to the institutions of liberal capitalism, however reformed' (ibid.: 46). But Marx in the third volume of *Capital* had referred to capitalism as a 'self-dissolving contradiction' (1966: 437) in which each regulative step forward is a step beyond.

It is precisely the market that abstracts individuals from their particular differences and 'equates' them. I concede that transforming the market is a protracted process, but to be uncritical of the market is to be uncritical of the mystification involved in the exchange process. Gray exhibits this mystification in his adoption of a traditionalist view of utopia and in the way he embraces the one-sided, abstract approach linked to the liberal tradition. Gray may have imagined that he has transcended liberalism, but in fact he has merely inverted it and remains prisoner to liberal abstractions.

In his early work on *Liberalism*, Gray defends neo-liberalism and the market explicitly. As he becomes more critical of liberalism, he continues (for some years) to make the case for individual autonomy and private property, although he now argues that not every culture is voluntarist, i.e. believes in free will (1993: 81). He appears to endorse Berlin's idea that all humans have a capacity for choice, and at this stage his argument is anti-determinist, interpreting determinism in its traditional, mechanistic form. One may, however, choose not to be autonomous, so freedom of choice need not mean the adoption of liberalism.

He then turns his abstract notion of free will on its head, arguing that the very notion of free will comes from religion, not science (2003: 109). In *Straw Dogs*, perhaps Gray's most nihilist work, he describes free will as an illusion (2002: 104) and sees humans as simply more rapacious forms of animals – machine-like in the way they operate and think. His critics have argued that *Straw Dogs* creates more philosophical problems than it solves, leaving such issues as personal identity, free will and the mind–body relationship in a chaotic intellectual condition (O'Sullivan, 2006: 302). Gray hops from one abstraction to another. Humans from being above nature are now indistinguishable from all other beings of nature. After all, Gray does not deny that humans have consciousness (although he sees this as a negative and problematic feature). But where does this consciousness come from? Gray claims to support Darwin but declines to give an evolutionary account of the birth of consciousness as humans emerged from the world of nature.

He holds that humans are different from animals (they are much worse), and yet at the same time they are animals themselves. Either they are different or they are the same – it is impossible for them to be both at the same time! Why can't humans be animals who produce and have social relations that they forge through their attempts to consciously organize their lives? Gray's thought is resolutely abstract and dualistic in character.

Transcending the market: the question of market socialism

Transcending the market is emphatically not the same as suppressing the market. Gray speaks of Marx seeking to abolish market competition (1996a: 79), but capitalism, like the market, is not a system to be suppressed: it is a system to be transcended. In the context of an analysis of Soviet totalitarianism, Gray argues that, for Marx, socialism and communism involved the abolition of commodity production and market exchange (ibid.: 171). But Marx, it seems to me, sought not to abolish commodity production and market exchange, but to go beyond them – to capture their advantages while discarding bit by bit the opacity that has historically accompanied them.

The market, Gray comments, is not a natural social phenomenon but 'a creature of law and government' (1993: 116, 135). If law and government are interpreted in a statist fashion, then I can only agree. The market arises because the exchange process has become central to economic life. It conceals the specific identities of the partners to the transaction, and therefore it presupposes class divisions and the state. Gray comments that unfettered markets tend to destroy or dissipate local knowledge and render the social world unintelligible – they deplete the stock of historical memory on which cultural identity depends (1995: 106) – but he fails to see that this is why the market is inherently abstract and must be transcended.

Gray's attack on central planning is well taken: the alternative to the market is, however, not a plan imposed from on high by geniuses who claim to have superior knowledge to the millions who buy and sell things every day. It is rather that, when we render the exchange process more and more concrete and thus *connected*, we begin to move beyond the market by examining the power and resources involved. To argue that 'cheap' airline flights waste fossil fuels, impact on the environment, disturb residents near airports etc. is to begin to render the exchange process concrete and, in my terminology, to move beyond the market.

Gray sees market socialism as a blind alley but this is because the market is suppressed in the provision of capital so that collective owners of productive assets cannot sell off these assets. Gray rightly notes that in this situation there is (albeit a rather more selective) denial of the dispersal of knowledge among the mass of the population who may wish to alter resource allocation (1993: 93). Gray assumes that we must either suppress the market or celebrate it: it is impossible to move beyond it.

The notion of a basic income

In *Beyond the New Right* Gray argues for 'a negative capital tax', as he calls it, the idea being that each citizen would receive a capital sum that would confer on him or her the possibility of independence and of self-provision 'against most forms of market-generated insecurity' (1993: 113). His argument is that such a sum would perhaps be index-linked against inflation and tax-exempt and would be redeemable for purposes of investment, savings, retirement etc.

The idea is an interesting one. Gray argues that it probably embodies 'one of the few viable means of reducing the systemic instabilities of market capitalism' and would, he comments, substantially dismantle the 'elephantine apparatus of the welfare state' (ibid.: 153). It is true that Gray is extremely hostile to the idea, much in favour among neo-liberals, egalitarian social democrats and market-oriented conservatives, of a negative income tax that would involve giving those with little or no income a sum allowing a decent basic subsistence. This, he argues, would be ruinously expensive and could be inflated as the result of the electoral process (ibid.: 25–6). It also fails to differentiate between different kinds of poverty, distracting from the poverty of the old, the disabled and the sick (1995: 54). It would create problems with incentives (1993: 110).

It is revealing that Gray himself acknowledges that there is a difficulty with 'market-generated insecurity'. The value of a basic income is that it would give people a real choice whether they were to work for another in paid employment. It would, as Faulks has pointed out, enhance their sense of community and individual autonomy (2000: 120), and it would dramatically improve the status of women whose precarious economic position makes them particularly dependent upon men or other women who are patriarchally minded. People often seek to work outside the home for social rather than purely economic reasons, and a guaranteed income would provide time and resources to be more involved in community-enhancing activities such as life-long learning, voluntary work and political participation.

It is true that the cost would be substantial. But it is worth noting that a universal basic income would markedly simplify the complex tax and benefit system. It is argued that a universal scheme would create dependency and undermine incentives but it should be pointed out that the British National Health Service is hugely popular precisely because it provides universal benefits. Increasing taxation would be much more palatable if people could see how the money generated would impact positively upon people's lives.

Gray also objects (1997: 44) that a basic income scheme would be exclusionary in the extra significance attached to citizenship (Faulks himself acknowledges that a scheme of basic income would be likely to mean excluding non-citizens – 2000: 120), and that it runs counter to the strongly held ethical belief that income should not be provided independent of need or merit (Gray, 1997: 45). It is true that Gray favours a negative capital tax as opposed to a citizen's basic income but his argument reveals some understanding that the market generates insecurity and anxiety. A basic income would detach rights from producing commodities for a market and would I think, for all its considerable difficulties, be the kind of measure that would enable society to move beyond the market. It would of course involve, as Gray implies, a dramatic change in popular attitudes.

Rights

Gray is correctly sceptical about abstract rights. Rights, he argues referring to Raz, are never fundamental or primordial in political discourse. Rights have what he calls 'an ineradicable open texture' (1993: 101), by which he means that they depend upon our perception of our interests – what we regard as our well being. This well being depends upon a whole host of conditions and the goal of enhancing autonomy cannot be squeezed into 'the Procrustean contours of rights theory' (ibid.: 102).

But it does not follow from this that, as Gray puts it, the discourse of rights is in its nature abstractly universalistic and monolithic, for Gray assumes that asserting a right necessarily involves disregarding questions of context and history. But this is an abstract notion of right: the challenge is not to reject the 'discourse' but to rework and reconstruct it. It is true that the appeal to abstract rights becomes a substitute for taking meaningful action to defend real interests. Rights should not be seen as theorems that fall out of theories of law and ethics (2000: 113). Gray is right to warn that the culture of unconditional rights can only speed the United States towards ungovernability (1998a: 109), but this is not the fault of rights per se. It arises from a classical liberal notion of rights as universal entitlements that exist outside circumstances and constraints. A person can only have rights that take account of resources and skills. When Gray comments that 'the effect of rights-discourse is to render political conflicts non-negotiable' (1993: 103), this is premised upon a traditional view of rights and a traditional (that is, statist) notion of politics. Asserting rights can be part and parcel of political negotiation if the assertion is realistic, and presented in a give-and-take manner.

The problem of sameness and difference

Gray does not differentiate between divisions and differences. Divisions violently exclude but (in my terminology) differences do not. Hence he fails to see that things that are different are also the same – that is to say, they have something in common and without this commonality it would be impossible to differentiate them. In my view, the confusion between division and difference arises from the tendency to view the world abstractly, and this in turn stems from an uncritical acceptance of the market and what Marx calls the 'fetishism' of commodities (1970: 72). Liberalism's penchant for abstraction arises from its belief that people are property – they are things rather than ensembles of relationships.

Liberalism is abstract because it ignores the fact that people become aware of themselves as individuals only *in relation to others*. A relationship implies that each party is both different from, and yet linked to, the other. If the parties to a relationship were simply the same, then they would not be different; if they were simply different, we could not speak of them as related. Liberalism is abstract because it ignores the factors that make people what they are. Parent and child, for example, are clearly different, but they are also the 'same'.

Individuals are of course different, but what distinguishes them – say their drive and initiative – itself only becomes explicable because individuals have a social and natural environment in common. An abstract (or non-relational) view of the individual arises from a belief that the relations between human and nature (that is, *human nature*) can only take the form of an exchange in the market. This exchange, as Marx's analysis indicates, privileges sameness over difference, so that the particular facts of each person's context (whether they are poor, female, Catholic etc.) is deemed irrelevant.

This abstraction bedevils Gray's treatment of the relation of humans to the wider world of nature, and can be seen strikingly in Gray's critique of humanism. It is perfectly true that humans not only differ from nature, but they differ among themselves. People have different cultures, religions and values, both between nations and of course within them. Each individual is unique. But does this mean that they have nothing in common? Liberalism treats individuals as either the same or different. Hence in its 'generous' moments, it speaks of an abstract humanity that, as subject peoples, women, the poor, the dissidents etc. know only too well, does not really embrace everyone in the world. In its restrictive moments, when liberals become aware of the emptiness of these universal abstractions, they turn against universalism and emphasize particularity.

Gray argues that realism claims that beliefs are either true or false (2000: 60), but this is realism (I prefer 'materialism') interpreted in a modernist manner. Beliefs are both true *and* false. They are true because they reflect objective reality but they are false because this reflection is of necessity partial, imperfect and historically conditioned. Even the most absurd of beliefs has a 'grain' of truth in it, and even the most solid of propositions has some falsity. Thus, racism would not be believed at all unless it were true that people look and believe differently, even though the causality that racism asserts is grotesquely false, and the notion, for example, that the world is round is generally true but aspects of the observation are continually being improved upon. The absolute truth can only manifest itself in relative form. It has become common to reject the truth, but this sceptical position arises because the truth is conceptualized in an ahistorical, abstract way.

Gray follows this dismal path. From the abstractly universalist position of liberalism, he moves increasingly to an abstractly particularistic position. Human identities, he contends, are never tokens of the universal type of generic humanity (1993: 79). Yet it is not difficult to see that without a notion of generic humanity it would be impossible to identify individual and unique humans. To argue that 'humanity' does not exist since there are only humans, driven by conflicting needs and illusions (2002: 12–13), is to see humanity as an abstraction – a static essence – that must be rejected (i.e. inverted). Gray contends that, because he rejects the attempt to realize abstract principles or ideals, he has adopted a post-liberal perspective (1989: 235). His task, he tells us explicitly, is to 'retheorize liberalism as itself a particular form of common life' (1995: 66). Hence, a commitment to liberalism remains at the heart of his work.

Gray's uncritical endorsement of the market means that he incorporates into his own analysis the very abstractions that he regards as ahistorical and false. The liberalism and traditions of the Enlightenment that he so righteously expels through the front door come slithering in through the back.

Conclusion

Initially Gray embraces Hayek's view of the market. He is impressed by Hayek's epistemological critique of social reality as ultimately unknowable and subscribes to the idea that the concept of planning presupposes a notion of transparency that is untenable. The market is central to the liberal tradition. Hobbes's state of nature is premised on the assumption that people follow self-interest and Locke's theory even assumes that money is discovered while people are still interacting in a state of nature.

It is true that later liberals abandon the notion of the state of nature but, although they ostensibly accept the social nature of the individual, liberals such as Smith and James Mill see market relations as natural and liberating. It is important, however, not to confuse neo-liberalism with classical liberalism, since the neo-liberals are reacting against the extension of liberalism in a social direction and vigorously reject the concept of equality as a motivating ideal. Earlier liberals were not enthusiastic about equality but they would never have presented inequality as a 'right'. Neo-liberals warn about the danger that democracy can pose to the market – whereas, for earlier liberals, democracy was either not an issue or something that was seen as compatible with middle-class hegemony.

Gray inherits some of the neo-liberal scepticism towards democracy and equality, and he fails to see that the market itself is an institution that generates abstraction and dualism. Of course, all ideas are abstract reconstructions of material reality, but the abstraction that underpins the exchange process distorts the material world in the way that it renders opaque the concrete realities involved when goods exchange or workers are employed. Emancipatory movements seek to make the exchange process more transparent by focusing on the gender or class of the people involved so that relationships that 'disappear' in market relations are rendered more visible.

This is the problem with linking the market with freedom, or choice, or autonomy. These notions arise within a particular context and set of constraints, and the market tends to conceal this context and these constraints. Although Gray is sharply and rightly critical of neo-liberal views of the market, he is not critical of the market itself and seeks to establish some kind of balance between human needs for security, on the one hand, and dynamism of the market on the other. He thus presents the opposition between free will and determinism in dualistic terms – we have to make a choice between them – and he moves from a one-sided defence of free will to a one-sided rejection of it. Determinism for Gray is always a mechanistic determinism, so that when he comes to embrace determinism, in *Straw Dogs*, for example, he insists that free will is no more than a humanist myth.

What is absent from his analysis is the distinction between abolishing the market and transcending it – that is, a gradual process of making the exchange process more and more concrete so that real people replace the abstract individuals of the market. This is why the notion of a basic income, payable to all as citizens, deserves a more sympathetic consideration than Gray gives it, and Gray's own support for a negative capital tax indicates that he is aware in part of the anxiety and insecurity that the market generates. His attitude towards the notion of rights is similarly one-sided. For, while he is right to warn that the concept of rights can abstract from context and undermine the need for the give-and-take of the political process, the notion needs to be reconstructed to take situation into account – not simply dismissed.

Overall, Gray seeks to retheorize liberalism (as he puts it) rather than go beyond it. He sees the market as necessary and inevitable and his rejection of universality arises out of his belief that sameness and difference form a dualistic coupling. Traditional liberalism has privileged sameness over difference: Gray seeks to privilege difference over sameness. Only humans exist – there is no such thing as humanity. This one-sidedness and abstraction reveal the uncritical attitude that he ultimately has towards the market itself.

6 • The Caricature of Marxism

Introduction

We will now examine Gray's critique of Marxism, and try to explore the reasons why it is inaccurate. Gray, we will argue, identifies Marxism with the Enlightenment because he is unable to distinguish between a static perfectionist theory and one that seeks to root itself in history and dialectics. After 1843, Marx sets out to go beyond the principles of the Enlightenment. Gray sees communism as wholly unhistorical (despite Marx's effort to present an historical view of communism); he misses Marx's view of progress as contradictory in character; and he ignores attempts to take ecology into account in the Marxist tradition. Gray treats Marxism as a form of modernism because he takes dualism for granted, and he does so because he is uncritical not only towards the market (as we saw in the last chapter) but (as we shall see in the next chapter) towards the state as well.

Marx's critique of the Enlightenment

Gray's knowledge of Marxism is seemingly impressive. The critiques he writes of Western Marxists are acute and pithy, so that it is both astonishing and disappointing that he should misrepresent Marxism in general so dramatically. In Gray's view, Marxism can be identified with humanism, Christianity and the Enlightenment. He describes Marxism as an Enlightenment ideology (1998c: 151). It is true that Marx was deeply influenced by the Enlightenment and up to about 1843 he subscribed explicitly to Enlightenment principles.

The young Marx, as has been frequently commented, was steeped in the traditions of the French Revolution. He consciously identifies his position with what he calls rather grandly 'the ever new philosophy of reason' (Marx and Engels, 1975b: 202) – a philosophy that extends back to Heraclitus and Aristotle, Machiavelli and Campanella, Hobbes, Spinoza and Grotius, Rousseau, Fichte and Hegel. Marx's position can be described here as Rousseauian in character, since he speaks of the state as 'the great organism, in which legal, political and moral freedom must be realised, and in which the citizen in obeying the laws of the state, only obeys the natural laws of his own reason, of human reason' (ibid.: 202).

Marx uses the notion of the 'rational state' as a stick to beat the state in the Rhineland where the government, by preventing peasants from collecting firewood, has become a mere 'instrument of the forest owner' (ibid.: 245). He follows Rousseau in seeing private interests as a violation of the 'universality' of the state's content (ibid.: 306). There is no doubt that the early Marx defends the Enlightenment, but by 1843 he becomes increasing critical. He no longer refers to partisan acts by the state as 'non-political', but in his critique of Hegel's *Philosophy of Right* he uses the term 'political' in a pejorative way, referring to the 'political state' as a narrow creation of special interests, 'the modern State as it is' (Marx and Engels, 1975a: 63). His critique is still transitional, for Marx contrasts the political state with the 'true state', and it is only in his work *On the Jewish Question* that the distinction between a political state and a true state falls away completely.

Marx now distinguishes between political and human emancipation and sees Rousseau as merely depicting the abstraction of the 'political man'. What was true in the *Critique of Hegel's Philosophy of Right* now becomes true of all states. They are all otherworldly embodiments of a divided world, and what the democratic state does is to perfect the separation of the general from the particular, the idealism of the state with its 'abstract, artificial man', and the materialism of civil society with its egoistic institutions of private property and money (ibid.: 167). Marx has broken from the Enlightenment and, although there are abstract echoes in the *1844 Manuscripts* (as already noted), from now on Marx seeks to place the notions of reason, freedom and emancipation on a dialectical footing. Critical of the Enlightenment, he attempts to establish what I have called a post-liberal view of the world.

Gray identifies Marx with Socrates, Plato, Aristotle, Descartes and Spinoza, saying that, 'for all of them, consciousness is our very essence' (2002: 111). Yet, from *The German Ideology* onwards, this is precisely the proposition that Marx vigorously combats! It is difficult to disagree with Kateb when he says that 'Gray's generalizations about consciousness are polemical and so broad and quick as not even to be productively satirical' (2006: 316). Gray cites Cioran: 'To turn from a metaphysical or theological conception to historical materialism is simply to change providentialisms' (Gray, 1995: 164). But Marx rejected providentialism – a belief that God or History rules the world and determines its fate. The critique of abstraction and the state is a critique of otherworldliness, and it is because Gray cannot sympathize with a dialectical standpoint that he assumes that Marxist theory must have some kind of abstract absolute at its base.

Communism as an historical society

Gray argues that Marxism looks to the 'final perfection of mankind' and 'the end of history' (2004: 1; also 2002: 167). It is a commonplace, he comments, that Marxism is a secular version of a Christian view of history (2004: 27). But, commonplace or not, this is simply untrue. I have already noted Marx's comment in which he describes communism as the solution to the riddle of human history (a comment that Gray wrongly believes is from the *Communist Manifesto*, 2007: 18); although this remark undoubtedly has a millenarian ring to it, it could be argued that after 1844 Marx goes beyond this kind of millenarian sentiment. Gray describes the end of history as 'an absurd idea' (2004: 44; 2007: 5) and it is difficult to disagree with him. But the idea was not Marx's.

The mature Marx regards communism not as the end but as the beginning of a human history (2000: 420). It is true that the historical nature of communist society requires more emphasis than Marx gives it, but Marx makes it clear that a communist society is a dynamic, contradictory one and that the conflict between the forces and relations of production would still continue under communism, even if revolutions themselves would have become a thing of the past. He declares at the end of his polemical response to Proudhon that in a classless society 'social evolutions will cease to be political revolutions' (ibid.: 232). Gray's contention that for Marx only prehistory (that is the history of class-divided societies) is law-governed (1993: 104) cannot be sustained textually. As we have seen above, the contradiction between the forces and relations of production operates under communism with a law-like regularity. Marx insisted, Gray tells us, that freedom from labour could be achieved without any restraints on people's desires (2002: 168). What then are we to make of the passage in the third volume of *Capital* where Marx insists that human potentiality can flourish only upon the 'realm of necessity as its basis' (1966: 820)? People will always enter into relations independent of their will, no matter how free they become. Restraints or constraints are part of human relations in general.

There is therefore a crucial distinction to be made between Marx and Hegel. Hampshire is cited approvingly by Gray to the effect that Hegelianism, positivism and Marxism see a social redemption leading to 'a final salvation of humanity' (1996b: 88). Whatever might be the case for Hegel and positivists such as Comte, Marx has an historical and not an abstract view of communism. Gray is wrong to argue that for Marx, like Hegel, there is a idealistic telos that is human emancipation, thus making communist society post-historical (1996a: 84). Marx, Gray argues, commits a fallacy of ethical naturalism by giving a moral term a wholly descriptive meaning (ibid.: 94) but, as I have argued elsewhere, the is/ought dualism is alien to Marx's argument. He assumes a relational view between facts and values that acknowledges distinction but rejects dualism.

Marx's hostility to traditional utopianism is premised upon a dislike of perfectionist notions of the future society. Marx, it is true, overemphasizes the discontinuity between capitalism and communism in order doubtless to make the case for dramatic and revolutionary change, and it can also be argued that Marx's equation between communism and the end of alienation erroneously (and undialectically) suggests a world without tragedy and loss. But Marx generally makes it clear that communism would be a real society, so that there is no reason to believe that communism would be without the kind of conflicts (including tragedies and losses) that require governmental (as opposed to statist) processes to tackle them. Barry complains that to ascribe to Green thinkers an Enlightenment-type vision of human mastery is completely false, since 'the Green vision stands for prudence, modesty and harmony' (2006: 260). For Gray, there is either realism (of his deeply pessimistic variety) or there is wild and unrestrained optimism of a traditional utopian kind. There is nothing in between.

The notion that communism is a society in which justice has been transcended (Gray, 1995: 123) rests upon the assumption that a stateless society is a society without conflict and dispute. Yet Marx makes it clear (in the *Communist Manifesto*, for example) that the end of what he calls politics would not mean the end of public power, contrary to Gray's argument (Gray, 2007: 20). Again, Marx could have put much more emphasis upon the historical character of communism as a society in which people have differences, dispute, die and conflict, but this is certainly *implied* in his writings. Marx is aware of what he calls the performance of common activities arising from the nature of communities, and of social functions 'analogous to present state functions' that exist in a communist society (Hoffman, 1984: 208). Although much work needs to be done on what might be called post-statist methods of conflict resolution, there is no serious textual evidence to support the argument that communism for Marx is a static, perfect society that lacks an historical character.

The contradictory character of progress

Gray characterizes progress as a modernist myth (1993: 138), the imposition of a plan of life in which the prejudices and anxieties of the late nineteenth-century European intelligentsia are made mandatory for all (1996a: 260). While progress is a fact in science, he argues, when it comes to ethics and politics it is a superstition (2004: 3). As an idea, it is usually accompanied by a vulgar and unreflective meliorism that assumes that progress entails endless economic growth (1995: 108). What is problematic in Mill's version of liberalism (towards which Gray at least in 1983 is relatively sympathetic) is Mill's view that moral and political theory depends upon a conception of progress – a dependency that Mill's liberalism shares with every other kind of liberal theory. Although it is tacit and unexpressed, post-war liberal theory in the English-speaking world – the American liberalisms of Rawls, Dworkin and Rorty, for example – have been reliant on a particular philosophy of history in which the idea of progressive cultural convergence on a universal civilization is central (1996c: 131).

From a pluralist view, Gray argues, history can have no meaning: it is, at best, a series of adventures in civilization, each singular and discrete, leading nowhere (1996a: 292). It is true that Christianity and the Enlightenment do have static views of the concept of progress, and this is because they postulate an ideal society embodying ahistorical notions of emancipation and freedom. Marx, on the other hand, emphasizes the contradictory and historical character of progress, and the case I will make later for a momentum concept derives from the dialectical character of Marx's argument.

Engels comments at the end of *The Origin of the Family, Private Property and the State* that 'every advance in production is at the same time a retrogression in the condition of the oppressed class'. What is a boon for one is necessarily a bane for the other (Marx and Engels, 1968: 592). Already Rousseau had argued in his celebrated essay on the arts and sciences that progress had brought with it deceit, superficiality, greed and above all inequality (Rousseau, 1968b) and Marx in his attack on the British rule in India draws out the contradictory argument of the *Manifesto* – that capitalism both advances and yet tramples upon humankind. The material basis of a new world has been created, even though the effects have been devastating. Only when a social revolution has mastered the results of the bourgeois epoch, comments Marx, 'will human progress cease to resemble that hideous pagan idol, who would not drink the nectar but from the skulls of the slain' (2000: 366–7). It is a gross oversimplification of Marx's views to say with Gray that he 'defended colonial rule' (2007: 61).

It is precisely this notion of contradiction that Gray's concept of progress lacks. The only notion of progress he can envisage is additive – one improvement after the other (2007: 188). The idea of progress, he complains, encourages us to view our lives 'as moments in a universal process of betterment'. Progress, according to Hayek, is movement for movement's sake, a nihilistic dictum that has led to the destruction of modern conservatism as a result of its embrace with neo-liberalism (Gray, 1995: 89). Gray quotes Santayana attacking 'mechanical progress' (ibid.). The idea involves an 'all but irresistible tendency to improvement' and, as one of the tenets of the modernist pseudo-religion of humanism, it is a sort of historical theodicy (1996a: 23).

But the point about a viable concept of progress is that it is *dialectical* and not mechanistic. It involves development and thus contradiction. Progress is not the linear vision of the Enlightenment – the idea that with the development of science comes a felicitous concomitant improvement in morals and social behaviour generally. Progress, in reality, involves the development of instruments of exploitation (at least under class-divided societies) and therefore the oppression of humanity, but the fact that progress is contradictory does not make it impossible. There is no doubt that capitalism provides the possibility of a world in which emancipation, self-government and freedom can be won – not as the end of historical development, but as an important step forward in the *infinite* progress that can be made.

Porritt in his recent work on capitalism cites the words of the Sustainable Development Commission, speaking of sustainable development as providing 'a framework for redefining progress' and redirecting our economies to enable all people to meet their basic needs. The Commission is acutely aware of the limits of the natural world but it still operates with a (post-Enlightenment) concept of progress (2006: 290). Elsewhere, Porritt quotes the words of Richard Reeves, who complains that our political systems and cultures have failed to adapt to a new world in which 'economics does not equal or even equate to progress' (ibid.: 309). Progress can be reworked as a concept so that it incorporates a critical view of Enlightenment abstractions. Greens, as Barry argues, should avoid rejecting the idea of progress (2006: 260).

In his work on Berlin, Gray insists that the pluralist rejection of perfection is fatal to the idea of human history as at least potentially progressive (1996b: 71). But why? The rejection of perfection is fatal to the notion of progress only if we assume that humankind is progressing towards a fixed goal beyond which no progress is possible. Once we challenge that abstract notion of progress, the argument falls. Gray is unable to distinguish between an abstract humanism that does indeed postulate a static notion of human emancipation, and a concrete humanism that recognizes difference and is rooted in history.

To endorse Kraus's dictum, which Gray quotes, that 'progress makes purses out of human skin' (1997: 161) is wrong. Kraus's comment involves a curious misreading of fascism and the holocaust: the Nazis may have believed that they were carrying history forward, but their policies were reactionary. They were reacting against progress – or the threat of it – not carrying history forward. They made their antagonism to the French Revolution and the Enlightenment crystal clear, and it is far better, in my view, to see Nazism as an extreme form of anti-liberalism in which the achievements of the bourgeois epoch are (almost all) rejected rather than built upon and transcended. Gray is fond of quoting the words of Koestler's Nazi intellectual who speaks of the grand enterprise upon which Nazism has embarked – 'there are no more impossibilities for man now' (Gray, 2003: 13) – but this is linked to a genocidal project that is profoundly at odds with the rationalism and liberal ideals of the Enlightenment.

Indeed, Kateb argues that Gray is forced, in order to make his case against humanity, to regard humanity as distinctive (although of course distinctively *bad*). This means that he even makes it possible to entertain the thought that evolution is progressive since humanity is the most complex, 'the highest species so far' (Kateb, 2006: 318).

The problem of production

Gray warns that, in so far as the left project remains wedded to 'growthmanship', it will suffer the same fate of political obsolescence that has befallen the market doctrines of the New Right (1995: 92). Marx, it is true, had a naïve and overoptimistic view about production and growth. In the *Communist Manifesto,* as elsewhere, he takes it for granted that the constant revolutionizing of production under capitalism creates the basis for a communist society. Although Marx is aware of the destruction of the environment through exploitation, he is, unsurprisingly, not conscious of the way in which even the most egalitarian production consumes finite resources.

In my view, Gray exaggerates when he says that the introduction of war communism by Lenin embodied 'an authentic Marxian vision' (1998a: 134), adding that, in their arrogant attitude towards nature, the Bolsheviks were faithful to Marx (ibid.: 149; also 2003: 8). Gray vividly documents the destruction of the environment wrought by Soviet planning (1993: 131). But did the USSR have Marxist credentials? Of course, there is continuity between classical Marxism and the Soviet experience, but there is also discontinuity as well. Marx assumed that communism would inherit the technological sophistication of advanced capitalist societies, and war communism resembles the 'crude communism' that Marx attacks in the *1844 Manuscripts* rather than the kind of post-capitalist communism that his theory presupposes. Marx, both in his treatment of other socialists and in his attitude towards liberalism, displayed leanings towards autocracy, but it has to be said, all the same, that, just as the dictatorial character of Communist Party states is in some tension with Marx's post-liberal values, so their rapacious attitude towards nature is hard to square with Marx's outlook. Bernstein was right to conclude that the Bolsheviks had 'brutalized' Marx's civilized doctrine (Gay, 1962: 295).

In 1993 Gray links Marxism to liberalism as a modernist political faith advocating the unlimited growth of population, production and knowledge (1993: 138). Yet there is nothing in Marxism that would oppose regulating population growth. Gray's argument that Marxism is a form of human imperialism in which nature is a mere object for human development cannot be sustained textually. Engels takes the view in the *Dialectics of Nature* that at every step we are reminded of the fact that we by no means rule nature like a conqueror as though we stand outside the world of nature. On the contrary, 'all our mastery of it consists in the fact that we have the advantage over all other creatures of being to learn its laws and apply them correctly' (1964: 183).

The whole concept of a dialectics of nature suggests that humans arise out of natural evolution, remain part of nature (despite their unique features) and are ultimately bound by natural limits. Gray's comment that 'Marx tends to treat the whole domain of nature as a precipitate of human activities' (1996a: 103; 2004: 37), making nature into an object simply of human will (1995: 179), is incorrect. To say of Marxism that it sees humans as being able to transcend the constraints of their animal ancestry (1997: 159) is not true. The idea that only human agency confers value onto a valueless world (ibid.: 172) cannot be squared with the concept of a dialectics of nature – that nature evolves and develops. Gray is right to argue that only if one subscribes to a view that value is created by persons can one imagine that value will disappear from the world when humans are no longer around (2006a: 341), but the whole point is that the world is not 'valueless' – as, in an era of ecological devastation, we are beginning to painfully discover.

Gray quotes Margulis approvingly: 'Gaia, the physiologically regulated Earth, enjoyed proprioceptive global communication long before people evolved' (2002: 60). Yet this is precisely the point that dialectical materialism has sought to establish in arguing that human evolution is conceptually possible only if we see nature itself as developmental and dialectical in character. Gray sees anthropocentrism as a belief that the human species enjoys a privileged place in the scheme of things, but it is quite possible to regard humans as special and different without regarding them as 'independent of nature' (1997: 151).

Humans are part of nature – both Marxism and Gray are right to stress this – but it does not follow that, because humans share many attributes of the rest of nature, they are simply the same. Humans are also different and, unless they respect and cherish the wider world of nature, they will put in jeopardy their distinctive characteristics – their capacity to speak, reason, produce and form social relationships. The point is that humans are *both* different *and* the same and it is because Gray espouses an undialectical view of nature that he adopts an either/or position that makes an emancipatory anthropocentrism, of the kind I have defended here, impossible. Gray argues that a genuinely naturalistic philosophy would not start by assuming that humans have attributes that other animals lack. 'Its point of departure would be that the evolutionary laws that govern other animals also govern humans' (2007: 189). This is certainly true but, because Gray interprets evolution in a mechanistic fashion, he fails to see how and why the distinctive attributes of humans are themselves the outcome of the evolutionary process.

Marx, scarcity and the individual

Gray argues that Marxism subscribes to a myth of a human essence shorn of religion, family, locality and all the accidents of time, purged of conflict and released from contingency (1996a: 254). But this is not only a caricature, it stems from Gray's dualistic view that the world of universals is spliced apart from the world of particulars.

The notion that emancipation involves a world without limits is alien to Marxism; although it is true that Marx's notion of technology is uncritical, he and Engels had begun to break from the Enlightenment view that humans could dominate nature as a mere thing. Gray argues that the anthropocentric belief sees the human species as independent of nature (1997: 150). Yet it is possible to see humans as important, not because they are independent of nature, but because they have specific features that distinguish them from the rest of nature. This is only 'anthropocentric' if one takes the view that distinguishing humans detaches them from nature and makes them conquerors. Such a view involves the same modernist logic here as elsewhere: either humans are different from nature or they are the same; they can't be both at the same time! Why can't we see humans merely as distinct from nature, and thereby 'privileged', not because they are conquerors of nature but because, as humans ourselves, we have a special concern for their well being? Gray argues that, like all other animals, humans have a common nature that is fairly constant in its needs (2000: 120). It is true that all humans have the need to produce and all enter into relations of production independent of their will. But this human nature also takes dramatically different forms, depending upon the relationship that humans have to nature at any given point in time. Human nature is both the same and variable, and the sociable, communitarian human nature that Gray approves of can only develop if we tackle the problem of the market and the state.

Gray sees Marxism, like other socialist liberationist movements, as hostile to tradition, characterizing the latter as 'shackles which repress our self-expression' (1993: 136). But this is one-sided. Marxism is hostile to repressive traditions, but not to democratic ones. Hence the interest British Marxists have in rediscovering the role of the Levellers and Diggers during the English Civil War, or the respect that Marxists have in general for early societies – societies that demonstrate the historical character of class divisions and the state.

Gray's reading of Marxism assumes that Marxism is simply a kind of Enlightenment modernism. To say that the more conscious humans are the more mechanical they become (2002: 133) is precisely wrong. Humans have become much more conscious of the limitations of a mechanical approach, and increasingly see the need to link the world together in a dialectical manner. It is because nature imposes limits upon humans that scarcity in some sense of the word is part of the human condition. To argue that 'Marx imagined that the end of scarcity would bring about the end of history' (ibid.: 167) is doubly problematic. Marx, as we have argued above, rejected the notion of the 'end of history', and he identified communism with the end of class divisions, not with the end of scarcity as such. Even the abolition of poverty cannot mean that nothing is scarce any longer, since the end of scarcity per se would imply that humans no longer have disputes or conflicts, and that would indeed be fanciful and, in the traditional sense of the term, utopian.

Gray ignores the dialectical character of Marxism and the attempt to move beyond liberal abstractions. He sees it as an anti-liberalism, arguing that 'an anti-individualistic animus' pervades the thought of Marx and Engels alike (1996a: 75). Yet the notion of communism as a society in which the free development of each is the free development of all shows that Marx was critical, not of individualism as such, but of the liberal notion of the individual. Gray persists with the view that, for Marx, liberal values were destined for the rubbish heap (2007: 58). Gray is quite wrong to argue that, for Marx, the autonomous individual with access to a variety of forms of life and modes of thought will vanish in a communist society. Marxism, he argues, has always been committed to the elimination of the modern expression of human identity as individuality (1996a: 256). Yet Marx makes it clear that a concrete individuality lies at the heart of his theory of emancipation.

Gray's reading of Marxism is linked to an uncritical attitude to the state, and he assumes that the only alternative to an existing liberal society is a static, perfectionist order in which abstract harmony prevails – in other words, a traditionally conceived utopia. To argue that 'Hegel and Marx followed Judaism and Christianity in seeing history as a moral drama whose last act is salvation' (2003: 7) is quite untrue as far as Marx is concerned.

The question of form

It is true that Marx's theory is sometimes presented in general terms that appear to neglect particularities. But even Marx's famous presentation of the base/superstructure analysis of society speaks of 'definite forms' of social consciousness, and argues that people become conscious of the conflict between relations and forces of production through 'ideological forms' of a legal, political, religious or philosophical character (Marx, 2000: 426).

There is no doubt that, when Engels conceded after Marx's death that he and Marx had placed too much emphasis on economic factors, he was also acknowledging an apparent neglect of form. Indeed, in an earlier chapter I have argued that class itself should be seen as a general category that only expresses itself in cultural, gender or religious forms. Form is important, but not more important than content. Gray tends to ignore content and elevate form as an independent, self-explanatory factor in his attack on rationalist and universalist movements, 'liberal as well as Marxist' (1995: 65).

He argues that class divisions are only one of the causes of conflict, and rarely the most important. Indeed, he tells Colls that he has never found the concept particularly illuminating. 'I have never been touched by, or particularly sensitive to, the culture of class'

(Colls, 1996: 71). 'Ethnic and religious differences, the scarcity of natural resources and the collision of rival values are permanent sources of division' (Gray, 2003: 9). But the challenge is to develop a notion of class (as noted above) in which ethnicity and religion, for example, are seen as the *forms* of class struggle, and do not exist outside class as 'permanent' sources of division.

It is true that the Enlightenment embraced an abstract view of universality, but it is not helpful to simply invert this rather than transcend it. Gray ends up with an abstract view of the form of particularity – a belief that cultural, ethnic and religious differences are themselves the source of conflict and war. Cultural difference, he argues, is 'a primordial attribute of the human species' (1995: 65). When Gray endorses the conservative's stress on the primacy of cultural forms (ibid.: 108), this implies a reductionism as one-sided as the economic determinism that he rejects.

Gray likens Marxism to what he calls market fundamentalism. Both theorize cultural and political life in the reductionist terms of economic determinism (ibid.: 101). But this is an inaccurate reading of Marxism, and Engels made it clear that when Marx actually examined concrete situations he took the forms of ideological struggle very much into account (Marx and Engels, 1975d: 396). I have already dealt with Gray's contention that Marx saw nationalism and ethnicity as 'epiphenomenal'. Indeed, class struggle always takes a national form, Marx argues, and he condemned those socialists who ignored language and other ethnic particularities. Whatever might be thought of the 'economic imperialism' of the neo-liberals, it surely cannot be said that Marxism does not take national and cultural forms and the individual seriously: Marx explicitly rejects the liberal idea that society is a mere abstraction.

Gray's attempt to identify Marxism with the Enlightenment and Christianity results in a caricature of Marxist theory.

Conclusion

It is true that the (very) young Marx supported Enlightenment assumptions about nature, the state and freedom and his position can be broadly described as Rousseauian in character. But from 1843 he begins a life-long process of challenging the Enlightenment, so that it is quite wrong for Gray to depict Marx and Marxism as a form of Enlightenment humanism. Marx explicitly rejects the notions of property, the state, human nature and freedom that underpin Enlightenment thought.

To argue that Marx sees communism as the end of history is to ignore Marx's attempt to present communism as an historical society – one in which the contradiction between the forces and relations of production continues, albeit without the revolutionary explosions that punctuate the history of class-divided societies. Nor is it correct to identify Marxism with a mechanical notion of progress. Marx and Engels acknowledged the tragic and contradictory character of progress and recent writers have tried to redefine the concept so that it is compatible with a strategy for sustainable development. It cannot be denied that Marx saw the production process as one that took place without regard to limited resources, but it is not true that Marxism is a form of human imperialism that ignores human dependency upon the wider world of nature. Indeed, the notion of a dialectics of nature that Engels expounded (but which I believe that Marx also endorsed) anticipates arguments within Green theory that nature exists as a force in its own right.

Gray's contention that Marxism is hostile to the notion of the individual ignores Marx and Engels's attempt to transcend liberalism by incorporating into the case for communism a richer and more concrete concept of individualism. Engels acknowledged a tendency to economic reductionism in the general expositions of historical materialism and I would argue that the notion of class in Marxism is too abstract in its tendency to separate exploitation from gender, national and religious oppression etc. But Gray subscribes to what Marx and Engels would have called the 'illusion of the epoch' by arguing that ethnic and cultural struggles should be taken at face value. If an actor asserts that religion is the root of a particular conflict, then that is the truth of the matter! But this kind of reductionism is not plausible, so it is not surprising that Gray's critique of Marxism is distorted and one-sided.

7 • The Problem of the State

Introduction

I have looked at Gray's uncritical attitude towards the market. Not surprisingly, his attitude toward the state is equally uncritical. He regards statism, if not the state, as existing in even the earliest societies, and sees the state as a 'civilizing agency'. He is conscious of the existence of social (as opposed to statist) sanctions, but never considers the conditions in which the latter could supplant the need for an institution claiming a monopoly of legitimate force. Even post-national developments of the kind occurring in the European Union are seen by Gray as taking a statist form.

Gray appears highly critical of the nation-state, and rightly sees it as trying to construct a 'homogeneous' nation where there are invariably many different peoples involved. He highly rates diversity and difference – yet he fails to see that the state is the enemy of diversity. He favours what he calls a 'modest' democracy but the notion of democracy calls for self-government and this is only possible in a stateless society. The state is necessarily shrouded in secrecy and embodies an authoritarian elitism. It institutionalizes and naturalizes the use of force as a way of tackling conflict and, although liberal attempts to limit this force are admirable, force itself is ultimately illimitable (hence inherently illegitimate). Nor is force a static problem: as democratic attitudes take root and technology becomes more sophisticated, force becomes increasingly dangerous for social development.

This is not to say that force is abhorrent in principle. Where conflicts cannot be resolved non-violently, force is inevitable, but it can be justified only as a method of cementing common interests. Gray pours scorn on the idea that the state can wither away, but not only is this necessary if humanity is to flourish, we need to chart the conceptual distinctions that make this process of the state withering away thinkable. The distinction between the state and government is crucial here – government being defined as a method of resolving conflicts of interest through arbitration and negotiation. Indeed, the recognition since the Second World War that universal rights can override state sovereignty points to a growing understanding that we have a global identity that transcends national interests.

The fact is that an uncritical attitude to the state enshrines dualism; this accounts for Gray's traditionalist view of utopia.

The nation-state and universal empire

Although Gray is frequently critical of the nation-state, he is unsure what to put in its place. He speaks of Santayana abominating the tribalistic passions associated with the nation-state, and Gray rightly contests the idea that the United Kingdom, for example, can be legitimately described as a nation-state. Most states are multi-national in character but Gray does not pause to consider the tension between an institution claiming a monopoly of legitimate force, and the multiple identities that people within states have. It is revealing, to stay with the British example, just how flexible the concept of national identity is. During the funeral of Princess Diana, not only was there much talk of a British nation, but this 'nation' appeared to embrace mourners from all corners of the world!

Santayana's argument leaves Gray uneasy. For, while Santayana is fiercely critical of the nation-state, he argues that the nation-state should give way to 'universal liberal empire' (Gray, 1996a: 25). Gray can see that this would be hopelessly impractical and a step backwards. Despite his huffing and puffing, he ultimately regards the idea of transcending the nation-state as futile and he praises Berlin for continuing with an older liberal tradition that recognized the principal embodiment of culture in the nation-state (ibid.: 99). But this, like all forms of statism, means enshrining a dominant culture at the expense of other cultures, since an institution that asserts a monopoly of legitimacy will inevitably press for a set of exclusive cultural values.

Gray's Hobbesian view of the world leads him to describe the sovereign state as a 'natural human demand', especially in the historical context of the modern world 'in which the nation-state is the pre-eminent political form' (ibid.: 115). It has to be said that Gray's argument is statist throughout.

A civilizing agency?

Gray takes for granted, as he puts it, that the practices of exclusion and subordination are constitutive of every community humans have ever lived in (1995: 8). Like the notion of conflict, the notion of inclusion and exclusion is ambiguous. The very notion of privacy implies some sense of exclusion, but the exclusion that is problematic is the exclusion that involves the use of force. It is not surprising that for Gray the political art is that of statecraft (1995: 128). Politics is more than the mere process of conflict resolution; for Gray conflict is necessarily violent, and politics involves the sanctions of force.

He identifies the withering away of the state thesis as utopian in the traditional sense (1997: 169), having described the state as a 'civilizing agency' (ibid.: 133). It is true that, if a society is riven with conflicts of interests of a kind that can only be tackled by force, then an institution claiming a monopoly of legitimate violence has an important and valuable role to play. After all, the state in general, and the modern state in particular, seeks to limit the use of 'unauthorized' force, and I agree with Gray that, where a state has broken down and war-lordism prevails, the establishment of the state is a crucial step forward. Gray makes this point graphically when he criticizes conservative libertarians for wanting a free market in, say, drugs while criminal mafias and mafia-controlled states still prevail (ibid.: 132). Clearly in this kind of context the state has an important role to play. Rights have to be enforced and, unless social sanctions are highly developed, that requires what Gray calls 'an effective modern state' (2000: 132).

But there is a difference between 'demonizing' the state (that is to say, rejecting it under all circumstances) and adopting a critical attitude towards it. My argument is that, where conflicts of interests cannot be tackled in a peaceful manner, states are inevitable even though the state can only suppress conflict, not resolve it. Gray argues that the state is a 'civilizing agency', but Rousseau had already argued that, with the development of the state, 'all ran headlong to their chains' (1968b: 205). States only arise because social sanctions are no longer effective in maintaining order. If by civilization we mean the use of negotiation and persuasion to settle conflicts of interest, then the state could well be described as an *anti-civilizing* agency, since the use of force to address conflicts of interest involves treating people as things. Gray himself comments, in his critique of

Thatcherite policies on the 'free market', that social cohesion has been undermined so that the informal sanctions of public opinion cease to be effective and only legal sanctions are left (1997: 141).

Yet this is surely the point. Non-statist sanctions can work where people can 'change places' and settle their differences through compromise and negotiation: a stateless society is not a society without sanctions – it is a society where institutional force is no longer necessary to tackle conflict. Revolutionary capitalism, as Gray calls it (ibid.: 142), undermines bonds of community and, with increasing economic insecurity, it 'downsizes' families. Over 10 per cent of the American population live in privately guarded buildings or housing developments. The figures that Gray gives on incarceration, violent crime and litigation in the United States portray a society in which (statist) law has become almost the only functioning social institution, and prison among the few remaining means of social control (1998a: 116, 119). Gray argues that law curbs freedom even when it is enabling (2006a: 333). But this assumes that law can only be statist in character and therefore must have violent sanctions attached to it. But what if laws are merely rules or norms with social rather than statist sanctions? Surely in this case they do not curb but facilitate freedom. Freedom, of course, needs to be defined in a relational, and not in an anarchic liberal, manner. Social sanctions are the kind of constraints that people have to recognize in order to be free. To take an example from our own society: traffic lights can hardly be said to restrict our freedom; it would be foolish, probably suicidal, to ignore them.

Crick defines politics as 'the public actions of free men', a civilizing activity in which we agree to disagree. Politics, he insists, chooses conciliation rather than violence or coercion (1962: 30). This is surely right (if one overlooks Crick's sexist language) and one could well argue that a political solution to a problem is at odds with a statist attitude to conflict. On the other hand, Crick also defines politics as centring on the state – an institution that has an acknowledged right to use force 'if all else fails'. Divided societies should, he tells us, be ruled 'without undue violence' (ibid.: 33) – a rather different proposition from the definition of politics as conciliation, as the hapless recipients of this 'moderate' violence can readily testify! Crick's definition naturalizes and normalizes violence even though he argues that such violence should be moderate in character.

Gray argues that since the Second World War organized violence has slipped from the control of states into that of other institutions. He instances the Palestine Liberation Organization, the African National Congress, tribal, ethnic and clan militias in Rwanda, Chechnya and Bosnia, etc., contending that this kind of institution has deprived sovereign states of their effective monopoly of violence (1997: 179). But the monopoly of legitimate force that the state claims has *always* been contested and it is not simply the state in late modernity that claims a monopoly that it does not possess. This problem is inherent in the state's troubled and contradictory identity. The Weberian view of the state became obsolete, Gray argues, 'by the end of the twentieth century' (2003: 72). But Gray misses the irony of Weber's definition. Weber does not say that the state actually possesses a monopoly of legitimate force: he says that it *claims* it. Not the same proposition!

Gray rejects the positive features of liberalism and Enlightenment, arguing that the vast majority of people do not wish to govern their own lives and are content to be ruled by others provided they have sufficient shelter, food and security (1996c: 130). Yet it was Hobbes who argued that there are few so foolish that they would not rather govern themselves than be governed by others (1968: 211, 225). It is this postulate that accounts for the critical character of the liberal tradition, and it is precisely this critical character that Gray rejects. No wonder he considers that the whole project of looking beyond the state is fanciful and mistaken.

The post-modern state

Gray has a fascinating section on the emergence of what he calls the post-modern state – an entity that we might see emerging in the institutions of the European Union. Such a state contains many cultural traditions and communities, and local and regional allegiances and supra-national institutions have replaced the exclusive loyalties of the sovereign nation-state. To say, however, that the European attempt to move beyond the nation-state 'is an attempt to move beyond democracy' (2003: 17), as Gray does, is to adopt an archaic notion of democracy, and to identify it exclusively with the nation-state. Why can't transnational institutions be democratic? Held has sketched at some length the model of a cosmopolitan democracy (1995).

Held's argument is that people in states are threatened by activities occurring across their borders. Whether it is the movement of interest rates, the profits that accrue to stocks and shares, the spread of AIDS, the movements of refugees and asylum seekers or the damage done to the environment, government is stretching beyond the state. What obstructs the notion of international democracy is the assumption that states are sovereign, and that international institutions detract from this sovereignty. Gray appears to share the view of his *bête noir*, George W. Bush, that institutions that look beyond the nation-state are a threat to democratic realities.

The post-war period has seen the development of what Held calls the UN Charter model (ibid.: 86). Although this has made inroads into the concept of state sovereignty, it coexists uneasily with what Held calls the 'model of Westphalia' – the notion that states recognize no superior authority and may legitimately tackle conflicts of interest through the use of force (ibid.: 78). A first step forward would involve enhancing the UN model by making a consensus vote in the General Assembly a source of international law, and providing a means of redress for violations of human rights in an international court (indeed, the International Criminal Court has already been established although the US authorities do not recognize it). The Security Council would be more representative if the veto arrangements were modified, and the problem of double standards addressed – a problem that undermines the UN's prestige particularly in the south (ibid.: 269). But, welcome as such measures are or would be, they still represent, Held contends, a very thin and partial move towards an international democracy.

Held's full-blown model of cosmopolitan democracy would involve the formation of regional parliaments whose decisions would become part of international law. There would be referenda cutting across nations and nation-states, and the establishment of an independent assembly of democratic nations (ibid.: 279). The logic of this argument implies the explicit erosion of state sovereignty and the use of international legal principles as a way of delimiting the scope and action of private and public organizations. These principles are egalitarian in character and would apply to all civic and political associations. The only problem with Held's argument is his assumption that enforcing these norms would be the task of the state as a permanent actor. While he contends that the principle of 'non-coercive relations' should prevail in the settlement of disputes, the use of force as a weapon of last resort should be employed in the face of attacks to eradicate cosmopolitan law.

This argument is residually statist in character since Held assumes that the idea of the state remains but it must merely be stretched across borders (ibid.: 233). Yet these statist assumptions are in conflict with the aim of this state force (seconded to international authorities), which is 'the demilitarisation and transcendence of the war system' (ibid.: 279). However, this is only possible if institutions claiming a monopoly of legitimate force give way to international government, and the logic of government is, I have argued, profoundly different from that of the state. Held quite rightly argues that we must overcome the dualisms between, for example, globalism and cultural diversity; global governance from above and the extension of grass roots politics from below. These polarities make it impossible to embed utopia in what Held calls 'the existing patterns of political relations and processes' (ibid.: 286).

Like Gray, Held is victim to what Bull called a 'tyranny of existing concepts' (1977: 267) – in this case, the idea that post-national developments have to take the form of, or be underpinned by, the state. Why call post-national entities states, as Gray does? Alas, because Gray assumes that nothing really has changed, and like any other state, the post-modern state 'must exist in a world in which threat of military force remains a pervasive reality' (1997: 180) – although Gray does speak at one moment of a renewal of the liberal project that needs to look beyond the sovereign nation-state (2000: 123). But the emergence of what I would call post-statal entities (governmental polities rather than post-modern states) can only be frustrated unless this emergence is accompanied by a recognition that diplomacy and negotiation must replace force as ways of addressing conflicts of interest.

Gray argues that the attempt to abolish the state results in unlimited government, and by 'unlimited government' Gray means totalitarian rule (2003: 9). Yet we are talking here not about 'abolishing' the state, but about its withering away. This would require conditions in which common interests are sufficiently cohesive to make negotiation and arbitration meaningful. Moreover, such a 'post-liberal' stage presupposes the development and consolidation of the liberal state with its ethical objections to the use of force to settle conflicts of interest.

The state and diversity

Gray is eloquent in his defence of difference and diversity, and yet it has to be said that the state is the enemy of diversity. The notion of an institution claiming a monopoly of legitimate force necessarily privileges sameness over difference, and the use of force involves a sharp division of society into friends and enemies. This makes it difficult to celebrate difference. On the contrary, when force is used, the target ceases to be regarded as a collectivity of different attributes, and one of these attributes has to be singled out and dealt with accordingly. Force is power that is monopolized and concentrated – it is the enemy of diversity. The fact that the person who throws bombs may be a gifted electrician, a good musician, a kind sister, a diligent parent etc. becomes irrelevant. She is a terrorist – a threat to society and must be crushed, carted away, put out of action as soon as possible. It is impossible to celebrate difference when force is employed as a method of tackling conflicts of interest.

Gray predicts in 1995 that the twenty-first century will be characterized by destructive conflicts as the twentieth has been, save that these will be fundamentalist, nationalist and Malthusian convulsions. But, even if we accept this, why does it follow that readiness to use military force is a permanent necessity (1995: 33)? Force is required when people cannot 'change places' – it is as 'permanent' as divisions are, and because gulfs exist between people that cannot be resolved by negotiation and arbitration. I will argue that the use of force to tackle conflicts of interest is becoming increasingly dangerous: the 'readiness' to use this force is itself part of the problem that humanity has to address if it is to have a future.

Democracy, force and the state

In *Liberalism*, Gray adopts the Hayekian position that a democracy is desirable only if it follows the rule of law and protects the free market. This is why 'an authoritarian government may sometimes do better from a liberal standpoint than a democratic regime' (1986: 74). Later Gray is in favour of a 'modest' democracy, and he argues that democratic government ought to be seen as an expedient to enable divergent communities to reach common decisions without violence (2000: 105); but surely this is only possible if 'democratic government' takes a post-statal form. For there is a tension between the notion of democracy as self-government and the state. To the extent that there is a state, there is secrecy, authoritarian elitism and arbitrariness and, although the recipients of state force are particularly affected, we all suffer as a result of the state. If laws are imposed through force, who is to say that obedience is based upon moral considerations alone?

Gray argues that justice and rights can be upheld, in the last resort, only by force (2000: 132); but why? In the first place, societies existed in the past (indeed for hundreds of thousands of years) in which justice was dispensed and rights upheld (albeit in customary form and where slavery had yet to develop), without the need for force, or certainly monopolizing and institutionalizing force as a way of tackling conflicts of interest. Second, it is worth noting that this form of 'anarchic order' still continues in the international community, where international law is enforced through moral and economic pressures, and not because there is a world state to impose order.

There is a third argument against the use of force as a way of addressing conflicts of interest. Gray is right to comment that it is impossible to prevent new technologies of mass destruction from becoming more easily available (2002: 12–13). But this is a powerful argument against not only war but the use of violence as a way of addressing conflicts of interest. With technological change, force becomes increasingly simple to employ, and we pay an ever-higher price if we naturalize and normalize the use of force. A society reliant upon computers for its networks of communication is supremely vulnerable to the use of force. After all, if states can use force, why can't terrorists? If parents can beat their children, why can't school students settle differences with machine guns and knives? Ask a beleaguered teacher in a British school about the effect that force has upon classroom discipline, and you will see why force is dangerous and destructive.

I am not arguing that force as a method of addressing conflicts of interest will disappear tomorrow. As long as sanctions of a social kind are ineffective, then the use of force is tragically inevitable, but we should not underestimate the cost involved in using force as a way of tackling differences. The use of force is likely to exacerbate divisions in society, despite the claims of liberals about minimum and legitimate force. It is, in my view, impossible to use force in a manner that harms the 'guilty' and not the 'innocent'. Mistakes are often made; moreover, those closely related to the individual are also harmed, and in a different way so is the perpetrator. Force is inherently arbitrary and illegitimate. Legitimacy involves the respect for limits, whereas force, by its nature, always goes to extremes. Of course, liberal societies are right to seek to limit this force but, while this is a laudable objective, it is impossible to successfully carry out.

The pacifist argument assumes that force is always wrong. Yet, where people or states are so brutalized that moral sanctions or diplomatic pressures are inadequate, then force is inevitable. Pacifism is effective where ruler and ruled share common moral values – Gandhi's campaign against the British in India is a classic example – but this consensus is surely atypical. Alas, those who resort to force have been socialized in a way in which force is usually the medium of intercourse, so that it would be naïve to assume that brutalized individuals, or rogue states, will comply with purely moral or social sanctions even though, in my view, we can 'justify' force only as a way of getting rid of force. If we have to use force in the present, this is in order to make it redundant in the future. Thus, using counter-force of the kind, for example, that makes it possible for residents to meet in a turbulent housing estate in order to discuss their problems, can be 'justified' only if the purpose of the meeting is to discuss measures that will strengthen common interests, and make negotiated solutions to conflicts of interest more plausible and viable.

The withering away thesis

This is why the idea of the state withering away is a valuable and important one. It is only utopian – in the traditional, negative sense – if we assume that the state is synonymous with order and that a society without the state is a society without conflict and dispute. Indeed, there is a strong argument for suggesting that the state actually undermines order since, when force is used, relationships are impossible, and those targeted seek vengeance. The great strength of Hobbes is that he recognizes that the state uses terror to secure compliance: his great weakness is the assumption that, without force, chaos prevails. As the war in Iraq grimly demonstrates, nothing is capable of generating chaos and disorder more quickly than the use of force! Using force to eliminate the regime of Saddam Hussein has provoked terrorism, insurgency and the deadly activities of rival militias.

The notion of the state *withering* away invites us to consider how we can and must look to alternative methods of tackling conflicts of interest. In my view, a distinction between the state and government holds the key to moving beyond the state. Government is inherent in society and involves the resolution of conflict through persuasion, negotiation and compromise. The state, on the other hand, is an institution claiming a monopoly of violence, and it seeks (usually vainly) to address conflicts of interest through the application of superior force.

Gray finds that it would be hyperbolic to claim that nation-states are withering away (2000: 125) and he argues that we are beginning a new era of state sovereignty (2004: 164). But this notion of state sovereignty is incoherent. Taking state sovereignty to embody the state's claim to exercise a monopoly of legitimate force, sovereignty exists in this context only because it is partial, challenged and ineffective. Not surprisingly, we are increasingly challenging state sovereignty with universal conceptions like the notion of human rights. Gray himself concedes that 'enforcing universal rights may mean overriding a sovereign state'; a situation that arose with the Nuremberg trials over the Second World War (2000: 115). The plea that judges were simply enforcing state law during the Third Reich was not accepted as a legitimate defence.

Individuals are now seen to enjoy entitlements that go beyond the claim of states to treat 'their own' subjects as they please. There is a growing recognition that democracy is not simply a national ideal. It involves developing institutions that are international in scope, and it is gradually becoming clear that governing your own life and living in the shadow of the state are objectives that pull in contrary directions. Bull points to a number of developments that constitute what he calls 'awkward facts' for the classical (i.e. state-centric) theory of world politics.

The first of these arise from the dramatic expansion of international law in the twentieth century. International law now extends to states outside the European tradition, and it has come to embrace a whole range of matters relating to the economy, society, communications and the environment that go well beyond traditional preoccupations with political and strategic affairs. The second of these 'awkward facts' has been the growth of regional associations in Asia, Africa and, of course, in Europe (we have already mentioned the European Union). A third 'awkward fact' is constituted

by the break-up of older states as secessionist movements or what
Bull calls 'disintegrative tendencies' become more marked. Indeed,
these trends led Bull even in 1977 to speak (somewhat confusingly
in my view) of the rise of a 'new medievalism' (1977: 264–6). Gray
objects to liberal legalism on the grounds that it rejects compromise
solutions and embraces judgments that yield complete victory on
the one side and complete defeat on the other (1995: 77). But is this
not precisely the problem when conflicts of interests are addressed
by an institution claiming a monopoly of legitimate force (that is,
the state)? For the state upholds the righteous law-abider and pun-
ishes the wicked law-breaker. Hence there is, in my view, a tension
between the state and the political process. Politics involves negotiation and compromise; the state employs force. Gray talks about
legalist liberals seeking to abolish politics, but surely this is just what
the state does!

Gray's view of the state is conventional and uncritical. His analysis invokes the views of 'realism' in international relations when
he argues that a transnational European political culture cannot be
constructed, and that the only likely future for Europe is that sometimes unstable sovereign states' relations with one another will be
governed by the classical logic of the balance of power (1996b: 29).
Gray talks of neo-conservatives repudiating the traditional practice
of diplomacy, which, he argues, aimed to contain and moderate the
sources of destructive conflict without imagining that they would be
eradicated (1998a: 102). But there is an important tension between
the practice of diplomacy – as the avoidance of violence – and the
actions of the state: diplomacy needs to be reconstructed as a source
of post-statal politics (Hoffman, 2003). But why is his view of the
state linked to his traditionalist view of utopia? The state, as Marx
once put it, is a 'theological concept' (Marx and Engels, 1975a:
119) because it postulates an ideal community that the divisive
practice of force belies. Those who uncritically embrace the state
necessarily embrace dualism – the divide between the ideal and the
real, theory and practice, community and the market. The idea that
utopias are unrealizable otherworldly ideals is a statist view – the
ethical alter ego of an intransigent empirical reality. It is impossible
to reconstruct the notion of utopia while subscribing uncritically to
a need for the state.

The neutrality of the state

Liberalism has generally argued for the neutrality of the state. Gray is sceptical about the idea that the principle of justice, as outlined by Rawls, is neutral to the particular claims of moral communities and their associated conceptions of the good. On the other hand, a private property regime can be endorsed by the principle of neutrality on the grounds that, should people not wish to be a capitalists, the choice is theirs! But this does not mean that everyone is equal, since neutrality can only be a question of intent, not of outcome. This is why neutrality is tied to value pluralism, and it cannot be a fundamental principle in liberalism (1989: 182–4).

Margalit and Halbertal argue that in their opinion the right to culture in the liberal state permits it to be neutral but only with respect to the dominant culture of the majority (1994: 492). But the whole issue of state neutrality assumes that the state is an unproblematic part of the political landscape. Once we argue that the state is inherently contradictory and seeks to realize communal ideals that its use of force necessarily belies, then the neutrality of the state becomes part of its mythology, not its real self. The use of force is by its nature *divisive* and therefore it discriminates against those who are victims of this force, and in favour of those who (in a limited sense) are beneficiaries.

Brian Barry argues that the notion of the good cannot be neutral, since autonomy cannot be seen simply as one good among many. He sharply raises the point of how non-liberals can respect, say, toleration when this is central to a liberal outlook (cited by Katznelson, 1994: 615). In other words, even the most liberal state is partisan in character. What is true of particular states is also true of the state in general. If the state is a necessarily disappearing necessity, then one cannot be indifferent whether the state stays or goes.

There is a revealing comment in Brink's novel *An Act of Terror* in which a key member of the South African security police (during the period of apartheid) reflects on the need to catch Landman, a 'terrorist' who has been involved in an attempt to blow up the state president. Kat Bester (the policeman) comments: 'If you're out to catch the big ones it's the struggle they put up that makes it worth your while.' He adds, speaking of Landman, 'perhaps that's how he sees me too. Strange to think of it that way: to do the job he needs me. This is the antagonist that gives him the reason to plant bombs

... if he and his kind hadn't existed there would have been no need for us. Neither can really do without the other' (1992: 459).

If the state depends for its very *raison d'être* upon the criminal and the terrorist, since their presence justifies the claim to possess a monopoly of legitimate force, how can it be neutral? The state is a contradictory institution that enshrines dualism and hypocrisy at its heart.

Conclusion

Gray appears critical of the nation-state. Somehow or other we must move forward, since replacing the nation-state with a universal empire would be a step in the wrong direction. He sees the nation-state as promoting a bogus and dangerous homogeneity, but for all this emphasis upon diversity he fails to see that an institution claiming a monopoly of legitimate force is a threat to this diversity. His logic demands that he should be looking beyond the state!

It is true that, where order has collapsed and divisions are so deep that negotiation and arbitration cannot work, states are inevitable, and it is no part of my argument to suggest that it is possible, or indeed desirable, to avoid institutionalized violence as a way of tackling conflicts of interest under all circumstances. But where we need states we pay a high price, and the use of force can only be provisionally justified if it is employed to make the use of force increasingly redundant. It is wrong to describe the state as a 'civilizing agency'. The use of force becomes easier and more and more lethal in contemporary society and, in treating people as things, we dehumanize them and eradicate their differences.

The case for looking beyond the state can be charted only if we make a clear distinction between the state and government – the process of utilizing social rather than statist sanctions in addressing conflicts of interest. It is revealing that, the more statist a society is, the less these social sanctions can be drawn upon in order to forge order and cohesion. Gray demonstrates that fundamentalist free market policies generate the kind of divisions that make prison, rather than community, the only institution that can tackle conflict.

It is important that we see post-war developments as exacerbating a contradiction that has always existed within the state. The state promotes an ideal of community that it is inherently incapable of achieving, so that when rival bodies of force develop in opposition to the state's 'monopoly' this merely aggravates a problem that stems from the state's very identity. The state only *claims* a monopoly of legitimate force – we should not make the mistake of thinking that it actually exercises it.

The development of supra-national institutions such as the European Union represents attempts to forge a political identity that is supra-statist in character. It is wrong to assume that, because those involved in the process are statists, the result can only be the development of a new kind of state. Gray assumes that the notion of the state is synonymous with the political process, and he fails to see that the concept of state sovereignty is fundamentally incoherent. The development of international law and a philosophy of human rights point to the need to rethink the concept of sovereignty itself. Democracy is increasingly being regarded as a post-statal concept.

The state is a theological concept that enshrines a division between the ideal and the material world. It is impossible to reconstruct the notion of utopia as long as analysis is bedevilled by the proliferating dualisms that derive from an uncritical acceptance of the state.

8 • The Inescapable Character of Universalism

Introduction

Gray is generally hostile to the existence of 'universals', arguing that these stem from the abstract vision of the Enlightenment. However, it is also clear to him that, without any room for the universal within an argument, relativism – the belief that all values are of equal merit – and nihilism, that no value matters anyway, are impossible to avoid, although Newey refers to the 'nihilistic anti-humanism of *Straw Dogs*' (2006: 276).

As a result, Gray concedes that there are goods that all humans value – peace, stability, community, sociability etc. What he calls universal evils do exist, but these constitute what he labels a 'minimal' universalism. He insists, therefore, that he has not constructed a universal theory. His theory is based upon a recognition of diversity and difference, and is thus particularist rather than universal in character. He champions what he calls pluralism and incommensurability: because values are different, there is no universal scale in terms of which they can be compared. In the same way, he argues that different moralities exist and that there is no universal morality. As Newey puts it, 'the line between asserting that there are "universal evils" and denying that there is a "universal minimum morality" seems vanishingly thin' (2006: 276).

His list of universal evils is persuasive, but the argument that there is a distinction between a legitimate 'minimal universalism' and an illegitimate 'utopian' universalism cannot be sustained. Gray rests his argument upon a dualism between the universal and the particular, and hence he takes the view that it is impossible to recognize particular differences within a theory that is universal.

The aversion to universalism is part of Gray's traditionalist view of utopia. In fact, when the notion of utopia is reconstructed, his own theory is itself seen to be utopian, but the problem is that his utopia is a rather feeble and vulnerable one.

Minimal universalism

Liberalism, Gray asserts, is intolerant because it denies that 'many different forms of government may, each in their own way, contribute to an authentic mode of human well-being' (1989: 239). This authentic mode of human well being would appear to constitute a purely minimal universalism, and Gray is anxious to distinguish between a 'minimal' universalism, which he defends, and a full-blooded universalism, which he rejects.

He tells us, for example, that a person who is indifferent whether he or she kicks a pebble or kills their family is 'insane and inhuman'. It is here, he says, that the ability to recognise universal – or almost universal – values enters into our analysis (1996a: 68). Indeed, Gray defines such values as 'generically human', and because they are universal, he says, they can be used to assess any particular way of life (2000: 8). Gray equivocates over the meaning of 'universal', for he also defines universalism as the metaphysical faith that local Western values are authoritative for all cultures and peoples (1997: 158), but it could well be argued that this 'metaphysical faith' is a perversion of universalism. It is a particularism masquerading in universal garb.

Gray himself concedes that there are universal evils – torture, fear of violent death, being cut off in one's prime (1993: 139). The common moral horizon of the species may disqualify the most radical forms of particularism – the thought that denies even minimal universalism (1996b: 158). Security from violent death, or from starvation, is not a 'good' that is culturally variable (1998a: 110) – in other words, everybody subscribes to them. Life and health can be said to constitute 'primary social goods', and Gray argues that 'in contemporary circumstances' all reasonably legitimate regimes require a rule of law and the capacity to maintain peace, effective representative institutions, and a government that is removable by its citizens without recourse to violence. Basic needs would have to be satisfied and minorities protected, and such regimes would need to reflect the ways of life and common identities of their citizens (2000: 106–7). This, in particular, would seem to suggest that a legitimate regime has to be liberal or post-liberal in character.

Rawls, however, is wrong to assume that these requirements extend to such goods as a rational life-plan. Rawls's attempt (in Gray's view) to erase culturally and historically variable forms of life from human wants is doomed to failure (1989: 35). There exists what Gray calls 'a common moral horizon' – 'a minimal universalism'– which, for example, the Nazis sought to destroy. Liberalism is one form of life, Gray tells us, among many that may flourish within the common horizon of the minimal values that are universal (1996b: 163). The point is that, although the moral horizon rules out creeds like Nazism, 'it leaves a vast range of regimes and cultures in the field' and, above all, it affords no particular privilege to liberal societies (1997: 94).

This is the problem with Nietzsche's rejection of Mill's Enlightenment view that all human beings can agree upon a single notion of what is good. He throws the baby out with the bath water. Nietzsche rejects the notion that there are generic human evils that arise from experiences that are 'much the same for all human beings' whatever their ethical beliefs might be (Gray, 2000: 66). Nietzsche lacks what Gray calls 'minimal universalism' and what I consider to be a dialectical notion of universalism in which every universal value must (and can only) express itself in particularistic difference.

The defence of pluralism and incommensurability

A common moral horizon, Gray argues, does not privilege liberalism since ways of life and our belief systems are incommensurable. Compromise – the mediation of value conflict – is the most reasonable application of the pluralist idea (1996a: 168). Gray does concede that in our historical circumstances, it may be that the universal minimum requirements for morality have the best chance of being met under liberal institutions. Yet there can be no universal priority of liberal values (1996b: 155).

This notion of universal or ultimate values is crucial in defending the notion of incommensurability against the charge of relativism. Gray would (rightly I think) reject the argument that he is 'in essence a cultural relativist who has lost his bearings' (Fukuyama's words cited by O'Sullivan, 2006: 285). We can know what the common moral framework of human thought is, and we can know that this generates undecidable dilemmas (Gray, 1996b: 65). The common framework of thought that assures the objectivity of reasoning also shows us that moral conflicts are insoluble by reason. This, Gray tells us, is the nub of Berlin's pluralism and what distinguishes it from every kind of relativism and subjectivism, as well as from all traditional doctrines of natural law (ibid.: 70). Gray thus endorses Berlin's concept of a universal minimum content of morality pointing to universal evils but denying that there can be any rational procedure for resolving conflicts. He sees himself as going further than Berlin by arguing that pluralism challenges even liberalism as a hegemonic theory. A regime does not have to be liberal in order to embrace this universal minimum. Indeed, a non-liberal regime may well meet this minimum better than a liberal one: what kind of morality, Gray asks, prevails in some US cities (1995: 82)? One could indeed argue that attempts to impose a liberal polity on Iraq have made a bad situation worse – in terms of stability, the provision of education, women's rights, the position of Christian minorities etc.

The pluralism that Gray defends (and he draws from the work of Berlin) is 'a species of value realism' (1996a: 66). By pluralism, Gray does not mean the kind of interest group theory that American political scientists advocated in the 1950s. Pluralism here denotes diversity within and between cultures and traditions as a permanent condition to be lived with and enjoyed (1996b: 12). It is important to stress diversity within cultures since relativists tend to assume that particular cultures are themselves homogeneous. While, for example, there cannot be a single British identity, it is hoped that 'within such a plural inheritance' there is enough common respect for the ruling ideas of civil society – toleration, responsibility and equality under the rule of law (1993: 57). Gray defines toleration as a universal value. By tolerating our differences, we come to discover how much we have in common (1995: 30).

But why does pluralism have to be at odds with an overriding theory? I would argue that pluralism need not deny a rationalist position. It is surely an abstract view of reason that assumes that rationalism means monism – that all values are ultimately the same. Gray's problem is that he assumes a static and absolutist notion of 'reason' and then abandons it. Surely rationalism, concretely conceived, involves both monism and pluralism, a 'post-modern' view that each notion presupposes the other. We do not need to make a choice between them. Crowder argues: 'if Gray's *modus vivendi* is a principled commitment to peaceful coexistence, what prevents it from amounting to a form of monism?' (2006: 178). This, it seems to me, confirms the fact that the minimal universalism that Gray defends is, in practice, a fully fledged morality. Crowder is right to insist that the *modus vivendi* is a universal principle (ibid.: 179). In the same way Gray continually argues for the polytheism of the ancients over the monotheism of the Christian and Islamic tradition: but again why do we need to reject one in favour of the other? If we need a conception of a deity, why can't it be some kind of universal force that only manifests itself in particularist forms?

Gray illustrates the question of incommensurability in terms of a discussion on friendship and money. His argument is that they are incommensurable: there may well be situations in which friendship is more important than money, and situations in which the opposite holds true (2000: 36). It is, however, possible to argue that what lies 'beneath', as it were, the question of incommensurability is the issue of development: we can adjudicate on whether money or friendship should prevail by assessing what best develops a person in a given set of circumstances. Of course, people develop in different ways and in different circumstances: but this surely is the 'universal' thread that underpins the infinite differences.

Why can't development be what Gray calls 'one all-encompassing human good' (ibid.: 39), provided of course we inject this good with a dynamism so that it is seen as not a static value but what I will call a 'momentum concept' – a notion that is infinitely progressive and is never realized at a given point of time. Kelly comments that in order to pursue the claim that there are genuinely incommensurable conflicts of value 'we need a theory of value and we need to do ethical theory' (2006: 146). The universal thread that Gray dismisses cannot be eliminated, and I have suggested that a dynamic concept of development can provide such an overarching principle. Crowder argues that if there is a common horizon (as Berlin and Gray contend) 'then it cannot be true that whole forms of life are completely incommensurable' (2006: 182). Generic concepts can be generic only if there is an underlying commonality between them.

Thus, take Gray's argument that the liberal and pre-liberal notions of marriage conflict as an example of 'incommensurability'. Here one could assert that the (apparent) incommensurability arises because arranged marriages cease to resonate with people in modern circumstances – that is to say, they cease to be 'developmental' and will change. Gray seems to acknowledge this universal thread when he says that the test of our ethical beliefs is not their consistency with one another but 'their fidelity to ethical life' (2000: 41). What Gray calls 'fidelity to ethical life' I call development. Take

Gray's example of the British minister during wartime who sacked all his typing staff because he knew that one of them (he did not know which) was leaking information to the enemy (ibid.: 47). We can surely acknowledge Gray's point that doing right also involves doing wrong without denying an ethic of development that makes an action justifiable on balance. Context is crucial.

A person, as Gray points out, can be both tall and short in different contexts (ibid.: 55). The contradiction arises because of difference. But what prevents differences from being simply relativistic or subjectivist is the commonality that links different values – and here we need something like a dynamic notion of development. Thus, the argument that women should be slim or well covered when displaying clothes is not simply a matter of taste. We can adjudicate by asking which aesthetic is most developmental under the circumstances. This is not, it should be stressed, the notion of development adopted by Mill, which is static and timelessly absolutist in character. Development as a concept is bound to be complex because it varies according to time and place.

Gray argues that 'there are many things the good life is not, but no one thing it is bound to be' (ibid.: 62). But again, this assumes a static view of oneness – a notion that, if something is one, it cannot also be multiple at the same time. But if all propositions are contextual then the contradiction between oneness and multiplicity, like the contradiction between tallness and shortness, dissolves. Different things can develop in different ways – here there is multiplicity and oneness. Development is not a notion that smothers difference: it is a oneness that expresses itself in multiple form. This dynamism is crucial to a post-modernist logic. Arranged marriages work in a particular set of circumstances, but these circumstances are always changing, so that, to generalize the point, everything is both itself and something else. This is not irrational and gobbledegook. The proposition arises from a fluid and relational view of the world. Everything exists in *relation* to everything else – a logic that is dialectical in character. Because Gray remains trapped in the modernist logic of 'either/or', this position eludes him.

The *modus vivendi*

What is valid about Rawls's insights in his *Political Liberalism* is the view that a liberal state does not promote the ideals of comprehensive liberalism, but enables rival ideals to flourish (Gray, 1997: 52). This notion of pluralism and tolerance is attractive, and Gray is surely right about the need to develop a *modus vivendi* through which people can resolve their differences without recourse to war. We need to break, Gray tells us, with the 'monist tradition in ethics and philosophy' that we have inherited from Platonic and Socratic rationalism (1989: 47). The problem is that Gray's notion of pluralism is riven with binary oppositions (as post-modernists call them) between diversity (good) and unity (bad) – conflict (our reality) and harmony (an impossible dream).

Gray describes this *modus vivendi* as a renewal of the liberal project – a guiding ideal of liberal philosophy (2000: 33, 35), indeed, as a political ideal (ibid.: 68). But a meaningful *modus vivendi* has to transcend liberalism and the institutions of state and market, since these are precisely the institutions that have generated the evils that humankind must escape from. Gray praises what he calls the 'circumstantial reasoning' aiming at the achievement of a *modus vivendi* but his notion of a *modus vivendi* assumes an historically variable view of the limits and functions of the state, not a serious challenge to the existence of the state as such. When Gray praises the character of political life as a practical art of mutual accommodation (1993: xii), he takes it for granted that by political life we can only mean the life of the state. Gray talks about a *modus vivendi* among different cultures animating the post-modern project, but his assumption is that this post-modern project is a post-modern *state* (1997: 181).

The problem of the state

Gray is right to argue that different ways of life must cease to be antagonists and simply become alternatives. But why are different ways of life seen antagonistically and not simply as alternatives? Because they are linked to the state and the market – the very institutions that Gray accepts uncritically. When he says that the *modus vivendi* arises as a political ideal (2000: 68), the problem is that the *modus vivendi* that he champions is unrealizable – an abstract ideal – since he leaves intact the very institutions that cause the universal evils he rightly condemns. Markets divide, and states employ force. If, as Gray says, the 'animating value of peace' runs through the political enterprise to which he subscribes, then that suggests not only that there is a universal value within his *modus vivendi* conception, but that the notion of peace is surely in tension with an institution that tackles conflicts of interest through force, and an institution that conceals the real relationships underpinning the exchange process.

To realize a *modus vivendi* between different cultures and peoples, we need to move towards a world in which differences are dealt with in a post-statal manner, and in which resources are distributed in a way that make it possible for different people to 'change places'. This requires a degree of equality that, in my view, is incompatible with liberal capitalism, and involves a strategy for transcending the market. To be sure, this is a long-term strategy, but we will never tackle the problems of pollution, terrorism, exploitation and violence unless we begin to chart a strategy that sees wealth creation and distribution as a social process that has to strengthen common interests, both within and between countries.

It is true, as Gray insists, that people pursue peace and avoid violence in different ways and through different cultural prisms. He is right to challenge what he calls the 'pan-cultural aspirations' of Rawls's theory (1989: 34) and we should all endorse Gray's rejection of the dictum that humankind is much the same in all times and places (ibid.: 38). It would be wrong to privilege one of the cultural prisms through which humans express themselves and demand that there is only one way to live and be fulfilled. But this insistence involves universal principles of a substantive and not 'minimal' kind. Such policies exclude fascism and racism and they point implicitly to the need to settle conflicts of interest in a post-statist manner, and through a strategy that transcends the market. It is the opacity of the unregulated exchange process that generates insensitivity and inequality. This is why the notion of incommensurability is problematic, for it is surely the idea of universal evils that provides the 'standard' in terms of which things can be compared.

It is impossible, Gray argues, for any one conception of human nature to be rationally preferable (ibid.: 82). But what if one argues, for example, that humans by nature dislike violence? All humans desire the kind of autonomy that enables us to dismiss the claim that there can ever be a contented slave (ibid.: 84). Gray argues that some of the injunctions of liberal philosophy – the aversion to torture, slavery or genocide – 'are plausible components of a universal morality' (1998c: 160). To say that universal evils do exist

– genocide, persecution, avoidable ill-health, poverty – is certainly true, but why does Gray argue that these evils cannot create the basis for a universal morality? Why does he assert that we lack universal principles to secure peaceful coexistence (1989: 235)? Gray must, Kelly argues, be working with a normative conception of value – a morality – if his argument is not to collapse into relativism (2006: 149). In his most recent work, Gray argues that 'there are some values that reflect universal human needs' (2007: 197).

It is because he takes a statist notion of oneness – of abstract universality – for granted that Gray argues that a political philosophy that is universal and rationalist has to be an illusion (1993: 47). But this kind of comment assumes that a theory can be universalist and rationalist only when it is necessarily abstract. If there are differences, then there cannot be sameness; when people express themselves in particular ways, there can be no universal that links them. 'Human beings', he remarks recently, 'have needs that cannot be satisfied by any rational means' (2007: 199). He comments that, with the abandonment of what he calls 'a hallucinatory perspective of universality', it is necessary to return theorizing to the particularities of our circumstances (1989: 235). Gray endorses a perspective of anti-universalism, without seeing that a rejection of universalism is as one-sided as a rejection of particularity.

For the point is this. Universality as such does not need to be 'hallucinatory', and in eternal contrast to the 'particularities of our circumstances'. On the contrary: a concrete universality asserts its general principles through, and only through, particularities. Gray praises conservatives for their insight that what is most essential about us is what is most accidental 'and what makes all of us what we are, is a local and not a universal matter' (1995: 105). But why should we assume that what is local cannot also embody universal truths and values? Democratic practices at the local level can be thus characterized only if they are seen as both universal and particular.

Universal values, Gray argues, are compatible with many moralities (2000: 66–7). Again, this is true but why should we assume that particular moralities exclude rather than presuppose a universal morality? It is because Gray subscribes to a dualistic view of the universal and the particular, that he takes the view that, if values are particular, then they cannot be universal. They must be one or the other!

The need for common institutions

Gray writes enthusiastically about Berlin, who was a great admirer of Russian writers such as Herzen. It was Herzen who describes, in his *Letters on the Study of Nature*, the word as the embodiment of the universal in the particular. By naming something, Herzen comments, the human wrenches things from his or her environment, 'doubles them and immediately introduces them into the sphere of the universal'. 'We are so accustomed to the word that we forget the magnitude of this grandiose act – the ascension of man on the throne of the universe' (1956: 137). The point is a dialectical one; even the most mundane object can be identified only if we abstract from it the sameness it has with others. Indeed, it is through this universality that we can point to particular things. To use the familiar and corny example: without the universal notion of 'tableness', we cannot identify particular tables.

It is true that Gray cites Herzen decrying the word 'humanity', on the grounds that it expresses nothing definite but merely adds to the confusion of all the remaining concepts. But Herzen's comment on the word 'humanity' suggests that, whatever strictures we wish to pass on what Herzen calls the 'piebald demi-god' (Gray, 2003: 1), we cannot dismiss it for being 'universal', since, as Herzen argues above, all words are universal while at the same time referring to an entity in particular. Although Herzen was staunchly opposed to dogma, fanaticism and abstract ideals, it is revealing that he saw the inevitability of the universal in the particular. Levinas comments that 'to comprehend the particular is already to place oneself beyond the particular. To comprehend is to be related to the particular which only exists through knowledge, which is always knowledge of the universal' (cited by Jantzen, 1998: 233).

Gray is right to warn that communitarians are inclined to situate identities in a single moral community (1996a: 262), an ideal form, not an historic practice, a denatured abstraction not to be found in the real world of history (1996b: 107). The notion of 'community' cannot be a recipe for returning to a vanished face-to-face society, for recovering lost forms of 'organic' social unity (1997: 81). Globalization has undermined communities – a point that communitarian thought has done little to illuminate (ibid.: 117). Communitarians may be tempted to overlook the fact that 'plurality and conflict are integral to our identities' (1996b: 103). People 'belong' to multiple communities, and Gray notes that all ways of life have some interests in common (2000: 136). This is certainly true, but this is the universality that binds divergent particulars. It enables us to list aversion to violence, ill-health, arbitrariness etc. as attributes that people share albeit in different ways and through different cultural values. It is not plausible to regard these shared attributes as a 'minimal' universalism. They are, as I have suggested above, substantial, and indeed it is on their basis that it is possible to look towards a world without war and thus without the state.

Gray is right to argue the dialectical point that we can be at odds only if we have something in common (ibid.: 43), but being at odds implies conflict, not violence and war. Conflict is inevitable in society, but conflict involves difference and diversity; it need not embrace violence and division. In fact, conflicts that rest upon violence and division cannot be resolved; they can only be suppressed. Hence the problematic nature of the state, and the need for what I have called government – the resolution of conflicts of interest through negotiation and arbitration. Honig refers to Haig, an evolutionary biologist, who attributes conflict to the ineliminability of difference from identity (Honig, 1994: 583). This link between conflict (in the sense of rivalry) and difference is essential to the human condition.

The common interests that (as Gray rightly acknowledges) exist provide the foundation for the kind of 'utopian' universalism that Gray rejects. Gray himself argues that common institutions are needed in which different cultures, communities and ways of life can find peace (1997: 160), and yet these common institutions must not only take a post-statist character; they point to a universal common interest that is hardly 'minimal' in character. If we have a common human nature, as Gray argues (1998c: 160), surely that suggests a universalism of a substantive kind. Gray's argument that common institutions should be distinguished from common values makes sense only if we assume that common values have to privilege one way of life and exclude all others (2000: 6).

It is certainly true that German capitalism, like capitalism in Japan, has certain unique historical features that make it unexportable to, say, Britain, but this does not mean that capitalism per se is the only system that we can envisage for modern human society. Gray is right to challenge and reject Mill's Eurocentrism – the notion that non-occidental societies can develop only by adopting Western institutions and moral beliefs (1996c: 132). But the point is that universality and particularity are not irreconcilable opposites, one of which we must choose and the other reject: on the contrary, both are required to make sense of either.

The issue of human nature

Where Gray does dissent from Hume is over the issue of a common human nature that is everywhere the same. What draws him to Berlin is the latter's view that 'diversity is the most evident expression of man's nature as a species whose life is characterized by choice' (1996b: 23). But when Gray speaks of human beings 'whose very essences are historical' (ibid.: 102) this surely implies that humans are both the same and different. If there are universal evils, as Gray acknowledges, then there must be something about humans that makes them opposed to torture, genocide, ill-health etc.

Gray himself argues, against Richard Rorty, that 'there are enduring human needs that are species-wide and largely resistant to socialization'. This, he adds, will not be disputed by anyone who accepts a Darwinian account of our origins and kinship with other animal species (1997: 58). It is this common human nature (albeit based on diversity) that underlies universal goods and evils (2000: 120). It is a clear advantage to Berlin's theory, Gray argues, that it recognizes that there are human needs that cannot be altered merely by changing our conception of them (1997: 92). It is true that humans are different, and Gray is on strong ground in resisting a view of human nature that thoughtlessly universalizes the behaviour patterns of one particular society.

But if we take the view that I do, that human nature is constituted by the relation between humans and nature, then human nature exists but manifests itself in radically different forms. There is no need to reject a notion of human nature – provided this conception takes full account of diversity and difference. Gray argues that a perspective that affirms the constancy of human nature is 'subversive of the modern idea of constant improvement' (1997: 177). But if this notion of improvement acknowledges the contradictory character of progress – that a step forward can also be a step back – then a dialectical view of human nature can embrace the notion of improvement (though not in a mechanist and purely linear fashion as it is depicted in modernist thought).

To say, as Berlin does, that human self-creation is always plural is to say something about all humans – it is human nature to be different. It is true that this is not the ordinary conception of a common or constant human nature (Gray, 1996a: 74), but it is still a conception of human nature all the same. If there is a 'primordial propensity' of the human species to embrace a plurality of diverse natures (ibid.: 75), that surely tells us something universal about human beings. We can accept that human identities 'are never altogether fixed or finished' (ibid.: 82) while seeing this as a universal truth about humans.

The notion that all human advance has led to devastation ignores the existence, as Barry notes, of human societies and cultures that have developed in harmony with their natural environment. The proposition is 'normatively objectionable' (2006: 252–3). Gray's argument is curiously ahistorical, a veritable counsel of despair – it universalizes exploitation and violence and ascribes it to human nature, rather than to particular types of historical society. Newey argues, in his critique of Gray, that 'there is no obvious political answer to the question, as there was for Aristotle: *what is natural for us?*' (2006: 280). Yet, while the concept of what is natural has to be placed in a historical context, why can't we argue that what is natural is what is developmental, so that whatever develops people's mental and physical faculties in ways that facilitate their progress towards governing their own lives is natural? When Newey says that human beings are by their nature creatures of politics (ibid.: 280), what makes this assertion problematic is Newey's apparent equation of political association with the state.

The problem of sameness and difference

To say, as Gray does, that 'humanity' does not exist (2000: 12; also 2003: 4) is to argue that because a universal entity manifests itself in different ways it cannot exist as a universal. Gray regards humanism as a doctrine of salvation (2000: 16), but this is only true if humanism is presented in an abstract and 'finalist' manner.

Why can't we present humanism concretely? A concrete notion of humanism is based upon the understanding that the *only way* in which humanity can express itself is through divergent cultures, life styles and values. These particular differences do not contradict a 'universal' humanity: on the contrary, one presupposes the other. The fact that people have common interests (as Gray rightly points out) does not mean that they are simply identical. Everyone is different – that is what people have in common! Gray is right to criticize the spuriousness of liberal notions of universality and abstract personhood (ibid.: 21). But these notions need to be rendered concrete: not simply abandoned. After all, the very notion of a generic human evil presupposes that people have a 'personhood' that torture etc. dramatically compromises.

Gray assumes that difference and sameness belong to conflicting worlds. 'The human mind', he tells us, 'serves evolutionary success, not truth. To think otherwise is to resurrect the pre-Darwinian error that humans are different from all other animals' (ibid.: 26). But the fact that humans and other animals have much in common does not mean that they are not also different. Humans form relationships in ways that other animals do not. They are rational toolmakers – animals in general are not. Humanity, as Kateb points out, does not make the world, but it does remake the world, as no other species can. Kateb also makes the telling point that in *Straw Dogs* there is a tension between placing humans on the same level as other animals and at the same time seeing humans as *uniquely* destructive. This makes humans unlike all the others (2006: 315–16). Indeed, he argues that Gray produces a veritable catalogue of what is distinctively human (ibid.: 318).

But this recognition that humans are both the same and different is implicit. Gray's approach is basically dualistic: he thinks that if two things are different then they cannot also be the same. This dualism stems from his uncritical view of the market and state. He embraces a modernist logic that assumes that, if things are different, then they cannot be the same; if an entity is universal, then it cannot manifest itself in divergent particulars. This is the modernist logic of 'either/or', whereas a post-statist reconstruction of the concept of utopia rests upon a post-modernist logic of 'both/and'.

The point is then that difference is not overcome by a 'monist' view of sameness: what makes Gray dualistic is his assumption that with the discovery of sameness we can no longer subscribe to difference. The two are separate, but Gray takes the view that therefore they cannot also be linked.

Gray's empiricist utopia

Gray contends that his post-humanist approach will not seek to contrive a utopia (a term that he uses traditionally as an Arcadia) (1997: 173). However, implicit in his argument is the case for a utopia. Colls comments that 'Gray has provided an alternative way to think about the way we live now' (1996: 66). In the sense that I use the term, Gray's thought is utopian, but Gray's utopia is not a particularly attractive one. Kateb refers to the fact that 'Gray's utopia would be a world population of half a billion to a billion' (2006: 308). The rest would have died through war, disease, overcrowding and disruptions wrought by climate change. Gray expresses in *Straw Dogs* a nihilistic nausea and, even although he veers between the literal extinction of humanity and massive depopulation, 'there is inconceivable murderousness in both' (ibid.: 312).

I call Gray's 'alternative' an empiricist utopia because Gray considers himself a realist but interprets realism in an empiricist way. Gray complains that Marxism is animated by a positivist creed (2003: 28) and that Western thought is fixated on the gap between what is and what ought to be (2002: 112). Yet it is Gray who adopts a classically modernist theory of dualism by contrasting his (rather cautious) 'ought' with what 'is'.

Like Hume and Kant, Gray divides the world into facts and values, ideals and reality, universals and particulars. Faced with what are seen as irreconcilable opposites, one has to choose. Gray sides with the growing tendency (exemplified, for example, by the argument of many self-styled post-modernists) to reject universalism, since he identifies universalism with the arrogant imposition of a single ideal that rides roughshod over local customs and cultures. Instead he chooses a particularism in which everyone follows their own way of life, even if this involves the oppression of women, backward attitudes towards nature, and an elitist attitude towards the vulnerable and the needy. Faced with this 'choice', Gray argues for particularism even though he accepts that universal evils exist, and that most humans are against poverty, ill-health, violence and torture. He describes the particularistic character of human identity as 'fundamental', contrasting a rational choice with a radical choice among incommensurables (1995: 67). As always, we have to have one or the other. It is interesting that Gray refers to the 'rational incomparability' among ideals (ibid.: 69) – but how can this incomparability be 'rational' unless there is some kind of universality (some 'rational' standard) to which reference is being made? The most radical pluralism requires a 'monism' to pull it together.

The distinction between facts and values that empiricism absolutizes is a meaningful one but, while facts and values are different, they are not divided but linked in a relational manner. Every fact implies a relationship and therein exists its potentially normative character. It is a fact that the poor tend not to vote in liberal societies, but this fact when contested becomes a value. It is potentially a value because it assumes a *relationship* between poverty and apathy. Facts are distinct from values only when the relationship they imply is not contested. Thus the relationship between the earth and roundness is normally presented as a fact because this relationship is not contested. It is because liberals see the world in an atomistic way that they deny the constitutive character of relationships ('I relate, therefore I am') and hence they necessarily naturalize anti-relational philosophies and practices, the state, empiricism, idealism, violence (to mention just a few things created by the market and division).

Gray argues that the emancipatory project of the left is inimical to the limits set for human hopes by humankind's place in the natural world (1997: 160). But this assumes that the left see the future as a form of putty to be constructed however they wish; but why can't one work towards the self-government of humanity within the constraints posed by social and natural structures? Gray is pessimistic about the future of the world because he identifies conflict and difference with division and violence. In our world, he comments in a passage that accuses communitarianism of idealizing communities, the shadow cast by community is enmity, and the boundaries of community must often be settled by war (1995: 7). Gray assumes that the claims for a good life are permanently irreconcilable and conflicts can never be resolved (ibid.: 9). As Barry puts it crisply, 'contemplation on the worsening human and natural conditions should be followed by action, not laments and mysticism' (2006: 259). Because Gray focuses on what he deems to be given and unalterable, the scope for effective political action is correspondingly narrowed (Newey, 2006: 268).

A collapse by civilized states into war, tyranny and anarchy would not, Gray argues, be apocalyptic, but a return to a very familiar historical terrain (1997: 175). Kelly refers to Gray's 'secular Augustinianism' (2006: 137) – a doctrine of the fall but no redemption. The twenty-first century will be dominated by 'ancient and primordial passions' associated with ethnic and religious loyalties (Gray, 1995: 32). There is a curious passivity about his argument when he endorses Heidegger's notion of 'releasement', in which we let things be rather than aiming to wilfully transform them (ibid.: 152). Gray assumes that to be an agent one must be an imperialist – one who dominates the lives of others. The notion of an agent who works within but seeks to change constraining circumstances is alien to his argument. Gray supports the view of the conservationist Aspinall that a 'demo-catastrophe' is necessary that will reduce population from 4,000 million to 200 million: if this is not done, the planet is doomed (1997: 168–9). Gray's focus on population control is, according to Barry, authoritarian and uncritical of the deeply skewed consumption of the world's resources. Barry complains that Gray ignores the normative implications of the idea of an ecological footprint – a notion that points to the dramatic inequality between the developed and the developing world (2006: 256–8).

The notion of freedom

It is no answer to our problems to replace one one-sided view with another one-sided view. Gray assumes that free will is incompatible with determinism. When he supports free will, he regards it as implying a rejection of determinism. When, in his later work, Gray rejects the notion of autonomy and choice, he comes to the (mechanically determinist) conclusion that free will itself is a myth. What is lacking is a dialectical view of determinism: that determinism involves a recognition of the forces that determine our conduct, in order to alter these forces.

In his earlier writing Gray champions autonomy, albeit as a 'pervasive and urgent' option in late modern Britain. This notion of autonomy will overthrow any communitarian policy that seeks a return to earlier modes of family or social life (1997: 81). But Gray assumes that autonomy and choice have to be formulated in opposition to constraint and differences. On discovering the latter, he then jettisons the former, but why should we assume that autonomy and freedom have to take an abstract form? When Gray says that humans may think that they are free, conscious beings, but in truth they are deluded animals (2002: 120), the problem arises because he assumes an abstract, static and idealist notion of freedom, which he then rejects. It is true that the idea that we can do as we please is deluded, but that is not a rational and coherent view of human agency. As Kateb points out, only human beings have minds. They are not the direct and unmediated result of instincts, impulses and programmed behaviour (2006: 317).

Gray rejects rather than concretizes the notion of the autonomous human subject on the grounds that the very idea of autonomy neglects the central role in human life of chance and fate (1995: 108). His argument is clearly mechanistic. If our actions are caused, he tells us (2002: 65), then we cannot act other than the way we do. In that case, we cannot be responsible for our actions. This would be true if humans were not agents, who are conscious of what causes their behaviour, and can therefore alter the cause. Of course, this 'new' cause still determines behaviour, but the determinism is 'dialectical': the action of the agent is both passive and active. Agents alter as they receive. This is why it is wrong to argue, as Gray does, that an account of robot behaviour applies no less to humans (2002: 72).

Freedom, concretely regarded, involves the recognition and transformation of constraints, just as autonomy is possible only because we are related to, and therefore dependent upon, others. Gray argues that we need both freedom and restraint, equality and liberty and this, he says, is a recognition that there is no simple and single solution to our problems, but the manner in which he elaborates this position is eclectic and flawed.

Take the example he gives of protecting people from racist abuse. This is a freedom. But to enshrine this freedom, he argues, entails curbing freedom of speech. The two freedoms are logically incompatible (2000: 79). This argument arises because freedom is interpreted in an abstract, non-relational manner. It is not surprising that judges in the USA have come to the 'old' liberal conclusion that so-called freedom of speech prevails over freedom from racist abuse. However to be free is not to do as one pleases – a point that Mill recognises in *On Liberty* when he says that you cannot be free to alienate freedom (1974: 173). Once we introduce the notion of freedom as development, then there is a basis for tackling the conflict between what are ostensibly rival notions of freedom. This notion of development needs to take account of Gray's important point that our conception of the good society must apply 'to the specific historical circumstances of particular regimes' (2000: 80).

Porritt argues that he is concerned to emphasize the inevitability of change, and the necessity of adapting economic and political systems to cope with that change (2006: 314). This does not mean that change must occur whatever humans do, but rather that change is necessary if humans are to survive and flourish. It is not a question of sacrificing the present 'in favour of a supposedly predetermined future' (Gray, 1996b: 87), but a question of living in the present in a productive and sensible way.

Freedom is linked to development – of oneself and others. Freedom to express racist abuse is therefore a contradiction in terms since no one can be free to harm others and, indeed, oneself. 'Free choice is worth little', Gray comments, 'if the life in which it issues is nasty, brutish and short' (1993: 60). It is questionable, in my view, whether a self-defeating 'free choice' can be called freedom at all. In the same way, Gray comments that 'autonomy is not worth much if it is exercised in a Hobbesian state of nature' (1993: 112). But is it autonomy at all if you cannot live in security and peace?

It is revealing that Gray argues that Marx views the human as 'an unconditioned and self-determining agent' (ibid.: 108). Not only is this incorrect as an assessment of Marx: it also assumes that if a person is self-determining then they must have transcended all historical conditions. If you are self-determining, then you cannot also be determined by external circumstances. This is to identify self-determination with the absence of constraint – an absurd idea that denies the existence of society.

A pessimistic scenario

Gray's rather limited and pessimistic vision of the future stems from the fact that he is still a liberal, and his argument is paralysed by dualism, statism and abstraction. He takes the view that ethnic and religious differences, the scarcity of natural resources and the collision of rival values are permanent sources of division. Such conflicts cannot be overcome; only moderated (2003: 9). But conflict need not be divisive, nor should we assume that the violence that scars the contemporary world is a permanent part of the political landscape.

Gray's argument is certainly pessimistic and ahistorical. But this does not mean that he is not utopian, for he does pose a vision of the good society. Nevertheless, his utopia is flawed. It assumes that the state and market are here to stay, that humanity will always be divided by class and that war is inevitable. In *Beyond the New Right* he argues that for our species the coming century looks like being one of wars, massacres and forced migrations, 'of which the holocausts of our century are but the precursors (1993: 174). It has been argued that he has outlined a programme for complete political passivity. As J. Barry comments, 'If war becomes more ruinous, if new diseases kill unfathomable multitudes, if technology renders our bodies immaterial – so be it.' Green political theory has analysed the unsustainability of an economic system based on the institution of private property (Barry, 2006: 254), but for Gray the market and private property are taken as read.

His *modus vivendi* is not plausible since the things that he rightly identifies as universal evils – poverty, genocide, violence – cannot be tackled by the institutions he takes for granted. On the contrary, he presupposes the very evils that he seeks to 'moderate' and, as a good Hobbesian, he laments the fact that the world is a cruel place and offers solutions that are unable to tackle the problems he exposes. Despite his apparent support for empiricism, his own theory contains an 'ought', but this 'ought' hangs lifelessly and impotently over a statically conceived 'is'. He has not avoided utopianism; he has merely produced a utopia that is inconsistent and unconvincing.

Gray does at one point acknowledge that perhaps he too subscribes to the need for a utopia. After a long quotation from J. S. Mill, he defends the need for a 'universal stationary state' that, he says, may well be a utopia, but it is 'a better measuring rod for attainable improvement in the human lot than the wholly unrealisable fantasy of infinite growth' (1993: 142). But this is a utopia that rests upon the modernist logic of 'either/or'. Why do we have to make a choice between infinite growth and no economic growth at all? Surely we can grow in a developmental way – a way that takes account of the need for environmental protection and increasing democracy.

Conclusion

Gray is concerned to avoid universalism since he believes that universal values underpin traditional utopias and stem from the Enlightenment and monotheistic religions. However, the problem he faces is this. If a theory is constructed without any universal dimensions, how can it avoid becoming relativistic and nihilistic in character? If pluralism simply means that every value is as worthy as every other, then killing Jews is as acceptable as saving them. Gray advances the concept of incommensurability – the idea that it is impossible to develop a universal scale in terms of which one way of life is, say, only half as meritorious as another. But what if one concludes from the concept of incommensurability that all values are worthless and that nothing matters?

It is to avoid relativism and nihilism that Gray argues that generic human evils exist. All humans whatever their culture and context abhor violence and seek stability, peace, cohesion etc. But this universalism is, he insists, purely 'minimal' in character since people are different, their cultures and belief systems differ radically and, although a liberal regime might be the best way of enabling humans to flourish, it might not. No set of values, liberalism included, can be privileged.

Gray is, in my view, right to argue that humans have goods in common, and he is also right to stress that humans are very different from one another. But why should this universalism be considered 'minimal'? Gray's problem is that he accepts a dualism between the universal and the particular: if the latter is emphasized, then it must be at the expense of the former. But this is a classical modernist outlook. If we embrace a post-modern logic of 'both/and' rather than 'either/or', then universality and particularity complement rather than exclude each other, and a universal value can only manifest itself through particular institutions that are necessarily distinctive and different in character.

Of course, the notion of humanity, like the notion of community, may be treated abstractly but that is a problem with abstraction, not the concept itself. When concretely analysed, the values we have in common are not minimal; they are substantial, and they account for the fact that a 'modus vivendi', as Gray calls it, is possible. Common values do not mean a way of life that is everywhere the same: it merely means that people everywhere want peace, prosperity, the avoidance of torture and preventable illness etc. and they will seek, in different ways and through different cultures and belief systems, to secure them. It is because Gray assumes that where things are the same they cannot also be different, and where they are different they cannot be the same, that he ties himself into knots. Why not construct a notion of development as a universal thread that enables us to differentiate between practices that are harmful and those that are helpful? This universal thread depends upon context and circumstance for its particular manifestation.

The dualism between sameness and difference bedevils Gray's discussion of freedom and autonomy. He comes in his later writings to reject the latter notions, but this is because he has defined them in a one-sided way and then substitutes their one-sided opposite. This problem is classically demonstrated by his discussion on free will and determinism, in which he rejects an abstract view of free will in favour of a purely mechanistic notion of determinism. Humans are certainly animals and Gray is right to stress that they are part of nature; but they are natural beings of a particular kind and they have attributes that set them aside from other animals. They are both the same as other natural entities, and they are also different.

Gray's notion of a 'modus vivendi' is certainly a utopia in the sense that it offers an alternative to the triumphalism and imperialism of many politicians. But it is not a particularly attractive utopia since it assumes that the market and state are here to stay, and with them war, violent conflict, destructive competition for resources, and overpopulation. There are, to be sure, daunting problems in the world today, but they are not insoluble if we adopt a strategy that is critical of market and state, and support a 'modus vivendi' that has a realistic chance of eliminating generic human evils. It is not difficult to see that Gray's ideals are undermined by his own pessimistic assumptions, and the dualistic approach upon which this pessimism rests.

9 • Globalization

Introduction

There is a good deal of scepticism about whether globalization is simply a new term for an old phenomenon or we are witnessing a transformation that is genuinely new. Gray is right to argue that, despite a good deal of continuity with developments in the past, globalization is something new. Indeed, I would argue that quantitative changes in the levels of trade and investment have been such that a change in kind has been produced, and the development of information technology has indeed created a global identity that is qualitatively different from anything that existed in the past. Globalization is cultural and political, as well as economic.

Gray is also right to argue that the neo-liberal version of globalization is radically flawed. It produces inequality, violent conflict and a fundamentalist reaction to American hegemony. Gray identifies the neo-liberal argument as a belief in hyper-globalization – I call it pseudo-globalization. Real globalization involves not only a respect for diversity, but policies that contribute to global justice and a spread of resources that is crucial if institutions for global government are to stand any chance of success.

Indeed, the neo-liberal or market fundamentalist arguments of writers such as Ohmae speak of the nation-state withering away under the impact of global markets, but this is not plausible. In fact, the move towards global markets increases rivalries, nationalism and inequality, and it is revealing that Ohmae is not against statism – merely the nation-state. It is also revealing that the belief in free markets is a dogma preached by the 'Washington consensus' but certainly not practised by the US in relation to its own economy.

Stiglitz's critique is particularly hard-hitting and, like Gray, he stresses the disastrous character that the policies of the International Monetary Fund (IMF) have had on post-communist Russia. The country has seen a dramatic collapse in living standards, health and security and the idea that it will become a US-style political regime is laughable. But, whereas Gray is pessimistic and inclined to blame globalization for chaos and inequality, Stiglitz (quite rightly in my view) argues that globalization has the potential for justice and fairness. He sees the rise of international terrorism as the product of a world order that is divisive and homogenizing.

In reforming international institutions such as the World Bank and the IMF, we need to move towards a system of global government or governance that is not modelled on the state but seeks to strengthen common interests between countries so that global regulations on the economy, the environment and the nature of government can bite. Gray is right to stress the importance of the universal values that underpin his *modus vivendi* but wrong to see that the necessary recognition of diversity works against universal solutions to global problems. The Huntington thesis – that we are witnessing a clash of civilizations – is rightly torn to shreds by Gray, but his pessimistic view that basically we are witnessing a future of violent conflict and self-destruction derives from a modernist view that universal values and political, social and economic realities inhabit different worlds. It is simply impossible to bring them together. The potential that globalization offers for overcoming chaos and division is ignored because, as always, Gray takes the market and state for granted.

The problem of a definition

Gray is much taken with the way in which the theory of globalization was initially developed by Marx in the *Communist Manifesto*. Even in 1848 Marx and Engels had stressed the cosmopolitan character of capitalism, arguing that it impacts upon every corner of the globe and cements 'the universal interdependence of nations' (Marx, 2000: 248–9). Indeed, in Gray's view the globalization of economic and cultural life began in Europe in the early modern period from the fifteenth century onwards (1998a: 23); although commentators do not usually go back that far, they argue that contemporary globalization certainly has its roots in the past. Turner makes the point that trade as a percentage of gross domestic product (GDP) is no higher in Britain now than it was in the nineteenth century (2002: 317). Gray comments that we can recognize in the pre-1914 world a precursor of today's global market (1998a: 61).

There is a good deal of scepticism about globalization as something new. Hutton has argued that the great bulk of trade is still between the leading industrialized countries; investment in the developing world accounts for only a tiny fraction of world output. If the economy were truly globalized, it is argued, then we would expect states to be subordinate to the imperatives of multi-national companies (MNCs) and the market. MNCs would no longer be based in a particular country, and international relations would involve corporations rather than states as central players (Faulks, 1998: 181).

A similar argument is advanced by Hirst and Thompson, who contend that national economies are still primary actors within the wider international economy (1996). Gray accepts that the sceptical argument is a useful corrective to what he calls the utopian view advanced by thinkers like Ohmae – that with globalization the world is becoming a single market and nation-states are for this reason withering away (Gray, 1998a: 64). But it is not a question of arguing that states have become redundant or that the economy has become international as opposed to national. There are decisive contrasts between the pre-1914 international economy and today's global market (ibid.: 65).

Gray defines economic globalization as 'the worldwide spread of industrial production and new technologies that is promoted by unrestricted mobility of capital and unfettered freedom of trade' (ibid.: 6–7), but argues that this undermines the global free market that American transnational organizations are seeking to construct. The differences between the pre-1914 world and contemporary globalization indicate that in fact power is ebbing away from Europe and towards the countries of the East. Gray is surely right to argue that globalization is not an end-state towards which economies are converging, and it is not a universal state of equal integration in worldwide economic activity (1998a: 56). But it is true that uneven and unequal development is accelerating and traditional societies are being drawn into the network of global economic relationships. This is also true of the former Communist Party states.

The question of globalization is normally discussed in economic terms, but it is, of course, a cultural and political phenomenon as well. The extraordinary innovation in communication and information technology has shrunk the constraints of geography in a dramatic fashion. This 'shrinkage' has important implications for the development of people with global (as well as national and local) identities and, although Ohmae argues for a neo-liberal, market fundamentalist view of globalization, he accepts that globalization has furthered the development of a global culture – a culture that undermines what Marx and Engels call 'national one-sidedness and narrow mindedness' (Ohmae, 1995; Marx, 2000: 249). Gray, although sceptical about the possibilities of a global culture, comments that the advent of modern information and communication technologies has meant that culture is far more deeply influenced than ever before (1998a: 57).

Gray sees globalization as delocalization – the uprooting of activities from local origins and cultures – and vigorously denies that globalization should be equated with a trend to homogeneity (ibid.). I will later distinguish between what I call globalization and pseudo-globalization, but Gray is right to see it as a fundamental mistake to conclude that we have returned to the international economy of the nineteenth century. Not only has there been a vast and unprecedented expansion in the volume of trade, but there is a world market in capital as never before. Nothing like a virtual market existed before 1914 (ibid.: 61–2).

Barry Jones makes a distinction between a 'strong' and a 'weak' globalization thesis. The strong thesis defends globalization as something new whereas the weak thesis argues that, while there has been a significant increase in internationalization, a new term is not warranted. Barry Jones examines the similarities and differences between the global situations at the end of the nineteenth and twentieth centuries in detail and notes some differences of substance. The micro-computer revolution has dramatically transformed information gathering, and he comments that the world of the twentieth and twenty-first century is enmeshed in a network of international organizations and transnational associations that is of far greater 'density and scope' than could have been imagined or sustained at the end of the nineteenth century (2000: 31).

Neo-liberalism and pseudo-globalization

Gray identifies globalization with the development of a global free market that the 'Washington consensus' has sought to engineer on a world scale, and America's claim to be a world civilization. An economic modernization seeks to impose the same thing everywhere.

I would prefer to call this pseudo-globalization but this version of 'hyper-globalization', as it sometimes called, is at stark variance with reality. In fact, new types of regime have developed and with them new types of capitalism. Thus, Gray analyses the character of Chinese capitalism, for example, arguing that it has more in common with Italian capitalism than it does with the economic culture of Korea, with the American market or with Japanese capitalism (1998a: 185).

Gray is sharply critical of Friedman, who, as a passionate neo-liberal, openly acknowledges that he is a technological determinist. Gray likens him to Marx (I think misleadingly), and argues that he consistently underestimates the power of religious and nationalist movements (2005: 13). However, whereas Marx saw capitalist development as necessarily accompanied by war and revolution, Friedman assumes that it is a peaceful process. A distinction needs to be made between a rapid and continuous technological innovation that links up events and activities throughout the world more quickly than before, and the 'groundless, ideological assertion' that a single worldwide system is resulting (ibid.: 14). Gray quotes a number of writers who see globalization as creating a uniform culture, the end of nationalism and the end of the nation-state, and yet, as Gray points out, most multi-national companies retain strong roots in particular countries and business cultures (1998a: 69). He argues passionately that sovereign states remain key players, and their leverage over business is still considerable (ibid.: 69).

Capitalism has become increasingly anarchic and disordered, so that even the former middle classes are debourgeoisified. Businesses have increasingly shed many of the responsibilities that rendered the world of work humanly tolerable. The present monetary regime has been termed the world of 'casino capitalism' (ibid.: 72). However, the effect of these trends is radically different in different societies.

Moreover, the idea that the earth is 'flattening' is hardly borne out by the inequalities that globalization generates. Russia, for example, suffered rising levels of absolute poverty and large increases in inequality of wealth (2005: 14). A quasi-authoritarian regime has resulted, with no prospect of a Western-style 'democratic capitalism' developing. Globalization has not only increased prosperity but, as China and India demonstrate, strengthened nationalist identities. The result of globalization is the production of a variety of hybrid regimes rather than convergence on a single model (2006: 20). The notion of uniformity is common both to the supporters and the critics of globalization. Cohen in his *Globalization and its Enemies* argues that the poor of the world are not so much exploited as neglected and forgotten (ibid.: 20). Yet more emphasis needs to be given to the fact that global warming and the struggle for resources are by-products of globalization. The completion of globalization, for which Cohen calls, may not be feasible (ibid.: 21). Globalization is not irreversible and over time its disruptive effects tend to result in deglobalization. Companies thrive or fail in different ways (ibid.: 22). Economic integration may result in liberal countries (such as the USA) propping up authoritarian ones (such as China) (ibid.: 23).

Of course, free market policies do not apply to the US itself. The USA has continued to keep quotas on a multitude of goods from textiles to sugar. The General Agreement on Trade in Services (GATS) prevents poor countries from defending their indigenous businesses, although that is precisely what the current industrial powers did during their major phases of development (Stiglitz, 2002: 15). Gray makes the point that large budget deficits were incurred in order to finance tax cuts and military expenditures, with much of American industry being protected by subsidies and tariffs (1998a: 108).

Globalization and the state

In Gray's view, the notion of the nation-state disappearing under the cut and thrust of the free market is absurd. Certainly the pseudo- or hyper-globalization thesis cannot tackle the role of the state.

This emerges clearly from Ohmae's argument that the nation-state has become 'a nostalgic fiction' (1995: 12) in the face of the global market. Ohmae rests his case on what he calls the 'Californization' of taste and preference. There is a ladder of economic development, he argues, upon which more and more societies climb, reaching the US$5,000 threshold of per capita development. The spread of information-related technology is infectious and Adam Smith's invisible hand now works in a global context.

But the neo-liberal argument is starkly inegalitarian and is hostile to democracy. Ohmae argues that the rules of electoral logic and popular expectations lead to general, indirect long-term benefits being sacrificed in favour of immediate, tangible and focused payoffs (ibid.: 42). The tyranny of modern democracy, as he calls it, seeks an equality of results, not of contributions (ibid.: 53). What he refers to as the 'civil minimum' is like a drug and takes the form of broad-based social programmes, welfare, unemployment compensation, public education, old-age pensions and health insurance. Established political systems have become the creature of special interests and the poorer districts. Whereas the nation-state solution assumes a zero-sum game for limited resources, the regional state model, he argues, open to the global economy, is a 'plus sum' as prosperity is brought in from without (ibid.: 55, 57, 62).

Yet Ohmae notes that huge disparities have opened up – disparities measured by a factor of 20 or more – between inland and coastal regions in countries like China. He concedes that the gap between the developed and developing world has substantially widened. Despite his defence of the 'trickle down' effect – that the poor ultimately benefit from the prosperity of the rich – not only is he hostile to democracy, but his argument is basically state-centric throughout. States are seen as having an unproblematic sovereignty, the European Union is described as a 'supernation state', and those worried about the most economically backward areas of the world are regarded as defending 'vested interests' that get in the way of global logic. Besides, regional states are seen as states that constitute 'natural economic zones' (ibid.: 80).

It is clear that, if so-called globalization aggravates and deepens inequalities in the world, then this will, as Gray argues, generate wars, fundamentalism and, of course, the need for states. Economic liberalization and religious fundamentalism go together (1998a: 103). As Gray notes, greater protectionism has already become apparent in the Bush administration. Friedman seems oblivious to the fact that energy autarky for the US – which he strongly advocates – would signify a retreat from globalization and actually advance the cause of radical Islam. Along with (supposedly) levelling the playing field, (pseudo-)globalization is inflaming nationalist and religious passions and triggering a struggle for natural resources. These conflicts are not grit in an unstoppable machine – they are integral to the process (Gray, 2005: 15).

Only if globalization cements common interests and allows conflicts of interest to be subject to governmental sanctions can it weaken the state.

Russia and the IMF

Stiglitz is highly critical of both the International Monetary Fund (IMF) and the World Bank, noting that, while almost all the activities of both are directed to the developing world, the heads are always chosen from the developed world (a European and an American). Stiglitz's most scathing analysis is reserved for the IMF.

Set up by Keynes after the Second World War to assist in the reconstruction of Europe, the IMF under the influence of Reagan and Thatcher began to adopt a rigid and blinkered view of the market – a market fundamentalism. Its functionaries took, and still take, the view that the market by itself leads to an efficient outcome. The notion that markets might work badly has been replaced by an ideological fervour that ignores the social consequences of policies that are imposed predominantly on relatively helpless developing countries.

Failure to be sensitive to the broader social context is the IMF's basic problem. Social costs linked to unemployment are simply not taken into account. Inequality has intensified and structural adjustment programmes often provoke hunger and food riots, inflicting a pain that Stiglitz sees as far greater than necessary. Over the last decade of the twentieth century, the gap between rich and poor has been growing and those living in abject poverty (less than US$1 a day) amount to 1.2 billion people.

Terrible poverty has been brought to Russia. Stiglitz devotes a whole chapter to the disastrous policies of the IMF here (as does Gray), noting that in 1990 China's GDP was 60 per cent of Russia's: by 2000, the figures were reversed (Stiglitz, 2002: 6). Income is lower than it was a decade ago and poverty much higher. The devastation – the loss in GDP – was greater than Russia suffered in the Second World War. Wage payments have fallen into massive arrears and workers are often paid with bartered goods rather than roubles. The IMF unwittingly connived with a new and wholly unscrupulous elite. The billions of dollars loaned to Russia showed up in Cypriot and Swiss bank accounts. The experience for the region has been a disaster. If Russia's GDP is two-thirds of what it was in 1990, Moldova's and the Ukraine's are just one-third of what they were ten years ago. Whereas in 1989 in Russia only 2 per cent of the population was in poverty, this had soared to 23.8 per cent in 1998 (less than US$2 a day), and some 40 per cent are now earning less than $4 a day. While a few friends of former President Yeltsin became billionaires, the country is unable to pay pensioners $15 a month (Stiglitz, 2002: 133–65).

Gray argues that the attempt to construct a free market in post-communist Russia has produced a species of mafia-dominated anarcho-capitalism (1998a: 133). On 2 January 1992 price controls were lifted on 90 per cent of traded goods. Prices rose by 250 per cent, wages by only 50 per cent. Living standards plummeted and people could survive only by growing their own food. Privatization enriched the few, not the many – former party members were particularly privileged. Gray argues that shock therapy 'criminalized the economy to an unprecedented degree', casting part of the population into utter destitution. Birth rates and life expectancy have fallen more sharply than in any other nation.

Gray calculates that in Russia 45 million people have fallen into poverty since 1991 (ibid.: 147). Unemployment has rocketed, and the recorded economy halved in size – a bigger fall than in America during the great depression. The number of people dying from alcohol-related diseases tripled between 1990 and 1995. The murder rate soared to three times that of the rate in the USA, and infant mortality rates dramatically increased (ibid.: 148–9). Male life expectancy fell from 62 to 59 and by 1995 it was lower than in China. Ill-health has increased as public services have sharply contracted. Gray quotes Cohen: for the great majority of Russian families, 'everything essential for a decent existence' has collapsed (ibid.: 151). Something like three-quarters of privatized firms and commercial banks are compelled to pay between 10 and 20 per cent of their turnover to mafia organizations. Contract killings are commonplace. No wonder Gray talks of Russia's Hobbesian problem of order (ibid.: 155).

Stiglitz also gives examples of the damage done by liberalization policies in East Asia, and makes the point that the dogmatic approach of the IMF reflects thinly veiled vested interests. A 'Washington consensus' incorporating the US Treasury has developed, with the IMF staff undertaking short visits and stays only in the capital cities of the countries they 'assist'. The Fund operates in considerable secrecy – democratic procedures and values are notable by their absence (2002: 40).

What we need

Stiglitz in his *Globalization and its Discontents* offers a positive critique that goes some of the way to presenting a view of the potential that globalization has for advancing the development of self-government. His argument is that if globalization is to enrich the poor then it has to be radically rethought. He accepts Gray's strictures of the free market and the theory of 'hyper-globalization', taking the view that the notion of the self-regulating market is naïve and dogmatic. But he argues that the events of 9/11 have brought home the need for policies based on social justice and decency so that we can live together and, far from rejecting or pillorying globalization (as Gray does), we should stress its potential for making the world a much fairer place. After all, the international landmines treaty was brought about through the interconnectedness that has been created by globalization (ibid.: 5).

Gray argues that 'a reform of the world economy is needed that accepts a diversity of cultures, regimes and market economies as a permanent reality' (1998a: 20). Democracy and the free market are rivals, not allies (ibid.: 17). But global regulation of environmental standards is not enforceable, and countries rich enough to protect the environment will find that, as a result of competitive pressures from the global market, they will lose capital unless they level down. However, Gray's argument is curiously uncritical. He argues that the case against the global free market is not an economic one since 'there is not much doubt that the free market is the most *economically efficient* type of capitalism' (ibid.: 82–3). But how can one abstract short-term economic gains from long-term social costs? How economically efficient is a regime that has to spend more and more on incarcerating the victims of its economic development? Gray himself concedes that neglecting social costs is 'a professional deformation of economists'; this surely means that the notion of economic efficiency that he earlier propagates is a misleading abstraction. Gray quotes the words of Lind – that 'civilized social market capitalism and unrestricted global free trade are inherently incompatible' (ibid.: 86).

Clearly, Gray is right when he argues that a return to traditional social democracy is not an option since this presupposed a closed economy (ibid.: 88). But why are egalitarian principles rendered unworkable in an open economy? Gray cites the freedom of capital to migrate; the impossibility of imposing high levels of taxation to expand the range of public goods; the way in which bond markets have knocked away the floor from under post-war full employment policies (ibid.: 92). World markets have already made inroads into the German social market model and ensure that it cannot prevail at EU level (ibid.: 99).

Stiglitz, however, argues that international economic institutions need to be reshaped. Global public institutions are required to set the rules (2002: 215, 222). Globalization has in fact enhanced the need for global collective action and global public goods. We have a system of what might be called global governance without global government, in which a few players dominate the scene. Globalization needs to be democratized with a change in voting rights so that it is not just finance and trade ministers whose voice predominates at IMF and World Trade Organization (WTO) meetings. Given the fact that the IMF and the World Bank are not directly accountable to the public, there should be more transparency. Secrecy allows vested interests full sway. Surveillance ought be done by others. A more balanced agenda for the WTO is crucial (2002: 214–52).

Globalization itself points to the need to regulate the market and thus subject it to a process of gradual and long-term transcendence.

The case for global government

If globalization is to be positively conceived – as an opportunity rather than as a source of violence and division – then it is crucial that we see free market fundamentalism, and the abstract similarity that it seeks to impose, as a distortion of globalization. If by globalization we mean a sense of interconnectedness between the peoples of the world, then we must distinguish between this and 'Americanization' (of which Gray is rightly critical), which inevitably creates a fundamentalist reaction.

Globalization, as we have already argued, is a cultural and political as well as an economic phenomenon. It is not simply that states are losing economic power; their claim to impose a monopolistic outlook is being more and more openly challenged both within and between societies. The value of the Stiglitz critique is that it explains why international institutions like the IMF have discredited globalization by making it appear synonymous with neo-liberalism and devastation.

We need to be clear that the case for global government is not a case for a global state. Barry Jones might speak of the 'functional equivalent' of the state but the point is that the state has no functional equivalent. Barry Jones's own list of the functions of governance – the provision of collective goods, the management of general externalities and the satisfaction of minority needs (2000: 176–7) – does not require institutional force as a sanction. What makes the state distinctive and specific is its use of force as a method of tackling conflicts of interest. The danger is that we either embrace a traditional utopianism in imagining a problem-free world or adopt an abstract realism by assuming that things can only go from bad to worse.

Sharp has distinguished between the 'no change' school, which argues that only professional diplomats as state functionaries can be taken seriously, and the 'all change' school, which sees state sovereignty as simply irrelevant. The state system is viewed as a town whose buildings have been burned down to shells (2001: 16). It is a false (and supremely modernist) choice to have to accept *either* that global government and the end of state sovereignty can be established tomorrow, *or* that the whole venture is an impossible dream.

If we are moving, as Barry Jones rightly supposes, to a world of 'complex, multi-layered' public governance (2000: 270), then it is crucial that we challenge the monopolistic pretensions of the state, and the statist view that diversity is the same as fragmentation. States will remain for the foreseeable future and the case for global government is one in which states become less important, and increasingly devote their energies to governmental activities, thus gradually transcending themselves. The problem with Kant's argument for perpetual peace is that it rests upon a liberal republican notion of a federation of states – whereas what is required is the development of global identities that go beyond the state.

I have already dealt with Held's argument for a cosmopolitan democracy. It is important not only to democratize the United Nations but in so doing to challenge the arguments of those who see the UN Charter as bestowing a kind of state sovereignty on the Security and General Councils. International law is already a stateless law, and it is vital to strengthen the common interest that makes it enforceable. The problem is that the UN is an organization with two souls. The one is certainly globalist in scope, since the Preamble to the Charter refers to the existence of universal human rights and Article 1 speaks of universal peace for the peoples of the world based on self-determination. But Article 2 speaks of sovereign equality for member states with Article 2 (7) declaring that no intervention is allowed in the domestic jurisdiction of any state. It is over ten years since the Commission on Global Governance referred to the 'crisis of legitimacy' (1995: 237) created by the unrepresentative character of the Security Council. Pressure needs to grow on the UN to boost its peace-keeping role and its post-statal activities, in which the plight of children, the spread of disease and problems of development are tackled imaginatively and effectively.

In the same way, the European Union has two souls – the market and democracy. The one can be particularist and short-termist, but the other is empowering and has tremendous potential – as in the concept of European citizenship that offers a wider identity, not in competition with but as a supplement to state identity. The European Court of Justice can uphold rights in opposition to narrow-minded actions of member states, and the right to petition Parliament and refer matters to the Ombudsman are bestowed on individuals who are not citizens of constituent states and therefore not eligible to be European citizens. It is difficult to disagree with Heater that the EU offers a new kind of citizenship that at the moment is a mere shadow of its potential (1999: 129).

A global civil society is also developing around non-governmental organizations (NGOs), which could be better called non-statist organizations, given the fact that NGOs within and between countries act in ways that help to cement common interests. NGOs such as the World Wide Fund for Nature, Amnesty International, Oxfam, Human Rights Watch and Christian Aid support a concept of order that stresses resource provision rather than military action, and they pose what has been called 'a serious challenge to the imperatives of statehood' (Faulks, 1999: 202). Heater argues that Amnesty International is of special relevance in terms of forging a global identity because it confronts national governments with transgressions of the UN Charter (1999: 144). It is true that some of the 29,000 NGOs suffer from problems of bureaucracy and authoritarianism, but they are becoming increasingly influential and they do represent proof that organizations can tackle problems without claiming to exercise a monopoly of legitimate force. They are no substitute for coordinated, collective global action to tackle the problem of global inequality but they do make a significant practical and theoretical contribution to the question of global government.

Globalization has demonstrated that humans face problems of a global kind and that global institutions have to be forged that, in conjunction with local, regional and national governments, are able to contribute positively to a world that recognizes difference, but works against division.

Global government and the Huntington thesis

Huntington's contention is that globalization is leading to a clash of civilizations. While he concedes that minorities in other cultures may espouse Western values – by which he means the values of what he calls 'democratic liberalism' – dominant attitudes in non-Western cultures range from widespread scepticism to intense opposition to Western values (1996: 184). Almost all the non-Western civilizations are resistant to pressure from the West – including Hindu, Orthodox, African and even Latin American countries – but the greatest resistance to the West has come from Islam and Asia (ibid.: 193).

Gray challenges Huntington's taxonomy of civilizations and argues that he tacitly reflects his American obsession with multiculturalism so that a people or culture is a civilization if it is politically active as an American minority (1998a: 122). But, as Gray argues, wars in our time are within civilizational groups, as in the millions who died in the Iraq–Iran war, or the genocides in Rwanda and Cambodia (ibid.: 122–3). It needs to be remembered that it was a US-led NATO that intervened in Kosovo to defend the human rights of people of Muslim faith against their Serbian (and Christian Orthodox) aggressors. This hardly fits the 'clash of civilizations' thesis. The notion of a Western civilization, as Gray points out, is highly questionable. The uniqueness to which Huntington refers is not that of the West; it is of the United States (ibid.: 125). What of the tensions between neo-liberal and social democratic strategies and values?

Huntington himself links what he calls 'Muslim assertiveness' to social mobilization, population growth and a flood of people from the countryside into the towns (1996: 102; 98). This is surely a social rather than a purely cultural explanation for antagonism. It is not that civilizational differences (however we categorize them) are not real and important, but it is wrong to see them as a necessary source of antagonism. Civilizations, in Huntington's view, are the ultimate human tribes and the clash of civilization is tribal conflict on a global scale. As a 'realist', Huntington sees all conflict as violent in nature, and he regards conflict as not simply between

Islamic fundamentalists and Christianity but between Islam itself and Christianity. Conflict is the product of difference: in civilizational conflicts, unlike ideological ones, kin stand by their kin (ibid.: 209–10, 217). Religion is the principal defining characteristic of civilization so that what he calls 'fault-line wars' are almost always between people of different religions (ibid.: 253).

In Huntington's view, it is futile and counter-productive for countries to integrate differing peoples. A multi-civilizational United States would, he argues, be the United Nations. We must reject the siren calls of multiculturalism (ibid.: 306–7, 310). Cultural identities inevitably collide in an antagonistic manner. 'We only know who we are when we know what we are against' (ibid.: 21). Although Gray sees Huntington's attack as directed against the Enlightenment conception of universal values, he refers to (a point that we explored in detail in Chapter 8) the evils and goods that are universally human. Indeed, Gray describes these as 'universal human values' that can be embodied in a variety of regimes (1998a: 124). It is these universal values that globalization has strengthened, since people meet others of different cultural and ethnic origin not merely when they travel abroad, but even at the local level. The media (at its best) presents people suffering and developing in other parts of the world as though they were neighbours, so that it becomes increasingly possible to put oneself in the place of the other. Modern conditions have contributed much to Kant's argument that 'a violation of rights in *one* part of the world is felt *everywhere*' (Heater, 1999: 140). What is needed is what has been called a 'differentiated universalism' (Gray, 1997: 197) – a universalism that is strengthened by a respect for particularistic difference.

Modernism and pessimism

Gray's problem is that he sees universalism and differentiation as opposites, at loggerheads with each other, inviting a choice between one and the other. This modernist stance makes it inevitable that he is unable to integrate his advocacy of universal values with his emphasis upon particularity. Globalization stands or falls on a recognition of difference – Gray is right to emphasize diversity – but wrong to assume that no universal values animate this diversity. Thus, whereas Gray argues that liberal democracy is not on the agenda of China (1998a: 189), it can be argued that capitalism will compel the regime not to imitate the 'West' but to dismantle its totalitarian controls so that a liberal political regime – albeit one infused with traditional Chinese values – emerges. Hutton has recently examined the career of one Zhang Yin (worth £1.9 billion), and takes the view that entrepreneurs like Yin can only push the economy so far. 'One day the party will have to let go properly. The issues are only how and when' (2006).

Gray argues that the result of globalization is not universal freedom but 'an anarchy of sovereign states, rival capitalisms and stateless zones [zones without effective government]' (1998a: 194). But how can we move to a world in which Gray's own *modus vivendi* becomes effective? All these differentiated regimes have a common interest in peace, ecological security and economic stability. Unless we can work towards a global government based upon these common interests, then humanity has no future. Gray himself comments that only a framework of global regulation – of global governance – can enable the creativity of the world economy to be harnessed to the service of human needs (ibid.: 199). I agree. But surely that means a strategy that goes beyond a world of sovereign states, rival capitalisms and zones without effective government? Gray mentions Tobin's tax on currency speculation as an example of the kind of global regulation needed (ibid.: 200). But that requires new structures to make this kind of regulation effective.

It is because Gray sees the solution in 'effective state institutions' (ibid.: 201) that he assumes that the institution that generates war and conflict, that normalizes violence and downgrades the importance of community and social sanction, is central to a world of peace. No wonder he is pessimistic and confused. For statism is part of the problem. A globalization that is based upon Gray's universal values must be critical of both state and market, even if the process of moving beyond them is a gradual and protracted one. Gray argues that people expect from their states security, both from violence and from destitution, unemployment and exclusion (ibid.: 201). But how is this kind of legitimacy possible unless we adopt a critical stance towards, not simply the free market, but the market per se; not simply the totalitarian state, but the state as such? The need for health care, economic stability, adequate transport and a safety net involves a radical rethink of the concept of government, freedom and democracy. There is no disagreement with Gray's objective of a global regulation that accepts a diversity of regimes, cultures and economies as a permanent condition (ibid.: 203); the question is one of linking this diversity with a critique of the state and market, for these are the institutions that work against peace and diversity.

Gray concedes that 'a basic shift in economic philosophy is needed' (ibid.: 234). But he underestimates the comprehensiveness and the depth of the shift that is needed. He links the free market with utopianism. But the notion of utopia needs to be reconstructed, and this is possible only if the conceptual tyranny of state and market is shaken. Globalization itself must be redefined so that its potential for making a reality of Gray's universal values becomes a real possibility.

Conclusion

Globalization should be defined in a way that emphasizes that, although the phenomenon has its roots in the past, it is indeed something new. Gray finds that, although scepticism about globalization is a useful corrective to those who see globalization simply in terms of global markets, such scepticism fails to capture the qualitative change that has occurred. We are talking about not just the dramatic increase in the volume of trade and investment that is taking place internationally, but the equally dramatic shrinkage in time and space that the revolution in information technology has made possible.

Gray is rightly critical of the neo-liberal or market fundamentalist view of globalization. Free market policies have increased inequality and the attempt to impose uniformity upon a diverse world has generated a fundamentalist backlash. Stiglitz is particularly scathing about the IMF and the way it has operated in terms of a 'Washington consensus' that seeks to propagate American hegemony. However, whereas Gray is pessimistic about the future and sees globalization simply in negative terms, Stiglitz stresses the positive potential that globalization has for establishing justice and global regulation.

It is naïve to imagine that globalization can lead to the withering away of the state if by globalization we mean free market policies that exacerbate inequality and make democracy more difficult to achieve. Ohmae's fundamentalist version is riddled with statism despite the fact that he argues that globalization is bringing about the end of the nation-state, for only if globalization respects diversity and strengthens the common interest between different countries can the state begin to be replaced by government. Stiglitz sees the need for global government, and his argument for reforming the IMF and the World Bank constitutes an important step in the right direction. Global government should be thought of not in statist terms, but rather in terms of international political institutions that will operate in cooperation with government at the national and local level. Although transcending the state and market is a gradual process, Gray's argument for effective states fails to see that the state (like the market) is part of the problem; it is not the solution to international chaos and conflict. A globalization that respects diversity requires a break with the modernist juxtaposition of the universal and the particular, so that the universal values underpinning Gray's *modus vivendi* can manifest themselves in regimes that are different and specific.

10 • Egalitarianism and Multiculturalism

Introduction

In this chapter I will critically examine Gray's treatment of egalitarianism and multiculturalism. He links egalitarianism to social democracy and he is correct to argue that traditional social democrats have handled the notion of equality in an abstract fashion. In the same way, communitarians have often constructed a notion of community that is purist and unreal. Equalities compete, he argues, and we have to make a choice between them.

But, like the notion of justice, equality can be treated as sameness. This is why Gray rejects it, but as always the problem is not with equality, it is with an abstract treatment of it. Local contexts are important, and Gray is right to emphasize them, but the local is empowering only if it is linked organically to the global. Gray's argument comes perilously close to relativism when he argues that the peasant and the courtier in authoritarian societies may have values as worthwhile as those of a liberal kind. It is true that liberal societies do not practise what they preach. But it is one thing to be critical of existing liberal societies; quite another to argue that roles that clearly depend upon patriarchy and the normalization of violence contribute to the flourishing of society.

Indeed, it is precisely this relativism that has undermined the credibility of multiculturalism. Multiculturalism cannot mean that different cultures are worthwhile simply because they exist. There must be criteria for assessing their contribution to human flourishing, and I argue that the question of violence is a meaningful way of differentiating between illiberal practices that should be tolerated and those that should not. Thus, arranged marriages that are accepted by the parties concerned should be tolerated, whereas arranged marriages that involve coercion and force are contrary to democratic norms and should be regarded as unlawful. As with equality, it is not multiculturalism that is the problem, but what I call a pseudo-multiculturalism that accepts practices that violate human development.

Autonomy should not be identified with the abstract notions of the liberal tradition. All humans are autonomous in that they are agents and change their environment. Of course, some are more autonomous than others, depending upon how comprehensively they can alter the world around them, but autonomy is a concept towards which we move, but can never reach. There are many different forms of family life and Gray is right to argue against those who would regard a heterosexual coupling as a universal norm. But, in deciding whether a family is tolerable or not, it is precisely what Gray identifies as universal evils that must be brought into play.

Again, Gray is correct to argue that religion is not itself a threat to human flourishing. Secularist fundamentalism demonizes religion and portrays the same kind of absolutist prejudices that conventionally religious groups have sometimes displayed. But this does not mean that belief in a supernatural god is part of the human psyche. Religious beliefs can be emancipatory and liberating if they take a positive view of human development but it can be plausibly argued that a tolerant secularism is likely to become more and more widespread as humans adopt more scientific attitudes towards their relationships with one another and the world of nature. It is fundamentalism that is the problem, and fundamentalism can never, in my view, be transcended as long the market and the state remain intact.

The critique of social democracy

In his *Beyond the New Right* (1993) Gray identifies himself with conservatism. A few years later, however, he argues that the genuine understanding of enduring human needs has passed to Green theory and, in Britain, to New Labour (1997: viii).

However, Gray argues that the central economic programme of social democracy has become unworkable, and social democracy itself is a bankrupt project. Its class base and its political vehicle have been marginalized (ibid.: 13). He defends a communitarian political morality that sees autonomy and fairness not as applications of universal principles, but as shared understandings arising from common forms of life (ibid.: 17). Norms of fairness should be substituted for the social democratic commitment to egalitarian principles, but norms that are local (1996b: 2). In going beyond Thatcherism, there is no going back to social democracy (ibid.: 5).

Gray seeks to advance 'a communitarian liberal perspective' – a perspective that seeks to enrich standard liberal thinking with the distinctive insights of communitarian thinking. Individuals are themselves creations of forms of common life. He rejects what he sees as the egalitarian imposition of a single conception of justice in all contexts of economic and social life (ibid.: 9). The notion of justice advanced here has purely local authority, matching goods to social understandings, as these arise in particular cultures (ibid.: 11). Gray warns that some communitarians seek a purist 'noumenal community' that, as he rightly points out, is as much a fiction as the autonomous subject of liberal theory (1995: 109).

We are confronted with 'uncombinable goods and choices among evils' (1996b: 12). There can be no across-the-board equality: there is a reality of conflict among equalities – between achieving equality of opportunity and social mobility, for example. Individual autonomy may not be particularly valued in some immigrant groups. In place of a monocultural liberal society, we must foster pluralistic common institutions that are culturally diverse (ibid.: 13). There is a real conflict of equalities that social democrats are shy of admitting (ibid.: 35). Market exchanges must be excluded from contexts in which non-market institutions and practices are protected as a matter of public policy (1997: 18). In place of full employment must be the fair distribution of work, and a benefits system that protects human interests without the classical social democratic commitment to equality (1996b: 14). Without an egalitarian political morality, social democracy is nothing. Gray identifies this egalitarian commitment with 'the imposition of a single conception of justice in all areas of policy and contexts of social and economic life' (1997: 16), but why can't we take a developmental view of justice that is sensitive to historical context and situation? Besides Gray is not always opposed to equality: he argues for equality 'as a safeguard against exclusion'; it is surely curious that this is deemed quite different from the requirement of any theory of justice (ibid.: 17).

Both the historic policies and the constitutive morality of social democracy have been rendered utopian by the ruling forces of the age, and in particular by the global freedom of capital (1996d: 18). Social democrats share with neo-liberals a 'utopian project of harmonising market institutions according to the requirements of an ideal model' (ibid.: 25). The European Union provides no *deus ex machina*. The social democratic project involves a rationalist disdain for local attachments and communities (ibid.: 29). Complex fairness has no 'overarching theory or principle' by which hard choices arising from conflicts can be arbitrated. There is a sort of moral scarcity that runs parallel with the finitude of moral resources (ibid.: 36, 38).

The human need for security must be reconciled with the permanent revolution of the market. We need a thinner, yet durable and resilient, common culture of shared understandings of fairness and tolerance. Politics is the negotiation of unavoidable conflicts (1997: 19–21). Equalities, like liberties, compete. Globalization undermines both the left project of egalitarian community and the right project of the free market. Markets are in fact integral expressions of histories and parent cultures (ibid.: 29–30). Egalitarian principles attach moral importance to purely relational properties when what has moral importance is well being (ibid.: 38). The goal of policy ought to be to enhance individual competences – participation in the world of work is, for us, a precondition of self-esteem and independence (ibid.: 47).

It is clear that, in rejecting egalitarianism as a mirage, Gray sees equality as sameness. If one person is blind and another fully sighted, why not transfer one eye from the sighted to the blind person so that both are partially sighted (1993: 87)? This is absurd, of course, but the example arises because equality is seen as an abstraction, as sameness, and not as a notion that incorporates difference. Treating people equally involves allowing each to develop. Hence it is egalitarian to help a five-year-old to cross a busy road; it is not egalitarian to do the same to a person three times that age. It is not egalitarianism that is a mirage; it is abstraction.

Gray concedes to Colls that some of his comments about social democratic settlements in Western Europe were unfair (Colls, 1996: 74), but he does not retreat from his basic critique of social democracy, nor does he ever move away from the one-sided view of equality that leads him to reject social democracy as an alternative to free market fundamentalism. What he never considers is a form of social democracy that challenges the existence of the state, looks beyond the market and is authentically post-liberal in character.

How diverse is diversity?

Gray rightly warns against trying to engineer traditional forms of family life. This seriously detracts from the task of enhancing individual competences so that people can choose the kind of family that meets the desire for lasting personal relationships (1997: 46). Gray argues that autonomy should not be seen as a universal ideal since recent immigrant communities make it clear that the latter is not necessarily revered as an ideal. To insist upon it would be 'a policy of liberal cultural imperialism'. 'We cannot restore a seamless monoculture animated by the liberal ideal of autonomy.' For the same reason, any attempt to restore the traditional family would be futile and counter-productive (1996b: 42). We harbour, Gray points out, a deep diversity of views and values as to sexuality and the worth of human life, our relations with the natural environment and the place of the human species in the scheme of things. Fundamentalism needs to be rejected whether it is of a cultural or marketing variety (1995: 109–10). The notion of the neutral state – so beloved by liberals – must be challenged (1996b: 43). Our chief danger is an asocial individualism (1996b: 45).

He argues that many virtues are absent from a liberal society, such as those of a 'courtier, a warrior or a pious peasant' (1989: 260). An authoritarian order may be more virtuous than a liberal society. It is true that momentary examples might exist such as Iraq, which was more stable under Saddam Hussein than it is under the 'liberal' rule of the United States. But in general this argument seems to me to be dangerously close to relativism. Of course, pre-liberal societies have values that are precious and that need to be incorporated into the post-liberal order. But how do we decide? It seems to me that we need recourse to Gray's universal evils. If violence is a universal evil, then the values of, say, a warrior are positive only if they are shorn of the support for violence that accompanied them in the past. The same is true of the values of the courtier and the pious peasant. These figures could convey powerful support for patriarchy – a dismissive and arrogant attitude towards women. They would contribute positively to human flourishing only if they no longer embraced the values of patriarchy. To say that human beings may have flourished better in such ages as medieval Christendom (1993: 50) than in secular modernity is to reject any notion of enlightenment or progress however historically nuanced.

In an essay on Santayana, Gray argues that the good life may involve bourgeois productivity or aristocratic leisure, religious piety or the pleasure of the senses: monarchy or republicanism, free enterprise or feudalism 'may be equally lawful facets of the human good' (1996a: 22). We return to Gray's own stress on generic human evils. What of those excluded, marginalized, oppressed and subordinated by these systems and values? Gray comments: 'who can doubt that human beings flourished under the feudal institutions of medieval Christendom? Or under the monarchical government of Elizabethan England?' (ibid.: 246). But who flourished in these systems: the ordinary people? And if the privileged depended for their identity upon the have-nots, can we really say that anyone flourished under these systems?

The same problem arises in Gray's argument that Singapore, China and Japan meet the criteria of a universal minimum morality even if they are non-liberal regimes (1995: 83). What if you are a woman in Japan in a traditional family, or a prisoner in China condemned to death, or a Tibetan wishing to develop indigenous culture, or a dissident in Singapore? Good life for whom? If violence is a universal evil, then where does this leave regimes that have a deplorable human rights record? Morgan rightly argues that, whereas feudal and early modern societies secured *some* people against 'generic evils', the modern liberal state takes the view that *all* have a claim to rights. One could equally say that under, for example, Duvalier's Haiti, Saddam Hussein's Iraq, or apartheid South Africa some 'flourished', but what of those who manifestly did not (2006: 235)? Where divisions exist, it is treacherous to make generalizations about societies. One group can flourish at the expense of another. Even this argument ignores the way in which privilege can be psychologically debilitating and personally corrupting, so that it could be argued that, unless all flourish, no one flourishes.

A self may be created or renewed, Gray says in his critique of Berlin, through participating in a form of life that is not liberal (1996b: 37). But this suggests that an oppressor or the beneficiary of privilege might have as worthwhile a life as people in a society where the governing norms point to freedom and equality. This is an anti-relational position – I can be free while you are a slave: a position that is quintessentially liberal in character. Gray argues that Hindu, Shinto or orthodox Jewish doctrine sustains authoritarian societies that 'harbour worthwhile forms of life' (ibid.: 151) – but again we have to ask, what of the victims of these societies, for example, women?

Multiculturalism, violence and democracy

The question arises: how to avoid imposing emancipatory values on practices that we regard as oppressive and unacceptable? The existence of universal values is crucial here, for while we should tolerate patriarchal practices where (as far as we can tell) they seem natural and normal to men and women – arranged marriage in liberal societies might be an example – we should not tolerate such practices where they involve violence or the threat of violence. Thus, a woman who wishes to marry a partner of her own choosing, to continue our example, should be free to do so and her relatives must be prevented from intimidation and violence.

Illiberal practices are tolerable where violence is not involved but, once violence is threatened, then we are entitled and duty bound to ensure that democracy prevails over what I want to call pseudo-multiculturalism, the kind of multiculturalism that is rooted in a relativistic acceptance of practices that subordinate individuals against their will. Gray speaks of multiculturalism as a fashionable form of paternalism 'which aims to embalm the dead or dying vestiges of submerged or occluded traditions and preserve their remains as public spectacles' (1996a: 261), 'the institutionalization of a cultural apartheid' (ibid.: 266). Yet how do we decide whether a tradition is worth preserving?

Gray himself argues for a common culture reinforced by laws and policies that resists pluralism 'when pluralism threatens the norms of civil society itself' (1993: 59). This common culture rests upon, Gray argues, the widespread acceptance of certain norms and culture – powerful notions of fair play and give-and-take (1995: 24). The central defining practices of toleration and compromise must be upheld. I would put it rather more strongly: any attempt to undermine toleration leads to a pseudo-pluralism since a meaningful pluralism assumes that diverse groups are *all* entitled to respect and the freedom of expression. One cannot be a pluralist if one advocates practices that suppress others.

What Gray is, however, unable to see is that, if violence and torture etc. are universal evils, then toleration of illiberal practices is only acceptable when there is no conflict with this universalism.

In this way we can combine toleration with democratic norms, accepting that people can act in ways we disapprove of, provided these practices are relational and thus genuinely non-violent. In the post-liberal world people are able to embrace any belief they like, provided they act in ways that enable others to believe as they please. A person must be free to practise Catholicism, Judaism, atheism etc. provided they do not prevent 'others' from having their own religious or anti-religious beliefs. Margalit and Halbertal point out that the ultra-orthodox in Israel react with violence against individuals who violate their rules. Anyone driving a car on the Sabbath in an ultra-orthodox neighbourhood may be stoned. The ultra-orthodox educate their children in schools that discriminate against female students (1994: 493). These violations of democratic norms are not only permitted, but massive financial support is given to the ultra-orthodox by the government (ibid.: 499). Margalit and Halbertal argue that the ultra-orthodox community does not have the right to force its members to remain within the community (ibid.: 508). This prohibition must surely extend to all practices that violate democratic norms. Kateb is right to insist that 'toleration cannot extend to crimes or to injurious blockages of potentialities of experience' (1994: 515).

What makes 'incommensurable beliefs' commensurable is that they need to be underpinned by the kind of universalism that Gray himself endorses but that he wrongly supposes is of a minimalist character. Gray identifies what he rightly calls the 'spurious universality of liberal principles' (1989: 262) with universality itself. But a rejection of universality is not an option. Hence we need a concrete universalism in the place of a spurious one. As Morgan asserts, Gray's argument for a *modus vivendi* rests upon the wide public acceptance of a multiculturalism (2006: 237), since otherwise different peoples would not tolerate the cultural practices and values they disapprove of.

It is one thing to be critical of classical liberalism; quite another to abandon, as Gray puts it, any expansive democratic project (1995: 141). Democracy must, in Gray's view, be limited if civil society is to survive (O'Sullivan, 2006: 297). The point about democracy, as defined here, is that it incorporates diversity and pluralism. Gray adopts an abstract notion of democracy (identified doubtless with the liberal democratic state) and then abandons the abstraction that he has created. To say that the Chinese regime should be criticized for undermining communities and cultural forms in Tibet is not to indulge in some kind of abstract critique: it is to invoke the question of democracy that Gray seeks to abandon.

The question of autonomy

Gray argues that autonomy is not a necessary element in human flourishing *tout court*. It is 'an essential element of the good life for people situated in our historical context as inheritors of a particular individualist form of life' (1993: 81). Yet what the discussion on multiculturalism indicates is that autonomy is crucial to freedom and democracy, but it must be an autonomy relationally conceived.

Autonomy is something towards which we move, but never fully reach: it is what I will call in my next chapter a momentum concept, and it is negated by violence and coercion. It is, therefore, a necessary element in human flourishing; but it has to be an autonomy that is not a liberal abstraction, but that arises from and works with the social relationships that exist at any given time. There is no need to reject a universal concept of autonomy, provided we identify this autonomy in concrete terms. To say that we should abandon the ideal of the autonomous chooser (1993: 137) is to identify autonomy only as an abstract liberal concept. This seems to be the problem with Kateb's response to Gray when Kateb argues that 'only now and then is someone, say, autonomous, fully there, fully active, fully self-possessed, fully aware or awake' (2006: 317). But the problem lies with the very conception of a perfectionist 'moment' in which a few people on a few occasions become fully autonomous etc.

Gray comments, in a critique of Raz, that 'the autonomous choice of a worthless life, if such there can be, is valueless even though it *is* autonomous' (1996b: 30). But this makes autonomy purely formal and, in my view, meaningless. It would concede that a person can act autonomously to end his or her autonomy – an absurd and self-defeating proposition.

Gray refers to Asian immigrants in Britain whose 'cultural traditions do not valorise autonomy' (1995: 142), but the case for toleration is much better based on the question of violence than the argument that such groups are often better off in terms of well being than liberal groups. After all, a lack of autonomy is problematic, and immigrants are likely to find that traditional hierarchies crumble under the pressures of a liberal society. In an argument with Raz, Gray quotes Parekh at some length where the latter comments that Asians in Britain have prospered 'because they do not set much store by autonomy and draw on the ample resources of a flourishing communal life and a readily available network on social support'. But Parekh is referring to autonomy as defined in liberal theory, and it is revealing that he proceeds to argue that Asians may even have less suffering and unhappiness than *allegedly* autonomous citizens' (Gray, 1996c: 154, stress mine). Parekh's language suggests that what is commonly seen as autonomy is not really a meaningful term.

To say that autonomy is 'the primary animating value of market institutions' (Gray, 1993: 82) ignores the fact that the market itself generates abstractions – a formal equality that does not address substantial differences. The market rests upon a dualistic conception between abstract autonomy and concrete subordination, so, if we seek to move towards real autonomy, we must render abstractions more concrete and differentials more visible, and in this way begin to move beyond the market itself.

Secularization

Gray makes the point that modernization does not imply secularization. Even in the West the USA points to a society in which a belief in the values of the Enlightenment coexists with devout religious beliefs. Even less can it argued that other cultures become secularized when they modernize. In Gray's view, we have no reason to suppose that secularism and modernity are connected, and indeed it could be argued that, for example, in Islamic societies modernization strengthens the influence of scholars – a social group that demonstrates its relevance through the interpretation of sacred texts (1995: 168).

Yet we return to Gray's universal moralities – all of which have a common antipathy to war, genocide, torture etc. To the extent that religion promotes universal evils, it conflicts with democracy. Gray is right to argue that a belief in religion as such does not undermine a civilized *modus vivendi*. To argue otherwise is to subscribe to a secularist fundamentalism. Morgan notes that modern liberal societies may in the main have abandoned conventional religion, but they have sacralized a whole range of other elements of the cosmos, including animals, the environment and even crystals (2006: 239). However the point is that faith can undermine science, just as belief in deities can promote absolutist and intolerant views. We should encourage the expression of religious views that accord with human emancipation – understanding that term not as an ahistorical abstraction, but to refer to a process in which people increasingly govern their own lives. Modernization does not mean, as Gray rightly points out, repeating the pattern of the development of European cultures, but it does have implications for the universal evils that form the bedrock of Gray's notion of a *modus vivendi*. Religion is not itself an obstacle to a dynamic view of emancipation, but it is a very ahistorical view to insist, as Gray does, that the need for religion appears to be 'hard-wired in the human animal' (2004: 45). 'The most necessary task of the present time', he writes recently, 'is to accept the irreducible reality of religion' (2007: 207). But why shouldn't religion be reconstructed so that its war with science and materialism is transcended?

As Jones has pointed out (2006: 201), Gray's notion of value-pluralism rests upon the assumption that ways of life are incommensurable – a conception that orthodox religious people are certain to reject. Why then should orthodox religious people be tolerant when they do not subscribe to value-pluralism? The whole theory of the *modus vivendi* is, it seems to me, premised on the view that religious people will become more pluralistic in the sense that, while believing that their own way is the right one, they will tolerate those whose beliefs they consider false. This process cannot simply be a cultural one: there have to be institutional changes that make this kind of toleration possible – economic security, respect for diversity and a rejection of violence as a way of tackling differences (in other words, the implementation of policies that move beyond market and state).

Conclusion

Gray argues that social democracy is flawed by its obsession with equality. Its bankruptcy is therefore not only social, but conceptual as well. It fails to see that invariably we need to make a choice between equalities – for example, equality of resources and equality of opportunity – and like the concept of community in some communitarian thought, the notion of equality is treated by many social democrats in a simplistic, purist and monolithic manner.

Gray's critique of (some concepts of) social democracy and communitarianism is valid although it would be considerably strengthened if he pointed to the uncritical attitude towards the market and state that social democrats and communitarians often espouse. The problem with his argument against egalitarianism is that it blames the concept of equality for what are deficiencies with abstraction, and Gray fails to see that the conflict between equalities is apparent, and arises out of the lack of a clear-cut universal value (such as development) that makes it possible to distinguish between policies that genuinely make people more equal and policies that divide people despite their honourable intentions. Gray assumes that the notion of equality excludes the notion of difference and is oblivious of the substantial body of feminist argumentation that seeks to transcend this particular dualism.

It is difficult to resist the conclusion that Gray, in rejecting an abstract construct of equality, privileges difference and ends up therefore accepting pre-liberal practices in the name of diversity. He argues, for example, that peasants, courtiers, warriors and aristocrats in authoritarian societies may contribute to human flourishing as much as liberal individuals, but the problem arises from the very universal evils that Gray argues are 'generic'. Pre-liberal societies may embrace aspects of 'minimal' universalism but they do so partially and selectively, and anyone concerned about, for example, women and the poor must see the problematic character of these authoritarian orders. Of course, liberal societies are also selective and partial as well, but postulating emancipatory values albeit as otherworldly ideals constitutes an important step forward.

Gray condemns multiculturalism as a form of paternalism, but it is not multiculturalism that is problematic, but the relativistic version that leads to the absurd and self-defeating conclusion that all cultural practices should be celebrated simply because they exist. I make a distinction between multiculturalism that is liberating and pseudo-multiculturalism that discredits toleration because it accepts practices that are divisive and contrary to democratic norms. Diversity is a strength when it increases the capacity of people to govern their own lives: otherwise it turns into its opposite, provoking a homogeneist backlash when policies promote practices that cripple and diminish people. I suggest that the employment of coercion and violence signals the divide between cultural policies that should be tolerated and those that should not. Arranged marriages, to take an example that has much exercised liberal commentators, constitute a difference when the parties involved are willing to follow the practice, and a division (that is, a 'difference' that is destructive) when coercion and violence are employed. A fundamentalist rejection of diversity is as damaging and counter-productive as a fundamentalist espousal of divisive and undemocratic practices.

The point is that people can be autonomous in different ways. It is because Gray interprets the notion of autonomy in a liberal and abstract fashion that he cannot accept that humans act autonomously whenever they act as agents, and that autonomy is an example of a momentum concept. We move towards it as circumstances allow but can never actually reach a situation in which we can say: 'Now we are fully autonomous.' Gray rightly argues that religion is not itself a barrier to the existence of a worthy life but, just as it is wrong to argue for the exclusive truth of a particular religion, so it is wrong to assume that conventional religion is somehow part of the human condition. There is plenty of evidence to suggest that the notion of God is being continuously reconstructed and that many find that religion itself is implausible and unnecessary.

11 • Reconstructing Utopia

Introduction

To reconstruct utopia is to make it a critique of the present. But it is more than this. It must be a critique of the present that arises out of the present and does not pose a perfectionist end – a culminating point that represents some kind of heaven on earth. Traditionalist concepts of utopia, like traditionalist utopias, are vulnerable to the charge that they pose a vision that stands outside of the existing society, offering an idealized alternative that invites rejection from those claiming to be realists. Manuel and Manuel argue that 'the great utopians have been great realists', but what they mean by this is that utopians have had penetrating insights into the society that they are criticizing. The term 'utopian' is still seen as a synonym for the 'chimerical, fantasic, improbable' (1979: 28).

Utopia, in its traditional formulation, starts from a position of established perfection (Goodwin and Taylor, 1982: 109). A reconstructed utopia could be an emancipated society in which humans relate to each other with sufficient equality that they can change places. Conflicts of interest would be settled without force – through negotiation and arbitration – and conciliation certainly involves constraints, but not force. Such a world is already anticipated by the liberal opposition to force – but an emancipated world has to be post-liberal in character because liberalism contradicts its commitment to freedom and equality by endorsing both the state and market as institutions necessary for society. An emancipated world must be classless and stateless in character.

Goodwin and Taylor argue that human nature is so diverse that, as far as the utopian is concerned, the empirical method would lead to no clear-cut conclusions about human needs, and no definite human values such as the social critic must work with (Goodwin and Taylor, 1982: 99). But this is, I have argued, an abstract notion of utopia that we need to transcend. Might it not be argued, however, that the notion of an historical utopia, a concrete utopia, is itself problematic? Does not, as some post-modernists assert, the very notion of emancipation imply a perfect world of freedom and autonomy? The problem here is that some post-modernists (as Gray himself does) operate with binary concepts. If a concept is absolute, it cannot be relative; if it is progressive, it must be ahistorical; if it is theoretical and abstract (in the non-pejorative sense of the term), it cannot also be practical and concrete.

This is why I argue for the notion of utopia as a momentum concept – a concept that is progressive, historical and unrealizable. There is no final goal since utopianism involves a process of change. This process is divided into an infinity of stages – each of which can be conceptualized as a utopia in its own right.

The primary agents in the struggle for greater emancipation are those who are suffer directly from the existence of the market and state, but a relational view shows that all who inhabit an alienated society are in different ways adversely affected. Men suffer from patriarchy albeit in different ways from women, for example, just as the lives of white people are impoverished by racist attitudes towards blacks. Although we would not expect the beneficiaries of the status quo to be in the forefront of the struggle for utopian change, it would be foolish to rule out contributions from any quarter. The realization of reconstructed utopias is inevitable but not in the traditional unconditional sense. The notion of inevitability here assumes not only human agency but a situation in which humanity is able to extricate itself from a threatened nightmare of social and environment devastation.

Gray ridicules utopianism for seeking to eliminate all tragedy and evil, but this is because he identifies utopianism with perfectionism and a religious-type salvation. Tragedy arises because humans enter into relations independent of their will. It is therefore part of the human condition. But it can be diminished, and a *modus vivendi* that rests upon policies that sought to move beyond market and state would surely reduce the sense of powerlessness and helplessness that generates tragedy. Likewise with the notion of evil. Evil is both an absolute and a relative term. Without some notion of evil, progress would be impossible: evil can be reduced as people are able to govern their lives more completely, but it can never be eradicated. An evil-free society represents a traditional but not a reconstructed view of utopia.

Prejudice arises from difference: it is because we are different from one another that we conflict, and these conflicts necessarily involve judgements that are variance with reality. Conservatives are right to argue that prejudice will always exist; where they are wrong is that they are often reluctant to work against more harmful prejudices in favour of judgements that are more conducive to human development and progress. An uncritical realism is as one-sided as an uncritical view of utopia; a reconstructed concept of utopia points to the transcendence of this particular dualism so that utopianism reinforces realism, and realism forms the basis for utopian thought.

Gray sometimes describes himself as a post-liberal. But post-liberalism is only possible if we go beyond liberalism and challenge the institutions that are central to liberal values. Gray, it seems to me, criticizes liberalism by inverting it rather than transcending it so that, for example, (in *Straw Dogs*) he rejects liberal notions of free will and autonomy. He is in danger of becoming anti-liberal rather than post-liberal, dismissing important values instead of building upon them.

Utopia as a 'momentum concept'

A reconstructed concept of utopia rests upon a concept of emancipation that is an example of a 'momentum concept'. A momentum concept is both absolute *and* relative: it is a concept that is infinitely progressive and egalitarian. It shuns the repressive hierarchy associated with patriarchy, violence, the state and class. It looks to the future but is rooted in the present.

The term derives from Tocqueville's celebrated analysis of democracy as a social form that has no stopping points – democracy can, Tocqueville argues, oppose feudalism but also declare itself in opposition to private property. It is true that Tocqueville's formulation is inconsistent: he assumes that a providentialist force – the hand of God – lies behind this momentum, and this, of course, points to an ultimately static and abstract reality driving democracy (1966: 8). Is it possible to formulate a momentum concept without such a 'foundationalist' (i.e. a static and abstract) base?

The point about momentum concepts is that they are *infinitely* progressive – they cannot be realized. They have no stopping point – they are part of the historical process. Tillich was to argue that his doctrine of the kairos differs from the dialectic in that there is no stage in which the dialectic comes to a final halt (Marsden, 1991: 115). But this unstoppability is precisely the point of the momentum concept and it is what gives this concept its dialectical character.

This is why we must insist that a world in which people can negotiate their conflicts of interest – with all the egalitarianism and celebration of difference that this implies – is in no sense an end of the road, although it is a world that is very different from our contemporary society. It is a utopian view in the reconstructed use of the term that is being proposed here. It is critical and dynamic. This means that it is impossible for us to see all the facets that are involved in this momentum towards emancipation, for we are part of history – our absolute goals can only be posed in relative terms.

Goodwin and Taylor argue that 'a half-realized utopia would be no utopia at all' (1982: 99). But this is precisely the absolutist concept of utopia that I seek to avoid. Progress is relative as well as absolute. Marsden takes it for granted that utopian awareness links to a 'final goal' (1991: 102), but it is just this notion of finality that the momentum concept contests. Twenty years ago, for example, we had a different view of patriarchy from the one that prevails today. In liberal democratic societies we are only now becoming aware of how sexual orientation, to take another example, can affect a person's capacity to be active and participatory. In authoritarian societies, different priorities prevail. The popular violence that is counter-productive in liberal societies may be necessary in illiberal societies where people have no constitutional right to protest and challenge authority.

Agency, reforms and the struggle for emancipation

But what of the agents who move in the direction of emancipation – the men and women who struggle to go beyond the state and class division? It seems to me that all who are victims of the state, capitalism and the market will seek to promote the kind of emancipatory utopia that is being advocated here. Notions of freedom, autonomy, equality and emancipation (to mention merely four) need to be reconstructed as momentum concepts, whereas violence, patriarchy, class and state are static concepts that cannot be reconstructed. Because they are divisive and exclusionary, they have to be overcome.

Of course, there is an infinity of stages in this movement forward. Some examples: to restrict smoking in public places in Britain or to move against private transport represents an important step in an emancipatory direction, since these measures seek at least to regulate individual actions (and their unintended consequences) in a socially responsible manner. The point about the momentum concept, as defined here, is that one thing leads to another – and small utopias make larger, more encompassing utopias possible.

Goodwin and Taylor argue that we could manufacture a utopia, not in the sense of a perfect society, but a utopia that is the best of all possible worlds in the circumstances (1982: 224). But the problem here is that utopia still has a static ring to it. It is the *best* world in the circumstances, whereas utopia as a momentum concept looks to a *better* world, an improvement in relation to the present, but certainly not a world that lies at the end of the road. Marsden argues that reforms that do not envisage the end of capitalist social relations are 'devoid of utopian content' (1991: 90). But this sets up utopia in abstract terms, and fails to see that utopianism simply involves the creation of alternatives to the status quo, however marginal and inadequate these alternatives may seem. To argue, as Gottlieb does, that the radical ideal goes beyond piecemeal improvements 'to a Utopian vision' (Merchant, 2005: xiv) is to mystify the way in which small 'utopias' collectively create larger ones.

Is it inevitable that people will struggle for a better future? In his critique of Berlin, Gray argues against any notion of inevitability that prevents people from making choices, since this smacks of determinism and science (1996b: 78–9). But determinism, as I note elsewhere, is compatible with free will provided it is a conditional and contextual determinism. If humanity does not destroy itself, then it is inevitable that it will increasingly seek policies that promote social responsibility and individual well being. If this proposition is rejected, nihilism follows: anything is possible.

The question of tragedy

Gray identifies with Hayek's view that we can never know our minds sufficiently to be able to govern them. Modern movements are based on rationalism and seek to achieve the impossible (1996a: 34–5). However, the fact that we cannot wholly eliminate prejudice does not mean that we cannot make significant inroads into ignorance and oppression. It is true that we cannot resolve problems once and for all, but this does not mean that we cannot engineer meaningful and provisional solutions. Gray supports the view that some of the dilemmas of practical life are basically insoluble, radical and tragic, and undecidable by rational reflection (1996b: 8). But this assumes that, unless we can resolve dilemmas once and for all, we cannot offer any kind of solution. We stand on the brink, Gray tells us, of a tragic epoch in which anarchic market forces and shrinking natural resources drag sovereign states into ever more dangerous rivalries (1998b: 206). But what is his solution? A notion of a *modus vivendi* that rests upon the very institutions that generate the generic evils that make the *modus vivendi* impossible.

Gray quotes Marx's comment in *Capital* that the 'religious reflex of the real world' 'can only finally vanish when the practical relations of everyday life offer to man none but perfectly intelligible and rational relations to his fellowmen and to nature' (Gray, 1996a: 104). But this comment overemphasizes the discontinuity between communism and a class-divided society, and it gives the impression that under communism all mystery can be banished, whereas it seems to me that Marx's dialectical approach points to a *process* of emancipation – not the realization of an abstract ideal. Gray is right to say that illusion will always be with us (2002: 53), but wrong to deny that we can replace greater illusions with lesser ones. Nor can it be said that Marxism promised a time when history's tragedies can be left behind (2004: 106). For tragedy is part of the human condition, and there is no textual evidence (that I know of) that Marx envisaged the elimination of tragedy under communism.

Scientific and technological advance, Gray declares, has not diminished and cannot diminish the realm of mystery and tragedy in which it is our lot to dwell (1993: 49). But, while it is true that it would be foolish to imagine that we can wholly erase 'the realm of mystery and tragedy', it does not follow that science and technology have made no impact upon this realm. Surely we understand more about the world than people did in medieval times? The fact that total change (that is change without continuity) is impossible hardly rules out particular and partial change. Gray sets up timeless absolutes as his opponent, and then proceeds to abolish them! But what if we regard the notion of a *timeless* absolute as itself hopelessly undialectical and ahistorical?

Gray argues that 'science promises that the most ancient human fantasies will at last be realised. Sickness and ageing will be abolished; scarcity and poverty will be no more; the species will become immortal' (2002: 123). But this is surely hyperbole. It may be that over the long term poverty will be abolished, and perhaps, in terms of certain material definitions, scarcity as well. But sickness, ageing and the realization of immortality? Certainly Marxism has never 'promised' this, and no scientist ought to make such claims.

Can evil be abolished?

Gray defines utopianism as the belief that the predicament in which people find themselves, a situation in which the elimination of one evil often discloses another, can be transcended (1993: 63). Gray argues that although there are generic evils – torture, violent death, being cut off in one's prime – which are obstacles to any sort of human flourishing, these evils are incommensurables, since the eradication of one evil typically spawns others (ibid.: 139). But surely these evils have something in common, and Gray makes it plain from the examples he chooses that violence against people, whether natural or social, is the root problem.

Evil itself is not a static category. The elimination may be of a greater evil and the inevitable consequence can be a lesser evil. That surely is progress! Gray speaks scathingly of a shallow optimism that sees human evils as problems to be solved rather than sorrows to be endured (1995: 18). He challenges Aristotle's view – defended by MacIntyre – that the conflict between right and right must be only 'apparent' (1996b: 41). Yet Aristotle is surely correct here: when two 'rights' clash, one must be lesser and the other greater, even though it may be extremely difficult to decide which contributes more to human development. Gray argues that 'to admit that genuine questions may not have a single right answer is to impeach a traditional concept of truth' (ibid.: 42), but the abstract absolutism of traditional thought is not transcended by an abstract pluralism that ignores the need for both the absolute and the relative in the concept of truth. As I have already argued, a true statement is not without its falsity, and false statements would not be uttered if they contained no truth.

The point is that it is not a question of abolishing evil: it is a question of tackling greater evils in the knowledge that only if goodness and badness are retained as analytical categories can human relationships exist. Of course, the notion that terror or violence or ill-health is an evil is hardly adequate as a mode of understanding how and why disagreeable things arise. To say that terrorism, for example, is evil does not demonstrate much understanding of the causality involved. But the point is that it is no part of a concrete view of emancipation to project a world without evil or badness. On the contrary, infinite progress is possible only if we can identify negative developments that we seek to overcome. The idea that a utopian society is frictionless – an idea that Gray takes for granted (1989: 65) – is precisely one that must be rejected.

The difficulty is evidenced, it seems to me, in the notion of incommensurability that Gray espouses. An option is incommensurable if – and here Gray quotes Raz – it is possible for one of the options to be improved without becoming better than the other. But this implies a non-relation between two things (1996b: 50). Of course, it is difficult to 'choose' between, say, Shakespeare and Aeschylus, but the problem arises because Gray juxtaposes a timeless and context-free absolute (which he rejects) to a non-relational set of options. Yet once we introduce context (say learning Greek) then Aeschylus is preferable to Shakespeare, although in other contexts (studying English literature, for example) the reverse might be true. Gray seeks to deny that human flourishing comes in only one form (ibid.: 53) but one can accept this without denying that goodness derives – in plural forms – from the development of the individual and society.

The question of prejudice

Gray argues that the project of abolishing prejudice is, in fact, closely akin to the Marxian project of rendering social life transparent by transcending alienation. Gray acknowledges that knowledge embodied in our habits and dispositions rather than in theories may contain tacit error as well as tacit knowledge. He gives the examples of anti-Semitic attitudes towards Jews. He ascribes to radical liberalism the project of abolishing prejudice (1995: 26–7). But while we need to tackle racism and patriarchy, for example, the notion that we can abolish prejudice as such is fanciful. Whatever the position of radical liberalism, the notion of abolishing prejudice (as noted above) is hopelessly undialectical. All societies involve conflict generated by differences, and this conflict must imply in part the kind of spontaneous and hasty judgements we associate with 'prejudice'. Without prejudice there would be no progress. Gray has set up an abstract absolute that he then knocks down.

What is utopian realism?

Mannheim takes the view that the disappearance of utopia brings about 'a static state of affairs in which man himself becomes no more than a thing' (Goodwin and Taylor, 1982: 28). But strictly speaking the notion of utopia can never disappear since the most intransigent conservative has some criticisms of the status quo – if only that it contains people who want change! The idea that there can be a literal convergence of thought and reality is an abstraction – it denies the dynamic character of the historical process. Ideals are always at variance with reality – and this is what accounts for their utopian character. Utopias seek alternatives to the world as it currently exists. Mannheim speaks of 'adequate realisation' but, as Levitas asks, who is to make this judgment (Levitas, 1990: 75)? All see reality in tension with ideals – indeed, it could be argued that, without this tension, progress and change would be impossible. Utopias, when reconstructed, are simply alternatives to the status quo, and it needs to be remembered that the status quo is itself in a process of change, so that it is impossible to support the status quo without being critical of something. In other words, the notion of utopia is inherent in all thought – from the most conservative to the most radical.

Berlin comments that 'it would be generally agreed' that the reverse of the grasp of reality is the tendency to fantasy or utopia (Gray, 1996b: 76). But it is precisely this 'generally agreed' view that a reconstructed view of utopia seeks to challenge. Bloch makes a crucial distinction between abstract and concrete utopia. The latter is linked to the power of anticipation as a possible future within the real (Levitas, 1990: 88–9). But is this concrete utopia static? Habermas was to say that Bloch had discovered the 'true consciousness' within false consciousness (ibid.: 90). Does not the notion of true consciousness have a perfectionist ring, particularly when it is seen as the transcendence of alienation? The argument here is that utopia is 'real democracy', the identity of 'men with themselves', a 'harmony in which they are postulated as one' (ibid.: 95–7). In the

Aesthetic Dimension Marcuse claims that the role of art is to keep alive the possibility of a 'historical alternative' – a utopia translated into reality. But is this historical alternative itself historical, i.e. a provisional world destined to change? Gray defends realism against the assumption that 'a mysterious process of evolution is taking mankind to a promised land' (2007: 195). But he takes it for granted that a theory cannot be realistic *and* utopian at the same time.

Bloch and Adorno refer to death as the ultimate problem for utopia (Levitas, 1990: 154, 181, 192). But, if death of the individual is necessary and inevitable, why is this a problem for utopia? It is only a problem if utopia is conceived in a fantastical way – a world that somehow escapes the world of necessity. Marin takes the view that utopia destroys itself when realized (Goodwin and Taylor, 1982: 89). It is true, for example, that with the abolition of formal slavery what was once a utopia becomes a reality. But the disappearance of a particular utopia hardly means that utopia per se disappears. Utopias are not abstract ideals – once and for all finalities – that supposedly exist outside the historical process. Morton contends that 'real socialism' (the socialism of the Communist Party states) constitutes the realization of utopia: imaginary pictures are no longer necessary, since what the workers and their allies have created is the real thing (Levitas, 1990: 30)! But this is a complacent and uncritical view, as the collapse of the Communist Party states demonstrates.

Gray accepts realities as basically unalterable – that externalities and scarcities limit economic growth, that reason is impotent to determine moral and political action and that *Homo sapiens* is a brief episode in the meaningless history of the planet (Newey, 2006: 268). What, in fact, is required is a notion of utopia that overcomes the dualism between the ideal and the real, so that utopianism and realism do not confront one another as irreconcilable opposites. On the contrary: a reconstructed concept of utopia projects a future that is rooted in the present and is an organic part of the historical process. We need to present the case for a utopian realism, so that each reinforces the other. Gray's attack on utopianism assumes that reality is simply the present world, frozen and unchanging in its 'essential' institutions – the state and market. To be utopian is therefore, in his view, to depart from reality, whereas a reconstructed notion of utopia stresses the dynamic character of a world whose most real property is that it is always changing.

Post-liberalism versus anti-liberalism

Although Gray is, as we have seen, critical of post-modernism, he is attracted by Rorty's notion that selfhood and the community are contingent (Gray, 1995: 84). He refers, as post-modernists do, to the logocentrism of Greek philosophy, and speaks of the 'post-modern condition of fractured perspectives and groundless practices'. However he is critical of both Rorty's post-modern liberalism and MacIntyre's anti-liberalism (ibid.: 146–7). Post-modernism aims to make the cultural fragmentation of the West a universal condition (ibid.: 157). Rorty's attempt to assimilate, for example, Britain, France and the USA to the category of 'North Atlantic democracies' is unpersuasive (ibid.: 173).

But, if Gray is not a post-modern, he certainly considers himself to be a pluralist who has gone beyond even post-liberalism (ibid.: 143). Although he is attracted by Nietzsche's attack on the Enlightenment, he sees him as a radical humanist, commenting that only some one steeped in Christian sensibility could have envisaged such an absurdity as the *Übermensch* (ibid.: 165).

Gray describes a post-liberal age as the exact opposite of those play-filled utopias that he identifies with ultra-liberals like Fourier (ibid.: 24). Gray's problem, however, is, it seems to me, an inability to coherently and systematically go beyond liberalism. He comments that a 'post-Pyrrhonian philosophy', as he calls it, involves not a return to Humean scepticism – Hume embraces a view of the world that rejects absolutes and necessity – but a 'return to history' so that we see our present forms of life as historical creations. Gray expresses support for Oakeshott's preference for the notion of theorizing over philosophy, because he argues that, if one adopts a position that is post-classical and post-modern, both the result and the subject matter are particularistic (Gray, 1989: 263). For Oakeshott, it is practice that is primordial (Gray, 1996: 41).

This argument would be fine if Gray sustained his post-classical and post-modern analysis. He speaks of the 'need to initiate a form of post-modern individualism that is fully conscious of its own historical particularity' (ibid.: 259). But how can (post-liberal) theorizing be subversive in its deflation of ruling fictions, if it does not tackle the market and the state? The post-Pyrrhonian, Gray argues, may adopt liberal positions on a variety of positions and 'even defend his own liberal order as one among the legitimate forms of political order' (1989: 264). Liberal institutions are fine; what is wrong is to see them as universally valid! Gray accepts the need for liberal societies in many Western countries (1995: 180). It is true that Gray argues in his latest book that there has been an unprecedented expansion of executive power in the USA as part of the 'war on terror' and this shift 'illustrates the delusive qualities of contemporary liberalism' (2007: 168). But ultimately this is a problem with what Gray considers to be utopianism; it is not a problem with liberalism per se.

It is revealing that, when Gray sets out his post-liberal order, it is inspired by Hobbes, 'who wrote for an age of religious wars and barbarous movements much like ours' and involves a state that is strong but small (1996a: 270). The argument is unmistakeably liberal-conservative in form. Gray makes it clear that, while he is opposed to the idea that liberalism is universally applicable, a liberal civil society is the best sort of society for those of us who live in late modern historical circumstances (ibid.: 288). If the essence of liberalism is a universal regime, then, Gray concedes, his argument is post-liberal (2000: 137). But it is here that Gray's argument runs into difficulties.

For this leads him to juxtapose the universal with the particular in a dualistic manner so that he either embraces liberalism uncritically or rejects it uncritically. At times Gray seems to embrace an anti-liberalism, as in his argument that post-liberalism must shed that spirit of individuality, virtually unknown to the Greeks and the Romans, that is the gift of Judaism and Christianity to our civilization. Indeed, Kelly refers to Gray as an 'anti-liberal' (2006: 138). The problem (of which Gray himself is acutely conscious) is that, in abominating the tribalistic passions associated with the modern nation-state, one might, like Santayana, look backwards to a 'universal empire'. Gray wishes to be critical, but not reactionary. Hence Gray also insists that we must return to the particulars of the liberal inheritance of civil society – limited government, private property, the rule of law (1996a: 24–5, 30). Gray is in favour of a liberalism that searches for the terms of coexistence between different moralities (2000: 138).

A genuine post-liberalism can be sustained only if it is neither pro- nor anti-liberal. We need to avoid this treacherous 'either/or' argument. The notion of utopia, the absolute, the ideal, the universal, needs to be reconstructed, rendered concrete, linked to and not torn away from the particularities of the real world. The notion of the momentum concept seeks to bring together continuity and change. The relationship of the post-liberal perspective and liberal societies needs, Gray tells us (1989: 264), to be dialectical. I agree. But how can it be dialectical if we have a love/hate relationship with liberal institutions rather than what I would call an authentically transcendental one?

Conclusion

Gray is right to resist the traditional concept of utopia. This notion is static, perfectionist and unrealizable. Whether it is admired or deplored, it is untenable. However, this does not mean that the notion of utopia per se is problematic. The idea can and must be reconstructed so that it loses its perfectionism and its static, ahistorical character.

A reconstructed notion of utopia is what I call a momentum concept. Momentum concepts are those that are dynamic and progressive – not only do they alter through context and circumstance, but they can never be 'realized'. This means that a reconstructed concept of utopia is rooted in the present. It is an alternative that represents an important step forwards and it is a revolution in the sense that it embodies a change in people's outlook. Thus, policies to banish smoking from public places are utopian because they embody a new realization that the actions of one person can unintentionally harm both oneself and others. These policies are context-bound; they are desirable because they can be implemented. This is why I argue that utopias must be rooted in the present: they must be practicable so that people's lives can actually change.

We would expect utopias to be supported primarily by those who are negatively affected by market and state; but, since the actions of individuals are all interlinked, even those who appear to benefit from a troublesome status quo are potentially supporters of transformation. To continue the smoking example: even the executives of companies producing cigarettes can die from lung cancer. It seems to me that it is unwise to exclude anyone from the struggle to promote change, and even the smallest change has wider repercussions and therefore deserves to be identified as utopian in character. Utopias are inevitable, using inevitability as a context-bound and conditional concept.

Gray argues that utopias seek to eliminate the notion of tragedy from social life, but this argument arises because Gray identifies utopia with its traditionalist and perfectionist formulation. It is no more possible to eliminate tragedy from human life than it is possible to eliminate death and decay. But it is possible to reduce tragedy, just as it is possible to enable people to live longer. To eliminate evil is to eliminate progress, since it is the overcoming of particular evils that makes it possible to improve human life; any vision of the future that seeks an absolute without a relative should be viewed with the greatest of scepticism. Prejudice derives from a perception of difference that is hasty and superficial; to imagine a society without any kind of prejudice is to imagine a world without difference and conflict. Violence can be eradicated, but not difference.

What discredits utopianism is the perception that it is unrealistic; a reconstructed concept of utopia must transcend the dualism between ideals and reality, theory and practice. There is necessarily tension between the two, but there is not a yawning chasm, an unbridgeable gulf. The case for a utopian realism rests upon post-liberal premises, for post-liberalism requires not a rejection of liberalism, but a transcendence, a building upon, a positive negation. Gray inverts liberalism by rejecting its values so that his theory is still built upon liberal abstractions. He challenges concepts of freedom and autonomy because he accepts their liberal formulation. He dismisses rather than reconstructs, and hence he sees utopia as a worthless idea rather than a proposition that should be built upon.

It might be objected that I simply see the reconstructed notion of utopia as a synonym for a political ideal. But ideals are not necessarily realizable; utopias, as I have reconstructed them, are ideals that are realizable. Of course, realities differ from ideals. The latter necessarily distort realities, so that utopias always contain an element of fantasy or abstraction. But this is true of all ideals. It is important that we understand that realizing ideals, enacting utopias, is an ongoing process. Today's utopia is tomorrow's reality. The latter might be more complicated than envisaged, but without the utopian 'vision', it would not have come about at all.

Conclusion

Gray is an important political theorist who tackles pressing political issues in a sophisticated fashion. He is initially a supporter of Hayek and what he will later call free market fundamentalism, but then moves to a traditional conservative critique of the market and notions of perfectionism. He comes to the view, however, that conservatism itself has been corrupted by neo-liberalism, and the Thatcher and Reagan administrations have subscribed to a market Bolshevism that has divided society and undermined community cohesion. What is distinctive about his argument is his insistence that humanism, the Enlightenment and traditional liberalism are flawed by a utopian impulse.

The term 'utopian' is traditionally used to designate a society that is static and perfect. This is the notion to which Gray himself subscribes, and he uses the term to denote a theory that is impractical and unrealizable. I concede that the traditionalist concept is untenable whether it is admired or deplored. Traditionalist utopias usually refer to pleasant and egalitarian regimes, sometimes religious, but always static and perfectionist. Critics invariably deplore them but some writers speak highly of traditional utopias, regarding them as a source of inspiration for an otherwise purely empirical and status-quo oriented political theory. I argue that the problem with traditional utopias is that they embody a dualism between what is and what ought to be – between ideals and reality – and therefore they end up as impotent and otherworldly. However, rather than abandon the notion of utopia, I seek to reconstruct it so that it is dynamic, critical and historical.

Gray is correct to identify the Enlightenment with abstraction. Its universalism stands grotesquely at odds with the policies that Enlightenment thinkers espoused in practice. Protestations of liberty and equality coexisted with patriarchy, colonialism, statism and support for the market. But Gray's attitude to the Enlightenment is one-sided. Instead of building upon the values of the Enlightenment, he rejects them, wrongly identifying the abstract humanism of the eighteenth and nineteenth centuries with Marxism.

There is much that is problematic within Marxism. The opposition that Marxism poses between science and utopia not only misrepresents the socialist thinkers who are deemed 'utopians' but continues with the traditional concept of utopia. I argue that this traditional usage probably arises from the residues of modernism that are manifest in Marxism: its support for revolution, its notion of class conflict, a tendency to underestimate the importance of form and the uncritical view of the state that manifests itself in practice in the concept (and grisly realities) of the 'dictatorship of the proletariat'. These modernist residues prevent Marxism from overcoming the dualism that a consistent or dialectical materialism transcends. Although Marxism implicitly presents communism as an historical society, its modernist view of politics assists its critics in misrepresenting it. Morris's *News from Nowhere* is a very interesting attempt to construct a vision that is apparently Marxist in character. In my view, however, *News from Nowhere* is basically utopian in the traditional sense although it does have arguments that could contribute to the reconstruction of the idea of utopia.

Gray's critique of Marxism leads him to seriously distort Marxist theory. He assumes that Marxism is itself a form of Enlightenment thought although it is clear that Marx challenged the liberal values of the Enlightenment in a radical and far-reaching way. It is true that Marx exaggerated the discontinuity between capitalism and communism, but he certainly sought to make the notion of communism an historical one. Classical Marxism is weak (as Engels himself acknowledged towards the end of his life) on the question of form, but if Marxism is prone to an economic reductionism (particularly in its general formulations) it is no answer to replace economic reductionism with the kind of cultural reductionism that Gray supports. Moreover, the argument that Marxism is a human imperialism that ignores natural limits cannot be sustained textually and, while it is true that Marx had an uncritical view of the resource implications of the production process, he had a notion of progress that was very different from the mechanistic and linear notion of progress that traditional liberal thinkers espouse and Gray fiercely contests.

Although Gray comes to challenge market fundamentalism, he remains uncritical of the market itself. Although he is (rightly) critical of abstract ideals, he fails to see that the market itself abstracts from social realities in the exchange process, and that it is impossible to transcend dualism while uncritically endorsing the existence of the market. Gray speaks of the importance of providing security to individuals and warns that the notion of 'rights' can be woefully abstract and empty, but he ignores the fact that these abstractions are generated by the market. This is the institution that he must challenge if a consistent and plausible critique of abstract thought is to be made. It is not a question of abolishing the market and replacing it with a system of Soviet-style planning (as Gray argues). Rather it is a question of making exchanges more transparent so that people become aware of the costs, unintended consequences and the real discrepancies of power involved in social and economic transactions.

Gray's problem is that, while he is on occasion critical of the nation-state, he is basically uncritical of the state per se. He extols the importance of the political process, but wrongly identifies politics with the state. Indeed, he even regards the state as a civilizing agency. I concede that states are inevitable in situations in which people are so divided that they cannot change places – that is to say, where they cannot negotiate and compromise over their conflicts of interest. In fact, in a society in which order has wholly broken down, establishing a state can represent an important step forward, and liberal states – states that seek to limit the use of force – are preferable to authoritarian ones. But the state is a contradictory institution, since it claims a monopoly of legitimacy only because it does not have one, and a monopoly of force in a context where rivals (terrorists, criminals etc.) use force themselves. It is, therefore, not merely 'failed states' in the post-war period that have not been able to successfully implement a monopoly of legitimate force. It is the state itself.

The state enshrines a dualism between ideals and reality. Gray is conscious of the existence of social sanctions whereby people are constrained by pressures that fall short of coercion and force, and he himself is critical of neo-liberal societies such as the USA where prisons and the police provide the only mechanisms seeking to achieve order. Gray speaks constantly (and rightly) of the need to respect and celebrate diversity and difference, but he fails to see that it is the state itself that crushes diversity and imposes monolithic and hierarchical identities upon people. Governing yourself – a meaningful definition of democracy – is only possible when common interests have become so cohesive that social sanctions suffice to maintain order. Gray dismisses the notion of the state 'withering away' as fanciful and utopian (in the traditional sense). Yet this argument needs to be premised upon a distinction between the state and government, with the state addressing conflicts of interest with institutionalized force, and government using constraints to underpin negotiation and arbitration. Like the market, the state is a source of dualism.

Gray's own theory can be called 'utopian' in the sense that he poses an ideal world. He refers to the need for a *modus vivendi* between different peoples, cultures and governments, and he is right to comment that even liberal capitalist societies are very different from one another. There is no 'model' that all should follow. The problem, however, is that Gray accepts uncritically the state and the market – and it is this uncritical acceptance that accounts for the dualisms that paralyse his theory and distort the logic of his argument. He is conscious that notions of pluralism and incommensurability can easily lead to a relativistic view that all values are equally valid and an assertion that nothing matters anyway. To rescue his theory from relativism and nihilism, he argues that all societies recognize generic human evils – such as torture, war and violence – but this is, he insists, a 'minimal' universalism. It coexists with diversity so that no way of life is superior to any other. Liberalism might be appropriate for certain kinds of society, but it is certainly not relevant to all.

But it is not difficult to see that Gray's argument hinges upon a mechanistic and abstract distinction between the universal and the particular. He insists that, while there are many moralities, there is no morality as such; there are different humans, but there is no humanity. Values are incommensurable and plural – no universal thread exists that enables us to link different values together. Yet why can't we postulate a notion of, say, development that enables us to assess different values and cultures? Of course, such a notion must be sensitive to context and situation so that we can acknowledge that in some circumstances illiberal institutions will develop people far more than liberal ones. But the idea that there are particulars without a universal to make them coherent and identifiable is absurd, and the notion of a 'minimal universalism' represents an attempt to shore up an argument through a linguistic sleight of hand. There is nothing minimal about the idea of generic human evils. The advocacy of a *modus vivendi* is a good one but it must be underpinned by a critique of the market and state, and a dialectical view of sameness and difference, so that we do not have to privilege one at the expense of the other.

Gray is right to be critical of traditional concepts of social democracy. Social democrats, he argues, are guilty of a simplistic and abstract view of equality, but it is not egalitarianism that is at fault. It is an abstract view of egalitarianism that ignores the problem of market and state. Equality is not sameness but involves respect for difference and, above all, a universal ethic (like the concept of development) that makes it possible to see beyond the apparent conflict of equalities like the idea of equality of opportunity and the equality of outcome.

This is why Gray is wrong to reject multiculturalism. Respecting difference does not mean accepting cultural practices that may be harmful and undemocratic (this is what I call pseudo-multiculturalism). But how do we distinguish between 'differences' as opposed to 'divisions'? The latter involve violence and coercion. They work against rather than in favour of integration and democratic norms, and they entail the very evils that Gray sees as universal in nature. Freedom and autonomy are not purely liberal ideals; on the contrary, these values are in tension with market and state and they need to be seen both as absolute and as relative. They develop as a process, taking many different forms. By rejecting rather than building upon traditional liberal values, Gray's utopia is pessimistic and flawed. It assumes that the market and state, war and overpopulation, ecological devastation and violent conflict are here to stay, so that the attempt to realize a *modus vivendi* between different societies seems doomed and futile.

The notion of utopia can only be preserved if it is reconstructed. The traditional concept is static and ahistorical; the reconstructed concept needs to be dynamic and historically informed. Utopia must become a momentum concept – an idea that is rooted in history, is sensitive to context and can never actually be realized. We move towards emancipation, sovereignty, the good society etc. but we never actually reach them. The momentum is eternally and infinitely progressive, so that what we consider freedom, for example, today will seem inadequate to future generations, just as earlier concepts of freedom seem to us to be lacking in various aspects.

A utopia is not, therefore, the end of the road, but a step forward. Utopias are multiple and transitional: they involve a movement beyond a greater imperfection towards a lesser imperfection. The idea that we can banish tragedy, evil or prejudice from our lives (as traditional utopias suppose) is absurd, for, if humans enter relations independent of their will, then built into social interaction is some element of powerlessness and disappointment. Just as there can be no progress without a consciousness and transcendence of a particular evil, so difference necessarily involves the kind of superficial understanding that generates conflict, and thus the need for politics. Moving beyond the state itself is not the end of history; it is a movement to a world with different problems and greater emancipation. It constitutes progress, but not finality. Moving beyond the market does not bring total transparency; it is a movement into greater self- and social consciousness in which we become more aware of the real character of our transactions.

Reconstructing utopia requires the adoption of post-liberalism. But post-liberalism is not anti-liberalism. Liberalism establishes universal values, the opposition between force and freedom, and the notion of the individual. But it also accepts the need for the market and state, and presents its values in an abstract and distorted fashion. Post-liberalism builds upon the positive features of the liberal tradition, and seeks to jettison its negative aspects. Above all, post-liberalism seeks to overcome dualism, while recognizing distinction. It aspires to analysis *and* synthesis so that realism is not at loggerheads with utopia. Of course there is a tension between the two in the sense that reality is always more complex than our ideals, but we seek to embrace a realism that reinforces utopianism.

References

Anderson, P. (1980) *Arguments within English Marxism*, London: Verso.
Arblaster, A. (1984) *The Rise and Decline of Western Liberalism*, Oxford: Basil Blackwell.
Bacon, F. (1974) *The New Atlantis*, Oxford: Clarendon.
Barry, J. (2006) 'Straw dogs, blind horses and post-humanism: the greening of Gray?', *Critical Review of International Social and Political Philosophy*, 9, 2, 243–62.
Barry, N. (1981) *An Introduction to Modern Political Theory*, Basingstoke: Macmillan.
Barry Jones, R. (2000) *The World Turned Upside Down*, Manchester: Manchester University Press.
Bauman, Z. (1976) *Socialism: The Active Utopia*, London: George Allen and Unwin.
Baumeister, A. (2000) 'The new feminism', in N. O'Sullivan (ed.), *Political Theory in Transition*. London: Routledge, pp. 49–69.
Bellamy, E. (1967) *Looking Backward 2000–1887*, Cambridge, MA: Belknap.
Berki, R. (1974) *Socialism*, London: Dent.
Bloch, E. (1986) *The Principle of Hope*, 3 vols, Oxford: Basil Blackwell.
Brink, A. (1992) *An Act of Terror*, London: Minerva.
Bull, H. (1977) *The Anarchical Society*, Basingstoke: Macmillan.
Carter, A. (2001) *The Political Theory of Global Citizenship*, London: Routledge.
Colls, R. (1996) 'John Gray and the condition of England question', *Northern Review*, 4, Winter, 66–82.
Colls, R. (1998) 'Ethics man: John Gray's new moral world', *Political Quarterly*, 69, 1, 59–71.
Commission on Global Governance (1995) *Our Global Neighbourhood*, Oxford: Oxford University Press.
Crick, B. (1962) *In Defence of Politics*, 2nd edn, Harmondsworth: Penguin.
Crowder, G. (2006) 'Gray and the politics of pluralism', *Critical Review of International Social and Political Philosophy*, 9, 2, 171–88.
Engels, F. (1964) *Dialectics of Nature*, Moscow: Progress.
Faulks, K. (1998) *Citizenship in Modern Britain*, Edinburgh: Edinburgh University Press.

Faulks, K. (1999) *Political Sociology*, Edinburgh: Edinburgh University Press.
Faulks, K. (2000) *Citizenship*, London and New York: Routledge.
Femia, J. (1993) *Marxism and Democracy*, Oxford: Clarendon Press.
Gay, P. (1962) *The Dilemma of Democratic Socialism*, New York: Collier.
Gay, P. (1967) *The Enlightenment*, vol. 1, London: Weidenfeld and Nicolson.
Gay, P. (1969) *The Enlightenment*, vol. 2, London: Weidenfeld and Nicolson.
Geoghegan, V. (1987) *Utopianism and Marxism*, London: Methuen.
Goodwin, B. (1987) 'Utopianism', in D. Miller *et al.* (eds), *The Blackwell Encyclopaedia of Political Thought*, Oxford: Blackwell, pp. 533–8.
Goodwin, B. and Taylor, K. (1982) *The Politics of Utopia*, London: Hutchinson.
Gramsci, A. (1971) *Selections from Prison Notebooks*, London: Lawrence and Wishart.
Gray, J. (1984) *Hayek on Liberty*, Oxford: Basil Blackwell.
Gray, J. (1986) *Liberalism*, Milton Keynes: Open University.
Gray, J. (1989) *Liberalisms*, London: Routledge.
Gray, J. (1993) *Beyond the New Right*, London: Routledge.
Gray, J. (1995) *Enlightenment's Wake*, London: Routledge.
Gray, J. (1996a) *Post-Liberalism*, London: Routledge.
Gray, J. (1996b) *Isaiah Berlin*, Cambridge: Polity.
Gray, J. (1996c) *Mill on Liberty: A Defence*, 2nd edn, London and New York: Routledge.
Gray, J. (1996d) *After Social Democracy*, London: Demos.
Gray, J. (1997) *Endgames*, Cambridge: Polity.
Gray, J. (1998a) *False Dawn*, London: Granta.
Gray, J. (1998b) *Voltaire*, London: Phoenix.
Gray, J. (1998c) 'Global utopias and clashing civilizations: misunderstanding the present', *International Affairs*, 74, 149–63.
Gray, J. (2000) *Two Faces of Liberalism*, Cambridge: Polity.
Gray, J. (2002) *Straw Dogs*, London: Granta.
Gray, J. (2003) *Al Qaeda and What It Means to be Modern*, London: Faber and Faber.
Gray, J. (2004) *Heresies*, London: Granta
Gray, J. (2005) 'The World is Round', *New York Review of Books*, 11 August, 13–15.
Gray, J. (2006) 'Reply to critics', *Critical Review of International Social and Political Philosophy*, 9, 2, 323–47.
Gray, J. (2007) *Black Mass*, London: Allen Lane.
Hayek, F. (1960) *The Constitution of Liberty*, London: Routledge and Kegan Paul.
Heater, D. (1999) *What is Citizenship?*, Cambridge: Polity Press.

Held, D. (1995) *Democracy and the Global Order*, Cambridge: Polity.
Herzen, A. (1956) *Selected Philosophical Works*, Moscow: Foreign Languages Publishing House.
Heywood, A. (1992) *Political Ideologies: An Introduction*, Basingstoke: Macmillan.
Hirst, P. and Thompson, G. (1996) *Globalization in Question*, Cambridge: Polity.
Hobbes, T. (1968) *Leviathan*, Harmondsworth: Penguin.
Hoffman, J. (1975) *Marxism and the Theory of Praxis*, London: Lawrence and Wishart.
Hoffman, J. (1984) *The Gramscian Challenge*, Oxford: Blackwell.
Hoffman, J. (1988) *State, Power and Democracy*, Brighton: Wheatsheaf.
Hoffman, J. (1995) *Beyond the State*, Cambridge: Polity.
Hoffman, J. (2001) *Gender and Sovereignty*, Basingstoke: Palgrave.
Hoffman, J. (2003) 'Reconstructing diplomacy', *British Journal of Politics and International Relations*, 5, 4, 525–42.
Honig, B. (1994) 'Difference, dilemmas and the politics of home', *Social Research*, 61, 3, 563–97.
Horkheimer, M. and Adorno, T. (1973) *Dialectic of Enlightenment*, London: Allen Lane.
Huntington, S. (1996) *The Clash of Civilizations*, New York: Simon and Schuster.
Hutchings, K. (1996) 'The death of the sovereign individual', in M. Griffiths and M. Whitford (eds), *Women Review Philosophy*, Nottingham: University of Nottingham, pp. 1–25.
Hutton, W. (2006) 'Thanks to Mao, she's a billionaire', *The Observer*, 15 October.
Jantzen, G. (1998) *Becoming Divine*, Manchester: Manchester University Press.
Jones, P. (2006) 'Toleration, value-pluralism and the fact of pluralism', *Critical Review of International Social and Political Philosophy*, 9, 2, 189–210.
Kateb, G. (1994) 'Notes on pluralism', *Social Research*, 61, 3, 511–37.
Kateb, G. (2006) 'Is John Gray a nihilist?' *Critical Review of International Social and Political Philosophy*, 9, 2, 305–22.
Katznelson, I. (1994) 'A properly defended liberalism: on John Gray and the filling of political life', *Social Research*, 61, 3, 611–30.
Kelly, P. (2006) 'The social theory of anti-liberalism', *Critical Review of International Social and Political Philosophy*, 9, 2, 137–54.
Kinna, R. (2000) *William Morris: The Art of Socialism*, Cardiff: University of Wales Press.
Kumar, K. (1987) *Utopia and Anti-Utopia in Modern Times*, Oxford: Basil Blackwell.
Kumar, K. (1991) *Utopianism*, Milton Keynes: Open University Press.

Lassman, P. (2006) 'Pluralism and its discontents: John Gray's counter enlightenment', *Critical Review of International Social and Political Philosophy*, 9, 2, 211–25.

Lenin, V. I. (1961) *Collected Works*, vol. 5, London: Lawrence and Wishart.

Levitas, R. (1990) *The Concept of Utopia*, New York: Philip Allan.

Locke, J. (1924) *Two Treatises of Civil Government*, London: Dent.

Lovell, D. (1984) *From Marx to Lenin*, Cambridge: Cambridge University Press.

Luxemburg, R. (1972) *Selected Political Writings*, London: Jonathan Cape.

Macpherson, C. B. (1973) *Democratic Theory*, Oxford: Clarendon.

Mannheim, K. (1960) *Ideology and Utopia*, New York: Routledge.

Manuel, F. E. and Manuel, F. P. (1979) *Utopian Thought in the Western World*, Oxford: Basil Blackwell.

Margalit, A. and Halbertal, M. (1994) 'Liberalism and the right to culture', *Social Research*, 61, 3, 491–510.

Marsden, J. (1991) *Marxian and Christian Utopianism*, New York: Monthly Review Press.

Marshall, P. (1993) *Demanding the Impossible*, London: Fontana.

Marx, K. (1966) *Capital*, vol. 3, Moscow: Progress.

Marx, K. (1970) *Capital*, vol. 1, London: Lawrence and Wishart.

Marx, K. (2000) *Selected Writings*, ed. D. McLellan, 2nd edn, Oxford: Oxford University Press.

Marx, K. and Engels, F. (1968) *Selected Works in One Volume*, Moscow: Progress.

Marx, K. and Engels, F. (1971) *On the Paris Commune*, Moscow: Progress.

Marx, K. and Engels, F. (1975a) *Collected Works*, vol. 3, London: Lawrence and Wishart.

Marx, K. and Engels, F. (1975b) *Collected Works*, vol. 1, London: Lawrence and Wishart.

Marx, K. and Engels, F. (1975c) *Collected Works*, vol. 6, London: Lawrence and Wishart.

Marx, K. and Engels, F. (1975d) *Selected Correspondence*, Moscow, Progress.

Marx, K. and Engels, F. (1976) *Collected Works*, vol. 5, London: Lawrence and Wishart.

Mendus, S. (1987) 'Introduction', in E. Kennedy and S. Mendus (eds), *Women in Western Political Philosophy*, Brighton: Wheatsheaf.

Merchant, C. (2005) *Radical Ecology*, London: Routledge.

Mill, J. S. (1974) *On Liberty*, Harmondsworth: Penguin.

Morgan, G. (2006) 'Gray's elegy for progress', *Critical Review of International Social and Political Philosophy*, 9, 2, 227–41.

More, T. (1992) *Utopia*, 2nd edn, New York and London: Norton.

Morris, W. (1970) *News from Nowhere*, London: Routledge and Kegan Paul.

Newey, G. (2006) 'Gray's blues: pessimism as a political project', *Critical Review of International Social and Political Philosophy*, 9, 2, 263–84.

O'Sullivan, N. (2006) 'Liberalism, nihilism and modernity in the political thought of John Gray', *Critical Review of International Social and Political Philosophy*, 9, 2, 285–304.

Ohmae, K. (1995) *The End of the Nation-State*, New York: Free Press.

Outram, D. (1995) *The Enlightenment*, Cambridge: Cambridge University Press.

Pateman, C. (1985) *The Problem of Political Obligation*, Cambridge: Polity.

Plato (1955) *The Republic*, Harmondsworth: Penguin.

Porritt, J. (2006) *Capitalism as if the World Matters*, London: Earthscan.

Porter, R. (2001) *The Enlightenment*, Basingstoke: Palgrave.

Riley, J. (2006) 'Utilitarian liberalism: between Gray and Mill', *Critical Review of International Social and Political Philosophy*, 9, 2, 117–35.

Rousseau, J.-J. (1968a) *The Social Contract*, Harmondsworth: Penguin.

Rousseau, J.-J. (1968b) *The Social Contract and Discourses*, London: Dent.

Sargisson, L. (1996) *Contemporary Feminist Utopianism*, London: Routledge.

Sharp, P. (2001) *Making Sense of Citizen Diplomats*, Leicester: Centre for the Study of Diplomacy, University of Leicester.

Smith, A. (1970) *The Wealth of Nations, Books I–III*, Harmondsworth: Penguin.

Stiglitz, J. (2002) *Globalization and its Discontents*, London: Allen Lane, Penguin.

Thompson, E. P. (1977) *William Morris: Romantic to Revolutionary*, London: Merlin Press.

de Tocqueville, A. (1966) *Democracy in America*, vol. 1, London: Fontana.

Turner, A. (2002) *Just Capital*, London: Pan.

Walker, R. B. J. (1999) 'Citizenship after the modern subject', in K. Hutchings and R. Dannreuther (eds), *Cosmopolitan Citizenship*, Basingstoke: Macmillan, pp. 171–200.

Index

abstraction 3, 6, 31, 36–7, 49, 54, 59, 67, 75, 78–81, 84–5, 88, 90–2, 95, 99, 105, 140, 142, 152, 165, 169–73, 183, 188–9, 191
Aristotle 19, 23, 41, 78, 93, 134, 181
autonomy 10, 44, 92, 104, 119, 129, 139, 163, 170–1, 174, 178, 193
see also Gray

Bacon, Francis 4, 27, 32, 34
basic income 87–8, 92
Berlin, Isaiah 12, 17–19, 85, 99, 108, 124–6, 131, 134, 167, 179, 183
Bernstein, Eduard 56, 101
Bloch, Ernst 59, 63, 71, 183
Bolsheviks 67, 100–1
Burke, Edmund 13

class 3, 29, 32, 53, 62, 65–70, 72, 76, 86, 91, 103–6, 141, 177–8
Colls, Robert 11–12, 75, 104, 136, 175
common interests 8, 47, 65, 69, 107, 113, 116, 129, 132, 135, 144, 150, 155–6, 159–60
communism 6–7, 30, 55, 59, 61, 63, 65, 69, 71–2, 86, 93, 95–7, 100, 103–6, 180, 190

determinism 33, 81, 65, 92, 105, 138–9, 143, 148, 179
development 9, 82, 126–7, 134, 139, 140, 142, 162, 164, 173
dialectical materialism 2, 56, 101, 190

difference 10, 23, 89, 92, 96, 99, 102, 114, 122, 125, 127, 129, 130, 132, 135, 165, 172–3, 177–8, 183, 186, 191, 194
as opposed to division 2–3, 89, 132, 156, 174, 183
dualism 2, 5, 8, 34–5, 37, 39, 45, 47, 49, 50, 55, 59, 70–2, 74, 96, 113, 118, 171, 173, 177, 184, 188–92, 194
see also Gray

emancipation 2–3, 54, 67, 80, 91, 93, 96–7, 99, 102, 104, 137, 163, 168, 172–3, 175–80, 182, 193–4
empiricism 46, 48–9, 54, 137, 141
Engels, Frederick 5, 70, 72, 98, 101, 104–5, 190
see also Gray
Enlightenment
defined 39–41, 53–4
and Gray 1, 5, 16–17, 19–20, 25, 39–40, 43, 50, 53–4, 91, 93, 103, 105, 111, 122, 188–9
problematic character of 39, 42–7, 50, 54, 97–8, 105, 189
see also Gray
equality 9, 30–1, 40, 45, 70, 75–8, 80, 119, 129, 139, 151, 171, 175, 178, 193
see also Gray
European Union 17, 107, 111, 117, 121, 150, 154, 156, 164

feminism 44–5, 80, 173
force 46–7, 66, 82, 107, 109–10, 113–16, 118–20, 129, 137, 155, 162, 175, 191–2, 194

Fourier, Charles 5, 70–1, 185
fundamentalism 9, 19–21, 25, 105, 114, 120, 144, 147, 150–1, 154, 160, 163, 165–6, 171, 174, 189–90

Geohegan, Vincent 34, 56, 60
globalization 8, 144–7, 149–50, 152–4, 156, 159, 160
see also state
Goodwin, Barbara 24, 28, 33, 35–7, 49, 59, 64–5, 70, 175, 178–9
Gray, John
  and anthropocentrism 20, 23, 25, 101–2
  and autonomy 10, 15, 26, 51, 83, 85, 88, 138–140. 143, 163, 166, 170–1, 174, 177, 188
  and communitarianism 21, 84, 103, 131, 137–8, 162–4, 173
  and conservatism 14–16, 20, 23–4, 36, 48, 75, 105, 109, 130, 163, 186, 189
  and democracy 22, 24, 91, 107, 111–12, 114, 153, 169–70
  and dualism 10, 37, 49–50, 74–5, 85, 91–3, 102, 108, 122, 130, 135–6, 140, 142–3, 186, 192
  early life of 11–12
  and ecology 9, 11, 15, 23, 84, 100–1, 134, 136, 138, 145, 153, 163, 166
  and equality 9, 17, 20, 75, 91, 125, 131, 160, 162, 164–5, 167, 172–3, 193
  and generic human evils 8–9, 19, 25, 122–5, 128–30, 132–3, 136, 141–3, 158, 163, 166–8, 171, 173, 180–1, 192–3
  and globalization 8–9, 144–8, 150, 152, 159–60, 165
  and incommensurability 18, 25, 122, 14, 126, 129, 132, 142, 169, 172, 181–182, 192
  and the individual 15, 50, 164–5
  and liberalism 2, 10–11, 13–15, 18–20, 25, 37, 53, 74, 77, 81, 84, 90–2, 111, 123–5, 128, 140, 142, 162, 169, 173, 177, 185–6, 188
  and the market 2, 6, 11, 14–15, 17, 20–1, 36, 74–5, 78, 81–7, 91–3, 107, 110, 128, 140, 143, 152, 159, 164–5, 192
  and Marxism 2, 6, 16–17, 19, 25, 37, 50, 55, 74, 85–6, 93–5, 98, 100–2, 104–6, 136, 140, 145, 148, 180, 189–90
  and modernity 3, 20, 24, 83, 90, 93, 101–2, 127, 135–6, 141–2, 145, 158, 161, 171–2
  and the *modus vivendi* 8, 21, 125–9, 141–3, 145, 159, 161, 169, 171, 180, 192–3
  and morality 8, 19, 25, 122–5, 129–30, 167, 192
  and multiculturalism 9, 162, 165, 173, 193
  and neo-liberalism 6, 14–15, 25, 37, 74, 85, 91–2, 144, 147, 160, 189
  and New Labour 4, 11, 20, 74, 163
  and the New Right 13–16, 20, 25, 50, 100
  and pluralism 8, 17, 25, 97, 119, 122, 124–5, 128, 137, 142, 168, 172, 181, 185, 192
  and the concept of progress 17, 21, 24–5, 39, 97–100, 105–6, 133, 190
  and rationalism 50, 125, 130
  and realism 2, 136, 184
  and relativism 8, 122, 124, 127, 130, 141–2, 162, 166, 192
  and religion 12, 163, 171, 174
  and rights 6, 21–2, 25, 88–9, 92, 117, 167, 191
  and social democracy 8, 20, 153, 162–5, 172–3, 193

and the state 2, 7, 17, 22, 36, 47, 83, 86, 93, 107–9, 111–14, 117–8, 120–1, 128, 140, 143, 159, 161, 166, 186, 191–2
and the distinction between the universal and the particular 8, 102, 122–3, 130, 132–3, 135–6, 142, 158, 161, 186, 192
see also autonomy, dualism, Enlightenment, Engels, human nature, equality, globalization, Green thought, Hayek, humanism, Marx, Mill, multiculturalism, state, values
Green, Thomas Hill 6, 76
Green thought 7, 15, 96, 105, 141, 163
see also Gray

Hayek, Frederick 6, 77–8, 98
and Gray 13–14, 20, 24, 74–5, 82, 91, 179, 182
Hegel, Georg 56–7, 84, 96, 104
Held, David 111–13, 155
Herzen, Alexander 131
Hobbes, Thomas 41–2, 44, 54, 91, 93, 111, 116, 186
human nature 18, 43, 47, 75, 89, 103, 129, 132–4
humanism 21, 23, 25, 39, 64, 90, 93, 98–9, 105, 122, 134, 185, 189
Hume 2, 5, 13, 44, 48, 50, 54, 133, 135, 185
see also empiricism
Huntington, Samuel 145, 156–8

international law 112, 115, 117, 121, 155

Kant, Immanuel 44–5, 74–5, 136, 155, 158

Lenin, Vladimir 16, 59, 66, 100
Locke, John 13, 41, 46, 54, 76, 91

Mannheim, Karl 36, 59, 183
Marx Karl
and the Enlightenment 6, 93–4, 103, 105, 190
and the individual 7, 104, 106
and progress 7, 93, 97, 105, 190
and utopia 1, 2, 5, 55–60, 64, 68, 71–2, 96, 190
see also Gray
Mill, John Stuart 45, 51–2, 127, 139
and Gray 5, 13, 15, 22, 45, 50–4, 74, 97, 132, 141
see also Gray
momentum concept 2, 10, 96, 126, 170, 176–9, 186–7, 193
More, Thomas 4, 27, 29–32, 37
Morris, William 5, 28, 55, 60–4, 72, 190
multiculturalism 162, 168–70, 173, 193
see also Gray

Ohmae, Kenneth 5, 57
Owen, Robert 5, 57

patriarchy 30, 37, 39, 42–3, 54, 87, 162, 166, 168, 176–8, 182, 189
Plato 4, 23, 27, 29–30, 32, 37, 94
post-modernism 2, 20, 24, 59, 127–8, 135, 142, 176, 185
prejudice 10, 17, 177, 182–3, 188

Rawls, John 16, 18, 22, 25, 77, 97, 119, 123, 127, 129
Raz, Joseph 18, 88, 170–1, 182
realism
and utopianism 5, 10, 35–6, 49
see also utopia
relationships 40, 49, 68, 80, 82, 88, 96, 102–3, 110, 127,

129, 135, 137, 163, 169–70, 176, 182, 194
Rousseau, Jean-Jacques 13, 41–7, 54, 93–4, 98, 109
Russia 24, 100, 144, 150–2

Saint-Simon, Claude-Henri 5, 56, 65, 71
slavery 30–1, 37, 41–2, 54, 115, 184
Smith, Adam 13, 75–6, 80, 84, 91
social contract 15, 76
state 2, 7, 42, 45–7, 54, 65–6, 76, 93, 107–21, 128–9, 132, 150, 156, 190–1, 194
 and the distinction with government 7, 66, 107, 120, 150, 192
 and globalization 144, 146, 148–9, 154, 156, 160
 and politics 7, 45, 69, 94, 109, 110, 118, 121, 134, 191
 and religion 42, 65, 118, 121
 see also globalization, Gray
Stiglitz, Joseph 9, 144–5, 150–2, 154, 160–1

Thompson, Edward 60–3
Tocqueville, Alexis 10, 177
tragedy 10, 17, 96, 106, 176, 179–80, 188, 194
truth 90, 181

United States of America 7, 20, 22, 25–6, 78, 88, 100, 125, 129, 144, 147, 149–50, 152, 157, 160, 166, 171, 185–6, 191
utopia
 and Gray 1–2, 24, 27, 35, 37–9, 84, 104, 108, 136, 140–1, 143, 160, 176, 181, 184, 186, 188–9, 192–3
 and perfectionism 5, 10, 16, 27–8, 30–8, 47, 61, 63, 96, 104, 175, 179, 187, 189
 reconstruction of 3, 10, 27, 34–5, 38, 65, 71, 118, 121–2, 175–8, 183–4, 186–90, 193–4
 and religion 1, 5, 16, 29, 31–5, 37–8, 62, 176, 189
 traditional view of 1, 27, 30, 37, 48, 55, 60, 62, 65, 68, 70–1, 74, 103–4, 116, 175, 187–90, 193
 and utopianism 28
 see also Gray, state

values 48–9, 101, 122–3, 130, 132, 142, 158, 161, 168
 in relation to facts 48–9, 71, 96, 137
 see also Gray

Weber, Max 7, 111
Wollstonecraft, Mary 45